PRESIDENTIAL SECRECY AND DECEPTION

Recent Titles in
Contributions in Political Science
Series Editor: Bernard K. Johnpoll

International Conflict in an American City: Boston's Irish, Italians, and
Jews, 1935–1944
John F. Stack, Jr.

The Fall and Rise of the Pentagon: American Defense Policies in the 1970s
Lawrence J. Korb

Calling a Truce to Terror: The American Response to International
Terrorism
Ernest Evans

Spain in the Twentieth Century World: Essays on Spanish Diplomacy,
1898–1978
James W. Cortada

From Rationality to Liberation: The Evolution of Feminist Ideology
Judith A. Sabrosky

Truman's Crises: A Political Biography of Harry S Truman
Harold F. Gosnell

"Bigotry!": Ethnic, Machine, and Sexual Politics in a Senatorial Election
Maria J. Falco

Furious Fancies: American Political Thought in the Post-Liberal Era
Philip Abbott

Politicians, Judges, and the People: A Study in Citizens' Participation
Charles H. Sheldon and Frank P. Weaver

The European Parliament: The Three-Decade Search for a United Europe
Paula Scalingi

Presidential Primaries: Road to the White House
James W. Davis

The Voice of Terror: A Biography of Johann Most
Frederic Trautmann

PRESIDENTIAL SECRECY AND DECEPTION

BEYOND THE POWER TO PERSUADE

JOHN M. ORMAN

CONTRIBUTIONS IN POLITICAL SCIENCE, NUMBER 43

GREENWOOD PRESS
WESTPORT, CONNECTICUT ● LONDON, ENGLAND

Library of Congress Cataloging in Publication Data

Orman, John M
  Presidential secrecy and deception.

  (Contributions in political science ; no. 43
ISSN 0147-1066)
  Bibliography: p.
  Includes index.
  1. Executive privilege (Government information)—
United States. 2. Deception. 3. Presidents—United
States. 4. United States—Politics and government—
1945–   I. Title. II. Series.
JK468.S4O75   353.03'2   79-8410
ISBN 0-313-22036-0

Library of Congress Catalog Card Number: 79-8410
ISBN: 0-313-22036-0
ISSN: 0147-1066

First published in 1980

Greenwood Press
A division of Congressional Information Service, Inc.
88 Post Road West, Westport, Connecticut 06881
Printed in the United States of America

10 9 8 7 6 5 4 3 2 1

for Renie Demkiw

CONTENTS

ILLUSTRATIONS

TABLES

PREFACE

This book examines presidential uses of secrecy and deception from the Kennedy through the Ford administrations by applying a framework to describe and explain such behavior in various case studies. The framework, which involves four components: personality development, bureaucratic politics, pragmatic calculations, and institutional constraints, is applied to the Kennedy administration program to eliminate the Castro regime, the secret war in Laos of the Johnson administration, the Nixon administration program to undermine systematically the legitimacy of the Allende regime in Chile, and the handling of sensitive information by the Ford administration in response to the Church and Pike committee investigations during 1975-76.

Political science on the whole has failed to deal systematically with potential abuses of presidential power. This research seeks to restore the investigation of secret and deceptive presidential behavior to its rightful place in contemporary scholarship. After attempting to explain why presidents engaged in secretive and frequently deceptive behavior, the case studies are evaluated as to their constitutionality, legality, morality, necessity, and justifiability. This book concludes by offering guidelines and reforms in the hope that disciplined and informed research on these highly controversial issues can help to clarify the complex problems associated with controlling secrecy and deception in the presidency.

The findings of this book suggest that the power of the presidency involves much more than just "the power to persuade." It also involves the power to issue unilateral commands for secret and deceptive actions.

The term secrecy, as used here, refers to a process that provides a capability to keep information from others. Deception, on the other hand, is defined as the intentional, deliberate misrepresentation of the facts, generally to further one's own ends.

A value framework to assess secretive and deceptive action is posited: presidents should not engage in secret or deceptive action that is unconstitutional, illegal, or unethical; when means and ends are not compatible; because "other nations do it"; when open action would suffice; or when an honest action would achieve the same goal.

Since presidential secrecy does have some societal benefit, however, the executive might be allowed to keep the following categories of information secret from Congress, the press, and the public: specific details about the development of ongoing diplomatic negotiations, covert means of intelligence gathering, defense strategy and military contingency and research plans, the nature of presidential advice, and the legitimate executive secrets of allied nations. Likewise, a president may legitimately deceive Congress, the media, and the public under the following circumstances: to save the nation from nuclear war, to protect the legitimate "executive secrets" listed above, and to avoid undue alarm during a constitutionally declared war. Other than these narrow cases of allowable secrecy and deception, the president cannot engage in unilateral secrecy and deception and remain consistent with the guidelines of the system of democratic accountability developed in the final chapter of this book.

After surveying various uses of secrecy and deception by the Kennedy, Johnson, Nixon and Ford administrations, which included an attempted assassination, secret wars, organized coups, paramilitary maneuvers, withholding information, and lying, it is necessary for researchers to advance some ideas about how such presidential behavior can be held accountable. The complex problem of accountability cannot be resolved by simply heeding the familiar presidential plea of "Trust me." Congress must reassert itself in an effort to gain access to presidential information. Moreover, this book suggests that Congress legislate allowable categories of presidential secrecy and articulate, after broad public discussion, some allowable categories of presidential deception.

Any project of this kind creates many debts and acknowledgments. I would like to thank Renie Demkiw for providing me with the Renie Demkiw Academic Scholarship for 1973-78 while I attended Indiana University. She also provided needed guidance on questions of style and title.

As usual, I owe a debt of gratitude to my manuscript readers. Kudos go to the following people for making perceptive comments on earlier drafts: my mentors Jeff Fishel, Maurice Baxter, Marjorie Randon Hershey, and John Lovell. The imperative cohort support was provided by Paul Hagner, Richard Hiskes, and John McIver. Moreover, I would like to thank the following people for improving the public record with respect to secrecy and deception within the White House. Without their contributions, this book could not have been written. The co-conspirators in investigative reporting include Daniel Ellsberg, Daniel Schorr, Seymour Hersh, Bob Woodward, and Carl Bernstein, to name a few.

I would like to thank Greenwood Press, including Margaret Brezicki, James Sabin, Dorothy Hoffman and series editor Bernard Johnpoll.

Finally, unlike Richard Nixon who would only accept the responsibility but not the blame for his actions, I gladly accept both the responsibility and the blame for this research. Any errors of scholarship and of interpretation are mine alone and they cannot be pardoned by any disclaimers, except perhaps Steve Martin's "well EXCUSE ME."

PRESIDENTIAL SECRECY AND DECEPTION

1. SECRECY, DECEPTION, AND PRESIDENTIAL POWER: JOHN F. KENNEDY TO GERALD R. FORD

One thing I want to tell you now and you can be sure of it. As your President, I will never tell you a lie.[1]

Jimmy Carter seemed to capture the mood of the electorate during the 1976 presidential primaries better than any other Democratic candidate. During the bicentennial presidential campaign, Carter promised the electorate a restoration of integrity and honesty to the White House. After the Vietnam experience, Lyndon Johnson's "credibility gap," Watergate, the CIA and FBI revelations, and the congressional sex scandals, Carter evidently thought the electorate would place great importance on a candidate's honesty, morality, and honor. Carter's stands on substantive issues were not important to some people, but his style, his image of morality, and his sincerity produced the appearance of an honest, truthful candidate.

It is a significant commentary on the state of the political system at that time that presidential aspirants scored their best political gains by convincing the public they would tell the truth. After experiencing the deficiencies of presidential leadership in the 1960s and 1970s, some people could only conclude that at times American presidents consciously lie to the public.

When a new president (Gerald Ford) spoke before Congress in his "crisis-inaugural" address in 1974, he received his greatest ovation for stating that he planned to tell the truth. The truthfulness of leaders would seem inherent in the concept of democracy, and yet the president of the United States received a standing ovation for simply restating the norm.

One wonders how Congress would have responded if Ford had stated such equally obvious principles as, "I expect to be held accountable for my actions," or "As President I plan to uphold the Bill of Rights."

In most democratic politics the notion of accountability in the linkage between leadership and the public is grounded in the fragile concept of "trust." Patterns of behavior by leaders that exhibit consistent lying and deception can easily disturb this relationship between follower and leader. More important, lying and deception distort the concept of representation, if by "representation" one is referring to delegate and symbolic representation.[2] When trust within the political system decreases, support for the regime also decreases; therefore, widespread presidential lying can weaken the foundations of a stable political system. Moreover, presidential lying interferes with accountability because citizens cannot be sure when the president is stating his or her views and accomplishments accurately, and thus citizens have a difficult time determining whether they held the president accountable.

Yet one might argue that even in a democratic polity the "rules of the game" assume that a fair amount of deception will occur.[3] In this view, it is only when deception becomes blatant, chronic, and coercive that norms of democratic practice are violated. This research will focus on the problem of presidential deception within the institutionalized presidency that developed in a blatant, chronic, and coercive way during the 1960s and 1970s.

Why Study Presidential Deception?

Presidential deception is one of the prime characteristics of the modern presidency, but it is an area of concern that has been overlooked systematically by most political scientists in recent years. Social scientists learn early that "human behavior is complex interaction" and one should be wary of simple-minded, single-causal explanations of behavior.[4] For political scientists in particular, most training is geared away from simple explanations that focus on deception as a primary technique of quasi-conspiratorial decision making. But a warning by some academicians to be wary of conspiratorial explanations in social science should not be taken to mean that conspiracies never exist. As Robert Lane has noted, "The application of this style of thought [cabalism] to the problems of the day is easy, too easy. But it is easy, too, to dismiss all imputations of 'deals,' of secret power, or discreet control. Somehow a balance must be achieved."[5] It seems that this balance has been lost within the discipline. Most political scientists are too willing to dismiss "deals" and the use of secret power. This book hopes to help restore that balance.

Another reason why political scientists have fallen behind in accounting for presidential deception is that the word "deception" implies malevo-lent motives on the part of the deceiver. To label a political action or process in a descriptive sense as "deceptive" opens up the possibility that the researcher will be accused of making highly biased, emotional value judgments. Value judgments, if made at all, should be posited with care in order to keep political science as "objective" as possible. Moreover, it is difficult to deal empirically with motives of any kind. Thus, many political scientists avoid the study of deception because the terms are so imprecise.

Perhaps a third, and some suggest the most important reason why most political scientists have avoided the study of presidential deception and covert power is that the data are so difficult to collect. The analysis of covert power relationships has been a controversial issue within the discipline since Robert Dahl made the case that one must be able to *observe* the exercise of power, and Peter Bachrach and Morton Baratz argued that power-holders can be said to be exercising power, even if one cannot observe the action, so long as the researcher can demonstrate the official's power to restrict the scope of the political process.[6] Since it is difficult to prove empirically in any systematic fashion that presidential conspir-acies to hide the truth from the public exist, many scholars have placed the study of presidential deception and covert action into an empirical "twilight zone" that should be avoided. In short, presidential deception has been overlooked for the most part because research on these manipula-tive themes has been viewed as too close to simplistic theories of human behavior, requiring speculation about motives and lacking necessary em-pirical evidence.

There have been some notable exceptions to this systematic bias within the discipline. Harold Lasswell, as usual, was ahead of his time with his concern for elite manipulation of the public. He attempted to show how elites use symbols to manipulate the public,[7] and Murray Edelman has ex-tended this concern with studies of the uses of symbols in American politics.[8] Edelman's works provide a theoretical framework for investigat-ing presidential uses of political symbols in manipulating the public. Yet

scholars working on various aspects of deception have not always agreed
on what constitutes elite deception, what is the effect on the public, or
how to measure political deception empirically.

If most political scientists have been reluctant to focus their research
on presidential deception and covert power, political journalists have not
suffered the same fate. Carl Bernstein and Bob Woodward produced excellent journalistic accounts of deceptive behavior in the White House in
All the President's Men and *The Final Days.*[9] Their prize-winning investigative reporting helped topple the Nixon administration. David Halberstam's
The Best and the Brightest gave a detailed account of Johnson's deceptive
actions in Vietnam as well as a look at John Kennedy's less than candid
role in publicizing his true position on Southeast Asia.[10] The investigative
reporting of Seymour Hersh brought to light domestic wrongdoing by the
CIA in violation of its charter and the My Lai cover-up in Vietnam, which
could certainly qualify as attempts at political deception.[11] Journalist
David Wise developed an extensive descriptive account of systematic
government lying in his *The Politics of Lying.*[12] The many examples of
government lying that Wise provides emerge as a regular pattern of behavior rather than aberrations.

Two popular accounts of executive political deception can be found
in Victor Marchetti and John Marks's *The CIA and the Cult of Intelligence* and in historian Arthur Schlesinger, Jr.'s, *The Imperial Presidency.*[13]
Marchetti and Marks explain how the cult of intelligence and secrecy
grew in the executive branch and Schlesinger documents the increasing
tendency for presidents to abuse their powers. For Schlesinger, Nixon's
presidency was not an "aberration but a culmination" of a long train of
expansions of presidential power.

Two other accounts of presidential deception are unique in that they
were written from within the inner circles of deception. These two seminal
accounts of presidential deception, which came to be published under
extraordinary circumstances, are *The Pentagon Papers* and *The White
House Transcripts.*[14] These books provided the public with a rare opportunity to read about deception from a primary source: the government's
own account.

Most of these accounts of presidential deception fall into the popular
journalistic category. They also have another common element: except
for portions of *The Pentagon Papers,* these accounts *were not* written by
political scientists. Although political journalists seem to have preceded

political scientists in writing about this important phenomenon, these journalists have only described the phenomenon. Political scientists should bring their analytical abilities to bear on the problem of presidential deception, moving beyond description to explanation and perhaps to prediction. Following is an analytical framework which can be used to explain why presidents in the 1960s and 1970s selected deceptive covert actions rather than public behavior.

Covert Presidential Power

The focus of this book is secrecy and covert presidential power as they relate to presidential deception, with selected covert programs in the Kennedy, Johnson, Nixon, and Ford administrations being examined to assess the relationship between secrecy and deception. The term "covert program" is not used in the narrow sense of only Central Intelligence Agency secret operations. Rather "covert program" refers to any foreign or domestic secret policy which the president establishes or approves.

With apologies to Lord Acton,[15] one might argue that "secrecy tends to corrupt and absolute secrecy corrupts absolutely." Unfortunately, such aphorisms are difficult to verify empirically. One must specify which acts covered under the secrecy system are abuses of power and not label all forms of secrecy as "corrupt" by definition. More important, one must distinguish between what is meant by secrecy and what is meant by deception, because even though the terms appear to be related they should not and are not being used as synonyms. The term secrecy is used here to refer to *a process that provides a capability to keep information from others.* Secrecy may be thought of as existing on a continuum ranging from *absolute secrecy,* when only the president and the program's executor know about the policy, to *absolute publicity,* defined as an intentional and nationwide (or widespread) advertisement of one's position. The term deception, on the other hand, means *the intentional, deliberate misrepresentation of the facts, generally to further one's own ends.* Deception is quite simply a conscious effort to make another person believe that which is not true or to disbelieve what is true. Deception may be thought of as existing on a continuum ranging from *total deceptive intent* to *no deceptive intent.* By intersecting the secrecy continuum with the deception continuum the following logical possibilities emerge.[16]

Figure 1: **Presidential Secrecy and Deception**

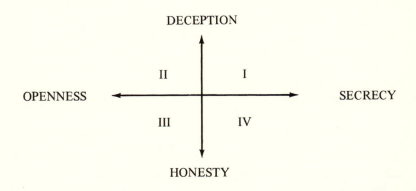

Quadrant I of Figure I represents presidential action taken in secret with an intent to deceive someone, such as Congress, the media, the public, or foreign leaders. If the president refuses to publicize a policy or program when specifically asked to account for his actions because he intends to mislead, the president is engaging in secret action which qualifies as deceptive. For example, if a reporter asks a president if he plans to take any paramilitary actions against a specific country and the president answers "No" or "I don't know" when in fact programs of a paramilitary nature are about to be carried out through presidential order, then the president is consciously trying to deceive and to suppress information.

Quadrant II represents full disclosure of a political problem with an intent to deceive. Here the president engages in cover stories, "plausible denials," and lying. The president consciously attempts to pass on false or partial information to get Congress, the media, the public, or foreign leaders to believe something which is not true. Nixon's behavior during the Watergate investigations in 1973-74 repeatedly fell into Quadrant II in that the president attempted to give the appearance that he was being honest and nonsecretive about his involvement in Watergate when in actuality he was lying about his involvement in and knowledge about the Watergate break-in.

Quadrant III presidential behavior is characterized by public statements that are not intended to deceive anyone. Misunderstandings about policy may occur after the transmission of a presidential policy, but in this case it is not because the president intentionally desired such a result or intended to deceive. Congress, the media, the public, and foreign leaders may feel that they have been deceived about presidential policy, but this may be because of their own misperceptions and problems with the communication channels rather than any deliberate attempt by the president to deceive. In a democratic polity, theoretically one would want to maximize Quadrant III presidential behavior because it includes honest and open messages conveyed by the president about his presidential policies.

Quadrant IV presidential behavior involves a high level of secrecy with no intention to deceive anyone. If the president is engaged in a secret program but is never asked by Congress, the media, the public, or foreign leaders to account for that program, then the president is not engaged in any deception. This quadrant includes so-called legitimate national secrets, which Congress, the media, the public, and foreign leaders recognize that the president has the duty to protect in the interest of national security. Information is withheld in this quadrant, but there is no effort to create any false impressions as to what the president is doing.

As Figure 2 indicates, presidential secrecy and presidential deception involves the president in relationship to someone or some group. When engaged in a secret act or a deceptive act, the president usually has a target group in mind. If secrecy is the process that provides a capability to keep information from someone, then the president must make a determination about which target groups should have what kinds of information withheld from them. Likewise when a president is engaged in a deceptive act, he is trying to deceive someone or some group.

There are basically four target groups that the president may decide to withhold information from or to deceive: elements in the *bureaucracy, Congress, foreign leaders,* and the *media-public group.* Figure 1, with its intersection of the secrecy continuum and the deception continuum, can be applied to each of the four presidential target areas. Such an application reveals that the president may choose to be open and honest with one target group, such as certain bureaucracies, while at the same time being closed and deceptive with another target group, such as Congress.

As an example of a president providing different information for different consumers of information, President Jimmy Carter decided to share his administration's secret assessment of the world situation, Presidential Review Memorandum 10, with officials from the People's Republic of China without informing Congress, the media, or the public of its con-

Figure 2: **Examples of Presidential Secrecy and Deception**

100% DECEPTION

Deceptive and Open II

1. JFK pre-Bay of Pigs statements

2. LBJ Vietnam antiwar statements, 1964

3. RMN Watergate comments, 1973-74

4. GRF confirmation hearings, "I will not run for President in 1976."

Deceptive and Secretive I

1. JFK Operation Mongoose to eliminate the Castro regime

2. LBJ ground war and air war in Laos 1964-68

3. RMN Track II to systematically undermine the legitimacy of the Allende regime in Chile

4. GRF handling of Congress in the Year of Intelligence 1975-76: the Angolan intervention

0% SECRECY ◄———————————————► 100% SECRECY

Honest and Open III

1. JFK steel price hike speech

2. LBJ Civil Rights support in speeches in 1964-65

3. RMN support for revenue sharing

4. GRF handling of Mayaguez affair

Honest and Secretive IV

1. JFK handling of the Cuban missile crisis 1962

2. LBJ secrecy surrounding new weapons development in the 1960s

3. RMN secrecy protecting the diplomatic breakthrough with the People's Republic of China

4. GRF and the SALT Negotiations

0% DECEPTION

tents.[17] The importance of differentiating presidential targets is that it helps one to understand who is being deceived and cut off from information and who is being dealt with honestly and openly.

Presidential deception can take many forms. For example, as a presidential candidate the president may promise to do things which he knows he will be unable to do while in office. In the normal course of presidential politics a president might make statements which he knows to be inaccurate in order to bolster the spirit of citizens. The president might announce to the American people, "I know that the economy is getting stronger," or "peace is at hand." The president may say that a member of his cabinet is one of the finest public servants and under no circumstances would he ever fire him for alleged wrongdoing, and then fire him within the week. A president may attempt symbolic deception by trying to wrap one of his policies in patriotic guise. A president may say that he will not seek reelection under any circumstances and then announce his candidacy. A president may cultivate the image that he is a happily married family man, while actually engaging in a number of extramarital affairs.[18] Finally, a president may try to present the picture of himself as a very righteous, church-going person who is above the use of vulgar language but in his everyday conversation with staff members engage in gross language.[19] However, these examples of presidential deception center on the president's rhetoric or his private behavior, and as such they are not the focus of this study. These kinds of presidential behaviors are accepted, understood, and often expected by the public in the normal course of American politics. This book will deal with deceptive presidential behavior that has *more* serious policy consequences for the political system.

One crucial form in which presidential deception and secrecy manifests itself is the covert program. If the policy adopted in a covert operation is substantially different from the articulated public policy, obviously someone is engaged in some form of deception. With the president maintaining some control over intelligence information, it is almost impossible to analyze all of his covert operations. If a covert operation has been successful, it is not usually made public by the president unless he is trying to defend the use of covert programs. However, if a covert program dramatically fails, there is a possibility that it will appear on the agenda of public discussion. The president then can be held accountable for the program that creates the dissonance between appearance and reality. The following examines presidential behavior that falls into

Quadrant I, which involves the relationship between presidential secrecy and deception.

A Framework to Explain Covert Presidential Action

The presidential decision to enter into a covert program rather than an alternative publicized policy can be better understood if one employs a framework that suggests four alternative explanations, both individual centered and situational centered. The four components of the framework carry explanations that have been labeled (1) personality-private motives, (2) bureaucratic politics, (3) pragmatic calculations, and (4) institutional. The four broadly competing but sometimes overlapping explanations which form this framework will be applied to limited data available from selected covert programs in the Kennedy, Johnson, Nixon, and Ford administrations. Some attempt will be made to evaluate which component of the framework provides the "best" explanation of the phenomena of covert program adoption, but the thrust of the analysis will highlight how the four components working together can more fully provide an understanding of the dynamics involved in covert program adoption. Before applying these components to the highly secretive and highly deceptive presidential behavior of Quadrant I, it is important to delineate them more fully.

The first component focuses on the personalities and private motives of presidents, contending that presidents turn to secret operations because of some personality flaw or trait. A president's decision-making style and the routines he selects to help him decide during crisis situations are reflections of the president's personality, according to this perspective. Harold Lasswell notes that the sources of political behavior for his Political Man could be viewed as "private motives displaced on public objects and rationalized in the public interest."[20] Under some circumstances, private motives can be expressed in covert operations and rationalized in terms of the public interest. Personality dysfunctions and characteristics may cause some presidents to develop a "passion for secrecy."

The interest in presidential personality greatly expanded during the Nixon administration from 1969 to 1974. Although Richard Neustadt introduced some personality variables into his bargaining model of presidential power in the early 1960s,[21] it was not until the late 1960s that

James David Barber focused students of the presidency on the importance of personality variables in explaining presidential behavior.[22] With the appearance in 1972 of Barber's classic work, *The Presidential Character,*[23] the popularity of presidential personality studies became firmly entrenched. A spate of psychoanalytic treatments followed as dozens of armchair analysts attempted to explain Nixon's presidency primarily in terms of his personality. A historian, a psychiatrist, a writer, and an English professor tried to explain Nixon's behavior using elementary psychoanalytic tools.[24] If personality variables had been overlooked in the study of the presidency until the 1960s, the 1970s ushered in an academic period in which personality variables may have been overemphasized at the expense of situational and institutional factors. The drama of Watergate and Nixon's bizarre actions were reduced to simple explanations in some circles by centering on Nixon's aberrant personality and character.

The personality-private motives explanation is a teleological explanation which posits motives, observes behavior, suggests tentative hypotheses about behavior, and tests hypotheses with motive as antecedent condition. The personality explanation maintains that certain presidential personality types are more attracted to secret and deceptive action than others. For example, if it can be demonstrated that a president is "paranoid" (has systematic delusions of being persecuted), one might be able to establish that paranoid personalities adopt secret and deceptive actions to a greater extent than do "normal," adjusted presidential personalities.[25]

If a president has a "manipulative" personality (a compulsive need to directly control his immediate political environment in every respect), he will tend to adopt covert programs more than a president who does not have this obsessive drive, since secret programs can be used as manipulative tools.[26]

In the same manner, an "authoritarian" personality in the White House might tend to engage in secret presidential behavior in order to establish stability and order. The "authoritarian" president is "made uncomfortable by disorder"[27] and covert operations afford the president the opportunity to try to control his environment secretly and to protect himself from the "weak" and the "inferior."

Likewise, a president who has a "cabalistic" personality (orders his political thought in terms of unofficial quasiconspiratorial groups perceived to manipulate and control public affairs behind the scenes) would tend toward covert programs to combat the cabals on their own level. The cabalist believes in "political goings-on" and he projects extraordinary and mystical powers to the cabals in their efforts to create revolutions, economic chaos, and war. As Robert Lane has observed, "It is only when [he] passes beyond reality limits and becomes suffused with projective and mystical thinking that he qualifies as a cabalistic thinker."[28]

Finally, an excessive use of covert programs might be characteristic of the "active-negative" personality type.[29] Of course, Barber would not necessarily equate excessive secrecy with "active-negatives," but his "active-negative" has a compulsive quality about him. He appears "ambitious, striving, power-seeking."[30] As Theodore Macaluso has noted, "[the active-negative] adopts an aggressive stance and has problems managing aggressive feelings. Self image is vague and discontinuous. The motivation is to get and keep power but the person tends to rigidify in its pursuit."[31] Covert programs could provide the active-negative personality types with opportunities to fulfill their compulsive power-seeking drives without suffering personal embarrassment.

The five personality types (paranoid, manipulative, authoritarian, cabalistic, and active-negative) that likely relate to the secretive presidential personality type are generally considered personality flaws. But personality traits need not be pathological before they can have an impact on the decision-making process and the decision outcome. As Herbert Kelman and Alfred Bloom have detailed:

The impact of the idiosyncratic dispositions of prominent decision makers and opinion leaders depends on the relevance of a given personality factor to decision-making behavior; on the centrality of the particular decision maker's position in the decision-making structure; and on the nature of the decision involved. . . . In general personality dispositions of important decision makers are *probably less likely to have an effect on the overall direction of a decision then on its qualitative characteristics, such as the style in which the decision is communicated and carried out.*[32] (emphasis added)

The personality traits of a president can be important when they help determine his decision-making style and more importantly his "modes of personal interaction."[33] If the president seems to deal with others in a secret and/or deceptive fashion because he is more psychologically comfortable acting in this manner, then his personality traits can be said to make a difference in the adoption of covert programs.

Personality and private motives explanations of presidential secrecy and deception have many problems. Besides the obvious difficulty of demonstrating that personality characteristics in some way determine political behavior, the analyst must verify that one's phenomenological account of a particular president's personality does in fact fit a particular personality type. This is a monumental task, since one researcher's "paranoid" may resemble another researcher's "obsessive-compulsive." Personality traits exist on a continuum, and an individual may have more or less of a particular trait over a broad range. Personality is a dynamic concept that contains many overlapping dimensions, and it should be considered multivariate. The analyst must demonstrate that in similar situations presidents with different personality types behave differently.

The problem of labeling a president as secretive is a difficult observational task. Does a president become labeled as a secretive personality if he engages in secret acts or are secret personality types identifiable independent of the knowledge of their secret acts? If the analyst cannot demonstrate that presidents with secretive personality types behave differently in the adoption of secret programs, then personality explanations lose their plausibility.

Regardless of the difficult problems of measurement in personality variables, personality should not be discarded as a possible variable in explaining secretive and deceptive behavior. Even though there are factors which tend to moderate the impact of personality at the level of presidential decision making (for example, presidential role demands, the recruitment process, role expectations, situational factors, bureaucratic politics, institutional structure, and the forces of accountability all work to diminish the articulation of idiosyncratic behavior), personality variables cannot be dismissed in the attempt to understand secretive and deceptive presidential behavior. Enough evidence has been presented by Barber and others to strongly suggest that personality characteristics of presidential role-occupants are important determinants of some forms of political behavior, particularly what Barber would call the stylistic aspects of presidential behavior.

The second component, a bureaucratic politics explanation, ought also to be part of any framework that seeks to explain secret and deceptive presidential behavior. The bureaucratic politics explanation is a "process" explanation. It argues that "what a government does in any particular instance can be understood largely as a result of bargaining among players positioned hierarchically in the government."[34] In analyzing the decision to adopt a covert program, one would look at (1) who plays and (2) what determines each player's stand. It is important to know whose interests and behavior have an important effect on the government's action and the reasons for each player's stand. Do national security interests, domestic politics, bureaucratic politics, or personal interests dominate the perceptions of the participants? Thus, according to the bureaucratic politics component, covert programs are the result of a bargaining process between the president, his top national security advisors, the director of Central Intelligence, other national security bureaucrats, and actors from other nations.[35] The bureaucratic politics explanation posits a bargaining environment, players and stances, outcomes resulting from bargaining and compromise, and the political nature of decisions surrounding national security.

As Morton Halperin and Graham Allison have observed, organizational interests are "often dominated by the desire to maintain the autonomy of organization in pursuing what its members view as the essence of the organizational activity."[36] For example, an administrator from the operations side of the Central Intelligence Agency (CIA) would be likely to push for adoption of covert programs which his bureau had developed. Organizations compete for various roles and missions that the president might assign during crisis situations, and covert operation developers compete to have their bureaucratic product accepted.

In this bargaining situation one's bargaining advantages, including the president's, "stem from control of implementation, control over information that enables one to define the problem and identify the available options, persuasiveness with other players (including players outside the bureaucracy) and the ability to affect other players' objectives in other, including domestic political games," according to Halperin and Allison.[37] Applying this principle to the adoption of secretive and deceptive programs, the CIA, the State Department, the National Security Council, and the Joint Chiefs could be viewed as the most influential bargainers in this bargaining situation.

The bureaucratic politics component carried to extremes would argue that some covert programs were adopted by the president after he acquiesced to their demands. Even when the CIA (or FBI) loses out in the bargaining over implementation of specific programs, the intelligence operators sometimes have been known to implement their secret programs on their own without presidential knowledge. This uncontrolled aspect of the bureaucratic politics component has been labeled by Senator Frank Church as the "rogue elephant" theory.[38] There is some danger, however, when presidents put too much emphasis on the runaway aspect of the bureaucratic politics model to describe political reality. It allows presidents to abandon the concept of presidential accountability by misusing an empirical description of reality for their own purpose.[39] The focus on this "roguish" quality of the national security bureaucracy often denies the importance of outside pressure groups, public opinion, norms, press, and counter players in the policy-making process. The focus also allows presidents to blame bureaucracies for their policy malfunctions rather than hold the chief executive responsible.[40] Thus, scholars should take great care in using bureaucratic politics descriptions of reality to be sure that the explanation is indeed accurate.

Perhaps the best known proponent of the bureaucratic politics and bargaining model to explain presidential decision making is Richard Neustadt in his *Presidential Power*.[41] Neustadt has guided presidents and scholars for almost two decades in his work, which instructs presidents on how to become strong leaders. His notion that in the American political system of shared powers "presidential power is the power to persuade"[42] is still the basis for any theory of presidential power. Neustadt portrays presidents as being essentially powerless unless they use their bargaining situation. The president is not viewed as a commander, but rather as a bargainer. He must realize, according to Neustadt, that he can use only his influence to get things done. To keep his influence the president must continue to make the "right choices," since, for Neustadt, "the power to persuade is the power to bargain."[43]

Many contemporary presidential scholars believe that Neustadt's work was a watershed in presidential studies because it provided an alternative to excessively constitutional/historical works on the presidency. His work presented a dynamic approach to the presidency that viewed the president as an actor in a bargaining system. The book took issue with the traditional chain-of-command view of presidential power, with the president at the top of the bureaucracy issuing rational, comprehensive policy dictates that are implemented by bureaucracy. Instead, bureaucracies would move only if the president could persuade them to move. As Fred Greenstein observed in Neustadtian fashion:

While the President can *in principle* act unilaterally to *tell* his "subordinates" what to do, in most instances peremptory command (as practiced for example when Truman dismissed MacArthur) is so politically costly as to be only a last resort.[44]

Neustadt felt that presidents must want to maximize their power. Peter Sperlich has noted that this desire to maximize one's power is Neustadt's most basic rule for presidents.[45] If presidents do not want to maximize their power, no matter what their other qualities might be, they are not "fit" for office. According to Neustadt, "Presidents must have a *will* to power."[46]

One response to such exhortations is to label Neustadt a champion of a strong presidency. Yet another school of thought contends that Neustadt's book helped form the academic rationale for the excesses of Johnson in Vietnam and of Richard Nixon in Watergate. Neustadt would vehemently deny this last charge, of course, since he would argue that Johnson and Nixon lost their bargaining advantages and had to resort to command. Whether Vietnam and Watergate were examples of the Neustadian model of presidential power carried to extremes is still an open question, but the important point to emphasize is that Neustadt's "bargaining approach" is only concerned with an *overt* orientation toward presidential power. Neustadt is not concerned with presidential power relationships that are not readily observed, but his approach *can be applied to understanding covert presidential power.*

Sperlich has detailed some of the fundamental weaknesses of Neustadt's "bargaining approach" as a framework for understanding presidential power. Although Neustadt does see command as a presidential resource, he has no sense of decisions stemming from unilateral direction, that is, Neustadt has no "unilateral manipulated field control."[47] Presidents operate with other than fellow Washingtonian bargainers, and in these situations presidential power is much more than just the power to persuade. The focus on politics as bargaining neglects compliance to presidential dictates through duty, pride, role conception, conscience, interpersonal identification, and symbolic attachments which are notoriously non-reciprocal.[48]

Neustadt's approach can be faulted on other grounds as well. His Machiavellian axiom to maximize presidential power can be conducive to creating a state of institutionalized paranoia within the White House. Neustadt argued:

> Our Constitution contemplated that such judgments (judgments of contemplated action vis à vis our world antagonists) should emanate from President *and* Congress. . . . But when it comes to action risking war, technology has modified the Constitution: the President perforce, becomes the only such man in the system capable of exercising judgment under the extraordinary limits now imposed by secrecy, complexity, and time. Therefore, as a matter not only of securing his own peace of mind but also of *preserving the essentials in our democratic order,* a President these days is virtually *compelled* to *reach for information* and to *seek control* over details of concrete plans, of actual performance, on "small" operations (to say nothing of large ones), where there often is a fleeting chance—sometimes the only chance—to interject effective judgment.[49] (emphasis added)

In other words Neustadt's modern president must attempt to control every operation from within the White House. He must guard against isolation by reinforcing "the dictates of common prudence for a man who bears the burden of that office in our time, namely, *to stretch his personal control, his human judgment, as wide and deep as he can make them reach*"[50] (emphasis added). As Greenstein has outlined, this ideal-typical Neustadtian president "behaves in ways which, if duplicated in the daily behavior of an individual not responding to similar situational imperatives, would seem to reflect excessive, perhaps even pathological, vanity and opportunism."[51]

In sum, presidential power is much more than just the power to persuade; it is also the power to issue unilateral, nonreciprocal commands and the power to engage in secretive and deceptive uses of covert presidential power. Keeping the limitations of the bureaucratic politics and bargaining component in mind, this bargaining approach can complement the personality-private motives component in the framework to explain secretive and deceptive uses of presidential power, as this research hopes to demonstrate. After all, bureaucrats have personalities too, and this influences how they enact their roles.

The pragmatic calculations explanation of secretive and deceptive presidential behavior, the third component, is an individual-centered explanation in contrast to the situational-based bureaucratic politics explanation and institutional explanations. At times during the 1960s and 1970s the active presidents may be said to have used a Machiavellian style of leadership that relied on pragmatic calculations. Kennedy, Johnson, Nixon, and Ford often presumed a congruence between their power stakes and the national interest, and, as they attempted to maximize power, Machiavelli's response to secrecy, deception, and lying still provided one form of guidance for strong presidents. Machiavelli's pragmatics included the following kind of advice:

1. The experience of our time shows that these princes who had little regard for their word and had the craftiness to turn men's minds have accomplished great things, and in the end have overcome those who governed their actions by their pledges.
2. It follows that a wise prince cannot and should not keep his pledge when it is against his interest to do so and when his reasons for making the pledge are no longer operative.
3. Men are so simple and so much inclined to obey immediate needs that a deceiver will never lack victims for his deception.
4. He must stick to good so long as he can, but being compelled by necessity, he must be ready to take to the way of evil.[52]

The pragmatic calculations approach considers cost-benefit analysis and rational decision making as key concepts in examining secret and deceptive presidential behavior. The president is viewed as a *rational, national actor;* covert policy becomes a rational choice to achieve objectives. By the term "rational" nothing more is meant than that the president has the ability to select an option from competing alternatives and that he can order his preferences in some way. If the president is faced with a national security problem, he examines his goals and objectives. He then considers the options and the consequences of each option and chooses among competing alternatives; his choice is, therefore, the result of "rational" decision making.[53]

Thus, in some circumstances the secretive and the deceptive covert programs are results of rational choice by the national decision maker because of the nature of specific problems and the political environment. In other instances the president may reject secretive and deceptive action after weighing the costs and benefits of that particular response. Since secret and deceptive programs have dynamics of their own, no two decisions about secretive and deceptive program adoption are alike. The president, as the rational, national actor, computes the costs and benefits for each program to determine whether or not the program should be open or secretive and/or honest or deceptive. Elements in the calculus include:

1. the need to promote national security;
2. the strategic advantages gained from secrecy;
3. ongoing foreign policy commitments;
4. the domestic political environment; and
5. the need to conceal incompetence, inefficiency, wrongdoing, personal embarrassment, national embarrassment, and/or administrative error.

In short, the pragmatic calculations component of the framework used in this study emphasizes the president as a rational calculator of costs and benefits of secret and/or deceptive action. Although the situation that the role occupant finds himself in is very important to understanding, the focus of this particular component is still essentially an individual-centered focus; that is, the individual's calculating processes, which vary from individual to individual and are ultimately subjective, are deemed more important than the situational aspects or the institutional aspects of the particular decision.

The final component in the framework is the institutional component. The institutional component argues that presidents turn to secret and deceptive programs because these various powers have become institutionalized within the modern presidency. As Edward S. Corwin has argued, the whole history of the institution of the presidency has been one of "aggrandizement."[54] Extending this theme, Arthur Schlesinger, Jr., argues that through various unusual exercises of presidential power, the advent of crisis diplomacy, the emergence of the United States as an industrial-military power in the twentieth century, and congressional abdication of their oversight responsibilities, the climate for the "imperial presidency" was created.[55] The rapid growth of the imperial presidency came after World War II out of "belief in permanent and universal crisis, fear of communism, faith in the duty and the right of the United States to intervene swiftly in every part of the world."[56] There came to be an extraordinary centralization of power over war and peace within the executive, and this concentration began to spill over into the domestic arena during the 1960s and 1970s.

Thus, institutional explanations of presidential secrecy and presidential deception contend that incoming presidents quickly learn what their predecessors have done about covert and deceptive policies and if previous presidents have not been criticized for such programs, they may come to believe that covert operations are not only permissible behavior for incumbents but even expected behavior. Managing secret programs and deceptive operations then becomes just one of the "awesome" responsibilities that have been posited systematically within the institution of the presidency. As the presidency developed, secrecy came to be institutionalized within the executive branch in the name of national security. (This development will be more fully detailed in Chapter 2.) The institutional component maintains that if presidents engage in secret and deceptive presidential programs to protect national security, they are just fulfilling one of the expected roles of the presidency.[57] Secrecy and deception are viewed as part of the role expectations that role occupants of the presidency must routinely engage in.

The four components of the framework (personality-private motives, pragmatic-calculations, bureaucratic politics, and institutional explanations) are not mutually exclusive. The bureaucratic politics component accepts personality and private motives of the president as important in the bureaucratic politics game, but it does not allow for the primacy of personality in determining covert program adoption. The institutional approach does not really explain why the practice developed in the first place. Perhaps personality factors, bureaucratic politics, and pragmatic calculations were at the genesis of the institutionalized secret presidency. The pragmatic approach is not purely logical, rational, or objective. Pragmatism rarely exists in such a state. The calculations that a president makes about covert programs are partly determined by personality, bureaucratic, and institutional factors.

The secrecy system presents many problems to scholars who are interested in doing foreign policy research, but, more important, the secrecy system deprives the electorate and strategic groups of the information needed to make intelligent choices over matters relating to foreign policy. The secrecy system as it has evolved is essentially a presidential system. By controlling the intelligence system through congressional neglect,[58] presidents have been able to control important foreign policy decisions with the following arguments:

1. There is a need to act swiftly in crises situations.
2. The president has superior expertise and information.
3. There is a need for unity.
4. The president is the only elected official who can speak for the nation as a whole with some legitimacy.

The major assumption of the system is that the president would be right more often than Congress in making foreign policy crises decisions. The secrecy system greatly helps to perpetuate the myth that the president has all the facts. The secrecy system expanded during the intense period of the Cold War years in response to the perceived threat of Communist aggression to the national security. There did seem to be some consensus among policy makers that some things had to be kept secret during the Cold War. Yet recent presidential abuses of the secrecy system for the deceptive purposes of the executive have called into question the *validity* of the current use of secrecy.

Strategy of Research

The purpose of this research is threefold. First, I intend to apply the framework to four purposively selected case studies that represent Quadrant I presidential behavior (highly secretive and highly deceptive) in an effort to explain *why* presidents, in these cases, engaged in such behavior. Second, I will evaluate the *justifiability* of presidential behavior. Who were the targets of presidential secrecy and deception? Was the behavior constitutional? Was the presidential action legal? Was the action necessary? Finally, the ultimate purpose of this study is to develop more precise *guidelines* to systematically delineate when secret and/or deceptive presidential behavior is justified in a democratic polity, if ever.

By selecting various covert programs that were adopted by Kennedy, Johnson, Nixon, and Ford in response to perceived national security threats, it should be possible to analyze the relationship between presidential secrecy, presidential deception and presidential power in these decisions. Each program that is selected on the grounds that it is Quadrant I presidential behavior will undergo the same analytical process developed in this section.

If one follows a research strategy that attempts to pursue the "weight of the evidence"[59] to explain secret and deceptive uses of presidential power, how can one give pursuit? One obviously has to devise ways to reconstruct meetings and events that were supposed to be kept secret. Bob Woodward and Carl Bernstein developed a radical methodology that used a "two source" rule to report "the best possible version" of Nixon's *Final Days.*[60] If at least two people's versions of events agreed, Woodward and Bernstein reconstructed the account as factual. Unfortunately, this agreement did not have to be among principals of the meeting which was reconstructed. Although suspect as a political science methodology to pursue the "reality" of past events, this methodology still produced a plausible and perhaps the best reconstruction one can obtain of Nixon's final days. Similarly, Fred Branfman used a "strengthened two-source rule" in his interviews to reconstruct the events of the president's secret army in Laos from 1962 to 1972.[61] Branfman tried to insure that material was confirmed by two independent sources who did not come from the same bureaucratic background and not contradicted by either common sense or documented data. Both of these works wrestled with the diffi- cult problem of trying to reconstruct secret meetings.

When one attempts to reconstruct "reality," one is engaged in an es- sentially descriptive process, which involves the use of testimony and observation. In recounting observations of the event, it is important to distinguish between direct observation and records. If one is using records of the event, are the records valid? Testimony about the event is much more difficult to process. Is the testimony corroborated? Were physical conditions favorable for an objective testimony from the observer? Was the sensory activity adequate? How recent was the experience that the observer is testifying to?

When dealing with the perceptions and interpretations of others, it is important to evaluate the possibility of undue bias because of the observ- er's emotional state, expectations, or lack of experience.[62] Has the ob- server avoided using emotive language if the description is to be factual? Does the language conjure up false analogies that could mislead? Is the insid- er's statement so significant that, if true, it would affect the decision that was being made?[63] All precautions must be taken to insure that the observer reports that may support one's hypothesis are not due to extensive observer error. One can never be methodologically sure in this regard, but the recognition that these problems exist in processing testimony about covert programs is the first step in devising methodological safeguards. Finally, if one can be certain to some minimal degree that the observations and the testimony are "correct," to what extent are they actually relevant to supporting or rejecting hypotheses?[64]

Of course, in trying to reconstruct the "reality" of a covert operation, one can never be sure that one has comprehended all of the intricacies and subtleties of the decision-making process. Using observation as a research technique, one can rely on "self-observation" by the political leader, informants, participant observation, and field observation. It is difficult for the researcher to ever really become an insider on a covert operation, but this should not preclude the possibilities of analyzing selected covert programs. Indeed, one can never fully insulate an investigation from one's own biases, but as Thomas Halper has noted:

> In a real sense, all studies must proceed with incomplete and imperfect data, and the reader, like a plaintiff in a negligence suit, must live with the doctrine of "assumption of risk." The truly relevant considerations then, are: first, are the questions asked in the study important to justify the assumption of risk; and second, are the available data so inadequate as to make a reasonably empirical approach impossible, and an assumption of risk merely a leap of faith.[65]

I would argue that the problems of presidential secrecy and deception are important areas of concern that require attempts to penetrate the inner web of presidential decision making. The questions posed in this study are important enough to justify the "assumption of risk," and there is enough data available to attempt a "reasonably empirical" approach to covert presidential power. The nature of the office makes it difficult for political scientists to construct a valid empirical picture of the presidency, but the office is important enough to require new approaches.

The four decisions, responses, or programs that will be analyzed are:

1. The program to eliminate the Castro regime as developed during the Kennedy administration, which took the forms of the Bay of Pigs invasion, Operation Mongoose, and the assassination plots against Castro.

2. The secret ground and air war in Laos that was fought during the Johnson administration.
3. The secret program to systematically undermine the legitimacy of the Allende regime in Chile, developed during the Nixon administration.
4. The handling of Angolan information by the Ford administration in response to the Church committee and the Pike committee investigations during the so-called "Year of Intelligence," 1975-76.

Each of these programs will be analyzed by using the following procedures and sets of questions:

1. In general, reconstruct the decision-making process for each selected decision.
2. Why was the decision reached to keep the specific program secret? Assess the utility of the framework as it helps to understand presidential secrecy in all of these cases.
3. Who were the targets of presidential secrecy?
4. Why did the president engage in deception? Assess the utility of the framework as it helps to understand presidential deception in all of the cases.
5. Who were the targets for the presidential deception? How did the outlines of the unarticulated covert response differ from the public statements of the president?
6. Finally, what were the consequences and implications for each covert response on the democratic political system when the president engaged in Quadrant I behavior? Was the response *justified?* Was the response *constitutional?* Was the response *legal?* Was the response *necessary?*

Obviously the nature of this kind of intellectual endeavor will not permit the researcher to establish the ultimate validity of his framework, but enough data has been generated in the form of inside accounts, investigative reports, hearings, documents, testimonies, memoirs, and confessions to tentatively apply each component of the framework to specific decisions. No outsider can exactly reconstruct the dynamics of a covert decision since each decision is unique. Covert operations by their very nature are not intended to be accurately reconstructed, but it is precisely this lack of traceable accountability that makes this analytical study of covert presidential decision making so compelling. Secrecy and deception by the president can be effectively hidden by covert decisions, and it is hoped that this research can contribute to specifying precise guidelines as to when the resort to secrecy and deception is justified and how this kind of presidential behavior can become more accountable.

Notes

1. Jimmy Carter, 1976 Presidential Campaign Trail, in Robert W. Turner, *I'll Never Lie to You: Jimmy Carter in His Own Words* (New York: Ballantine, 1976).

2. For a seminal work on representation see Hannah F. Pitkin, *The Concept of Representation* (Berkeley: University of California Press, 1967).

3. A certain amount of deception is assumed, for example, in the rhetoric that candidates use while running for office. The act of running for president is not the same as actually being president. About one-third of the electorate believes "quite a lot of the people running the government are a little crooked." See Arthur H. Miller, "Public Policy and Political Cynicism: 1964-1970," in *Public Opinion and Public Policy*, ed. Norman Luttbeg, rev. ed. (Homewood, Ill.: Dorsey Press, 1974), p. 455. Even in the 1976 presidential election which was characterized by the media's obsession with presidential character, an NBC poll taken on election day found that only 30 percent of the voters described Carter as an "honest man" and 33 percent thought Ford could be described as an "honest man." See *Newseek*, November 15, 1976, p. 28. In a Harris Poll in 1971, 54 percent of the respondents believed that "most politicians take graft," in News Release, *The Harris Survey*, December 4, 1971.

4. Hubert M. Blalock, *Social Statistics* (New York: McGraw-Hill, 1972), pp. 442-50; Margaret Conway and Frank Feigert, *Political Analysis: An Introduction* (Boston: Allyn and Bacon, 1972); M. Brewster Smith, "A Map for the Analysis of Personality and Politics," *Journal of Social Issues*, 24, no. 3 (1968): 15-28; and Milton Yinger, *Toward a Field Theory of Behavior* (New York: McGraw-Hill, 1965), Chaps. 3-8, in which Yinger focuses on "the totality of coexisting facts which are conceived of as mutually interdependent."

5. Robert Lane, *Political Ideology* (New York: Free Press Paperback, Macmillan, 1962), p. 118.

6. Robert A. Dahl, "The Concept of Power," *Behavioral Science* 2 (1957): 201-15; Dahl, "A Critique of the Ruling Elite Model," *American Political Science Review*, 53 (1958): 463-69; and Dahl, *Who Governs?* (New Haven, Conn.: Yale University Press, 1961). For the counterpoints, see Peter Bachrach and Morton Baratz, "Two Faces of Power," *American Political Science Review*, 56 (1962): 947-52; and Matthew A. Crenson, *The Un-Politics of Air Pollution: A Study of Non-decisionmaking in the Cities* (Baltimore, Md.: Johns Hopkins University Press, 1971).

7. Harold Lasswell, *Politics: Who Gets What, When and How* (New York: World Publishing, 1958). *See also* Lasswell et al., *The Language of Politics* (Cambridge, Mass.: MIT Press, 1965) and Lasswell, D. Lerner and Ithiel de Sola Pool, *Compara-*

tive Study of Symbols (Stanford, Calif.: Stanford University Press, Hoover Institute, 1952).

8. Murray Edelman, *The Symbolic Uses of Politics* (Urbana: University of Illinois Press, 1964), and his *Politics as Symbolic Action: Mass Arousal and Quiescence* (Chicago: Markham Publishing, 1971). *See also* Kenneth Dolbeare and Murray Edelman, *American Politics: Policies, Power and Change*, ed. 2 (Lexington, Mass.: D. C. Heath, 1974) Chap. 18, "Symbolic Politics and Political Change."

9. Carl Bernstein and Bob Woodward, *All the President's Men*, (New York: Warner Paperback Library, 1975); *see also* their *The Final Days* (New York: Simon and Schuster, 1976).

10. David Halberstam, *The Best and the Brightest* (New York: Random House, 1972). Halberstam in a lecture at Indiana University's Poynter Project Lecture on April 25, 1975, replying to a query about the message from his book, said, "Quite simply, American presidents consciously lie to the American people."

11. Seymour Hersh, "The Rolling Stone Interview," *Rolling Stone*, April 10, 1975, pp. 48+. *See also* Hersh, "Huge CIA Operation Reported in U.S. Against Anti-War Forces and Other Dissidents in Nixon Years," *New York Times*, December 22, 1974. Hersh also covered other forms of political manipulation in his *Cover-Up* (New York: Random House, 1972), on the My Lai story.

12. David Wise, *The Politics of Lying: Government Deception, Secrecy and Power* (New York: Vintage Books, 1973). Perhaps Wise is the best chronicler of the "invisible government" in the United States. See his *The American Police State* (New York: Random House, 1976): *and see* Wise and Thomas Ross, *The U-2 Affair* (New York: Random House, 1961); their *The Invisible Government* (New York: Random House, 1964) and their *The Espionage Establishment* (New York: Random House, 1967).

13. Victor Marchetti and John Marks, *The CIA and the Cult of Intelligence* (New York: Dell, 1975) *and see* Arthur Schlesinger, Jr., *The Imperial Presidency* (New York: Popular Library, 1974).

14. See *The Pentagon Papers* (New York: New York Times-Bantam Books, 1971), and *The White House Transcripts* (New York: New York Times-Bantam Books, 1974).

15. Lord Acton in G. Himmelfarb's *Lord Acton: A Study in Conscience and Politics* (Chicago: University of Chicago Press, 1952), p. 161, from the following context: (To Creighton) "I cannot accept your canon that we are to judge Pope and King unlike other men, with a favorable presumption that they did no wrong. . . . *Power tends to corrupt and absolute power corrupts absolutely.* . . . There is no worse heresy than that the office sanctifies the holder of it."

16. Marjorie R. Hershey suggested this intersection to me.

17. Bernard Gwertzman, *New York Times* Wire Service, "Brzezinski Briefed Chinese on Arms Talks, Secret Memos," in Louisville, *The Courier-Journal*, May 28, 1978, p. A-4.

18. John Kennedy apparently had a close relationship with Judith Campbell Exner while he was in the White House. The Church committee in the course of its investigation revealed that a close friend of the president's was also a friend of

mobsters Johnny Rosselli and Sam Giancana. Later, Judith Exner admitted that she was the unidentified friend of Rosselli and Giancana. For an account of these relatively shocking associations, *see* Wise, *The American Police State,* pp. 217-19; an Interim Report of the Select Committee to Study Governmental Operations with Respect to Intelligence Activities, the United States Senate, "Alleged Assassination Plots Involving Foreign Leaders," November 1975; and Judith Campbell Exner, *My Story* (New York: Grove Press, 1977).

19. *The White House Transcripts.*

20. Harold Lasswell, *Psychopathology and Politics* (Chicago: University of Chicago Press, 1930, and New York: Viking Press, 1960), p. 75 (Viking ed).

21. Richard Neustadt, *Presidential Power* (New York: John Wiley & Sons, 1960 and 1964).

22. James David Barber, "Classifying and Predicting Presidential Styles: Two Weak Presidents," *Journal of Social Issues,* 24, 1968. Yet Barber had some impressive forerunners. See Alexander George and Juliette George, *Woodrow Wilson and Colonel House* (New York: John Day, 1956), and particularly Erwin Hargrove, *Presidential Leadership, Personality and Political Style* (New York: Macmillan, 1966). For the best general overview of the problems involved in personality and politics research, see Fred Greenstein, *Personality and Politics* (New York: W. W. Norton, 1975).

23. James David Barber, *The Presidential Character* (Englewood Cliffs, N.J.: Prentice-Hall, 1972 and 1977).

24. See Bruce Mazlish, *In Search of Nixon* (New York: Basic Books, 1972); Eli Chesen, *President Nixon's Psychiatric Profile* (New York: Peter Wyden, 1973); Arthur Woodstone, *Nixon's Head* (New York: St. Martin's Press, 1972); and Alan Rothenberg, "Why Nixon Taped Himself: Infantile Fantasies Behind Watergate," *The Psychoanalytic Review,* 62, 2, 1975, 201-23. *See also* Stanley Renshon, "Psychological Analysis and Presidential Personality: The Case of Richard Nixon," *The Journal of Psychohistory,* Winter 1975, and Lee Rangell, "Lessons from Watergate: A Derivative for Psychoanalysis," *The Psychoanalytic Quarterly,* 45, 1, 1976.

25. For a discussion of the paranoid symptoms exhibited by Nixon, see Mazlish, *In Search of Nixon,* pp. 84-85, and William Saffire, *Before the Fall: An Inside View of the Pre-Watergate White House* (New York: Belmont Towers Books, 1975), pp. 307-15.

26. Erwin Hargrove labeled Franklin Roosevelt as the "manipulative" leader in the presidential personality typology found in Hargrove's *Presidential Leadership, Personality and Political Style,* 1966. Later Hargrove categorized FDR's Personality and leadership style as "the self-confident leader" in Erwin Hargrove, *The Power of the Modern Presidency* (New York: Alfred Knopf, 1974), pp. 49-58. Evidently something happened between 1966 and 1974 to give the label "manipulative" a bad name so that Hargrove felt he could no longer use it for Roosevelt. Perhaps the presidencies of Johnson and Nixon gave new meaning to the term. For other descriptions of "manipulative" personalities, see Richard Christie and Florence L. Geis, *Studies in Machiavellianism* (New York: Academic Press, 1970). They define "Machiavellianism" as "the psychological capacity to treat other human beings as

objects and thus to feel free to manipulate them," in Greenstein, *Personality and Politics*, p. xxv.

27. A description of the personality traits for the authoritarian personality can be found in Theodore Adorno, Else Frenkel-Brunswik, Daniel J. Levinson, and Nevitt Sanford, *The Authoritarian Personality* (New York: Harper & Row, 1950), Chap. 7; *and see* Greenstein, *Personality and Politics*, pp. 102-18.

28. Lane, *Political Ideology*, p. 118.

29. "Active-negative" is Barber's concept in his *The Presidential Character*.

30. Theodore Macaluso, "The Presidential Character and Presidential Action in Conflict Situations" (paper delivered at the Southern Political Science Association Annual Meetings, Atlanta, Georgia, November 1976), p. 8, Table 1.

31. Ibid. p. 8, Table 1. For important critiques of Barber's typologies, see Alexander George, "Assessing Presidential Character," *World Politics*, 26, January 1974 pp. 234-82, and Erwin Hargrove, "Presidential Personality and Revisionist Views of the Presidency," *American Journal of Political Science*, 17 (November 1973): 819-35. More recently, see James H. Qualls, "Barber's Typological Analysis of Leaders," *American Political Science Review*, 71 (March 1977): 182-211, and Barber's abrasive comment following, called "Quall's Nonsensical Analysis of Nonexistent Works," pp. 212-25.

32. Herbert Kelman and Alfred H. Bloom, "Assumptive Frameworks in International Politics," in Jeanne N. Knutson, ed., *Handbook of Political Psychology* (New York: Jossey-Bass, 1973), p. 271.

33. Margaret G. Hermann, ed., *A Psychological Examination of Political Leaders* (New York: Free Press, 1977), p. 22.

34. Graham Allison and Morton Halperin, "Bureaucratic Politics: A Paradigm and Some Policy Implications," *World Politics*, Spring 1972, 42; *and see* Allison's *The Essence of Decision* (Boston: Little, Brown, 1971), Models II and III.

35. Although Allison and Halperin usually receive credit for establishing the bureaucratic politics paradigm in the 1970s because of Allison's *Essence* and Halperin's *Bureaucratic Politics and Foreign Policy* (Washington, D.C.: The Brookings Institution, 1974), their work actually synthesizes bureaucratic themes that were sounded earlier in the 1950s and the 1960s. *See* Neustadt, *Presidential Power;* Gabriel Almond, *The American People and Foreign Policy* (New York: Praeger, 1960); Charles Lindblom, "The Science of Muddling Through," *Public Administration Review*, 19, 1959, and his *The Policy-Making Process* (Englewood Cliffs, N.J.: Prentice-Hall, 1968); Warner Schilling, "The H-bomb: How to Decide Without Actually Choosing," *Political Science Quarterly*, 86 (1961); and Samuel Huntington, *The Common Defense* (New York: Columbia University Press, 1961), for example.

36. Allison and Halperin, "Bureaucratic Politics," p. 49.

37. Ibid., p. 49.

38. Senator Frank Church labeled the CIA as a "rogue elephant" during testimony of CIA abuses while he acted as Chairman of the Select Committee to study Governmental Operations with Respect to Intelligence Activities of the United States Senate, 94th Congress.

39. Stephen Krasner, "Are Bureaucracies Important? (or Allison Wonderland)," *Foreign Policy*, no. 7, 1972, 159-79. I. M. Destler makes a similar point in his

Presidents, Bureaucrats and Foreign Policy (Princeton, N.J.: Princeton University Press, 1972), when he argues that the bureaucratic politics approach has undermined the notion of presidential responsibility for policy. For other critiques of Allison and Halperin's bureaucratic politics model, see Robert Art, "Bureaucratic Politics and American Foreign Policy: A Critique," *Policy Sciences,* 4 (December 1973): 467-90; Ernest Yanarella," 'Reconstructed Logic' and 'Logic-in-Use' in Decision-making Analysis: Graham Allison," *Polity,* 8 no. 1 (Fall 1975): 156-72; Bertel Heurlin, "Notes on Bureaucratic Politics in National Security Policy," *Cooperation and Conflict,* 10 (1975): 237-59; *and see* John P. Lovell's review of Halperin's "National Security Policy-Making" *Society* (July/August 1976), 88-90.

40. For example, a president may claim that the CIA is running out of control or that the FBI was controlled by "Mr. Hoover and not me." This allows presidents to accept the responsibility "but not the blame" since ignorance or presidential unawareness is supposed to pass as an excuse. See Daniel Ellsberg, "Quagmire Myth and the Stalemate Machine," in his *Papers on the War* (New York: Pocket Books, 1972), pp. 41-141, in which Ellsberg argues that United States involvement in Indochina was not that of a stumbling giant who took incremental steps into a morass of quicksand in Vietnam. Rather, American involvement can be explained in terms of presidential awareness, presidential planning, presidential choice, presidential manipulation, and presidential responsibility.

41. Neustadt, *Presidential Power,* 1964.

42. Ibid., p. 10.

43 Ibid., p. 36.

44. Fred I. Greenstein, "Political Psychology: A Pluralistic Universe," in Knutson, ed., *Handbook of Political Psychology,* p. 458.

45. Peter Sperlich, "Bargaining Overload," in *The Presidency,* ed. Aaron Wildavsky (Boston: Little, Brown, 1969), p. 171.

46. Ibid., p. 171. Of course, the phrase "will to power" was Friedrich Nietzche's, but Neustadt's use of the phrase is central to understanding the strong presidency literature. As Woodrow Wilson once put it, "A President must be as big of a man as he can." More recently, the strong presidency has been touted by Louis Koenig, *The Chief Executive* (New York: Harcourt, Brace, Jovanovich, 1964); Clinton Rossiter, *The American Presidency,* rev. ed. (New York: Mentor Books, 1962); Rexford Tugwell, *The Enlargement of the Presidency* (Garden City, N.Y.: Doubleday, 1960); Wilfred Binkley, *The Man in the White House* (Baltimore, Md.: Johns Hopkins Press, 1959); James M. Burns, *Presidential Government* (Boston: Houghton Mifflin, 1965 and 1973); and Theodore Sorensen, *Watchmen in the Night* (Cambridge, Mass. The MIT Press, 1975). For critiques of the strong presidency thesis, see Schlesinger, *The Imperial Presidency;* Thomas Cronin, "The Textbook Presidency and Political Science" (paper presented to the 1970 Annual Meeting of the American Political Science Association); and Cronin, *The State of the Presidency* (Boston: Little, Brown, 1975); George Reedy, *The Twilight of the Presidency* (New York: New American Library, 1970); Henry Commager, *The Defeat of America* (New York: Simon and Schuster, 1974); and Alfred de Grazia, "The Myth of the President," in Wildavsky, ed., *The Presidency.*

47. Sperlich, "Bargaining Overload," in Wildavsky, ed., *The Presidency,* p. 186.

48. Ibid., pp. 188-92.

49. Neustadt, "Afterword on JFK," *Presidential Power* (1964), p. 212.

50. Ibid., p. 213.

51. Greenstein, "Political Psychology" in Knutson, ed., *Handbook of Political Psychology,* p. 458.

52. Machiavelli, *The Prince and Selected Discourses* (New York: Bantam Books, 1966), pp. 62-63.

53. See Anthony Downs, *An Economic Theory of Democracy,* (New York: Harper and Row, 1957); Thomas Schelling, *The Strategy of Conflict* (Cambridge, Mass.: Harvard University Press, 1963); Anatol Rappaport, *Two Persons Game Theory* (Ann Arbor: University of Michigan Press, 1966); Herbert Simon, *Administrative Behavior* (New York: The Free Press, 1951); Allison, "Model I," in *The Essence of Decision; and see* Earl Ravenal, "Logic or Psycho-logic? Nixon and Kissinger Move to a Balance of Power Policy" (paper delivered at the 1976 Annual Meeting of the American Political Science Association, Chicago, September 2-5, 1976).

54. Edward S. Corwin, *The President: Office and Powers* (New York: NYU Press, 1957), pp. 29-30.

55. Schlesinger, *The Imperial Presidency.*

56. Ibid., p. 205.

57. For a classic discussion of the various roles that a president is called upon to play, see Rossiter, *The American Presidency,* pp. 14-40.

58. Regarding congressional neglect of its oversight function with respect to the intelligence community, see Morton Halperin, Jerry Berman, Robert Borosage, and Christine Marwick, *The Lawless State* (New York: Penguin Books, 1976), pp. 276-78; Arthur M. Cox, *The Myths of National Security* (Boston: Beacon Press, 1975), pp. 150-80; Marchetti and Marks, *The CIA and the Cult of Intelligence,* pp. 351-52; and Stanley Futterman, "What Is the Real Problem with the Classification System," in Norman Dorsen and Stephen Gillers, eds., *None of Your Business* (New York: Penguin Books, 1975), p. 104.

59. C. Wright Mills, *The Sociological Imagination* (New York: Oxford University Press, 1959).

60. Woodward and Bernstein, *The Final Days,* pp. 12-13. For some standard techniques of investigative reporting, see David Anderson and Peter Benjaminson, *Investigative Reporting* (Bloomington: Indiana University Press, 1976).

61. Fred Branfman, "The President's Secret Army: A Case Study of the CIA in Laos 1962-1972," in *The CIA File,* ed. Robert Borosage and John Marks (New York: Grossman Publishers, 1976), pp. 46-78.

62. John O'Shaughnessy, *Inquiry and Decision* (London: George Allen and Unwin, 1972), p. 187.

63. Ibid., p. 187.

64. William Stephens, *Hypotheses and Evidence* (New York: Thomas Y. Crowell, 1968), p. 22.

65. Thomas Halper, *Foreign Policy Crises* (Columbus, Ohio: Charles E. Merrill, 1971), p. iv.

2.THE PRESIDENTIAL SECRECY SYSTEM

The problem of secrecy in a democratic political system is an area of concern that is not new. The difficult balancing of the people's "right to know" with the requirements for a strong national security and effective government is a complex constitutional and practical task. This delicate balancing process between publicity and honesty and the competing tensions of secrecy and deception has been with the United States since the founding of the Republic. Indeed, the proceedings of the Constitutional Convention of 1787 were held in secret because the framers did not want day-to-day interference from dissident groups. Were it not for James Madison's prolific diary of the secret proceedings, which became available long after the adoption, some of the intricate floor arguments and the rationale for adopting some sections of the Constitution might not have been known today. The Constitution itself only mentions secrecy once when it grants the power to determine what should be kept secret in the Congress's "Journal of Its Proceedings" to the Congress.[1] John Jay later provided arguments for executive secrecy in certain areas in his Federalist 64. As Jay noted, "It seldom happens in the negotiation of treaties, of whatever nature, but that perfect *secrecy* and immediate *dispatch* are sometimes requisite. There are cases where the most useful intelligence may be obtained, if the persons possessing it can be relieved from apprehensions of discovery."[2]

If Jay provided a rationale for executive secrecy in some very restricted instances (negotiating treaties), George Washington as practitioner established the early precedents for executive secrecy. A president could present secret treaties to the Senate and refuse to give details of the agreement to the House or to the public. Washington presented the Senate with a secret article for the treaty with the Creek Indians in 1790, and later in 1795 he refused to supply the House with details of a treaty that Jay had negotiated with Great Britain.[3] In the latter treaty the House was asked to appropriate funds to carry out the terms of an agreement which it knew nothing about. In responding to the House's request for information, Washington replied:

It is perfectly clear to my understanding that the assent of the House of Representatives is not necessary to the validity of a treaty. . . . It is essential to the due administration of the Government that the boundaries fixed by the Constitution between the different departments should be preserved, a just regard to the Constitution and to the duty of my office, under all the circumstances of this case, forbids a compliance with your request.[4]

However, the competing tension for disclosure also became well established by early precedents. Virginia Senator Stevens Mason felt that the House and the people had a right to know the terms of Jay's secret treaty with Great Britain. Mason leaked the document to publisher Benjamin Bache who published it in his Philadelphia *Aurora,* and a new "leaking-publishing" tradition developed.[5] For example, later in 1844 Ohio Senator Benjamin Tappan leaked President John Tyler's attempt to secretly annex Texas to his brother Lewis Tappan and William Bryant who published it in the *New York Evening Post.*[6]

Throughout the nineteenth century the confrontations that would develop over presidential secrecy and the people's right to know centered on diplomatic moves by the president. Ironically, during the great threat to national security that the Civil War posed, a presidential secrecy system did not exist. The war was fought without espionage or sedition laws, and as Arthur Schlesinger, Jr., has noted, the war was fought to "a remarkable degree in the open."[7] Schlesinger makes this point even though he realized that Lincoln did suspend *habeas corpus,* intercept the mail, and suppress newspapers. Moreover, the conduct of the war was certainly characterized by secret plans, secret missions, and espionage, but no formal system developed to keep information about war activities from the public.

An official presidential secrecy system did not develop until the twentieth century. By "presidential secrecy system" I mean the formal and informal sets of institutional and bureaucratic arrangements within the executive that systematically keep information from others by classification. With the rapid rise of the United States as a world economic and political power in the early 1900s, and with the technological explosion in weapons development, the secrecy arrangements began to develop into a system and to broaden in scope. The War Department announced in 1912 that the following records would be considered confidential: *submarine mine projects, land defense plans, tables, maps and charts showing defense locations, number of guns,* and *character of armament.*[8]

The United States' participation in World War I brought on a classification system and an Espionage Act. In 1917 information could be classified as "Secret," "Confidential," and "For Official Circulation Only," and the Espionage Act provided for the imprisonment or the death penalty for communicating a document or information relating to the national defense to any foreign government or citizen with the intent to injure the United States or to benefit the foreign nation. Specifically during war time the Espionage Act forbade the communication, publication, collection, or elicitation for the enemy of any information "with respect to the movement, numbers, or disposition of armed forces, ships, aircraft, or war materials or military operations, plans or defenses or any other information relating to the public defense which might be useful to the enemy."[9] The Espionage Act was worded so that the government had to prove that the person who disclosed the information had "reason to believe" that the disclosure would injure the United States, and the mere fact that a document was marked with a certain classification had no bearing on espionage statute violations. A jury would decide whether the information, regardless of the government's classification, did in fact relate to the national defense.

In 1940 President Franklin Roosevelt issued an executive order that brought the system of military secrecy under the direction of the president through executive authorization and furthered the process of institutionalizing governmental secrecy. Roosevelt's order allowed secretaries of Navy and War to label documents "Secret," "Confidential," or "Restricted."[10] His order provided a basis for the World War II classification system. The system of secrecy that developed during World War II was not dismantled after the war. It protected such projects as the Manhattan Project and the actions of the Office of Stategic Services during the war. The need for presidential secrecy in the conduct of the war was never seriously challenged. The very survival of the nation was thought to be at stake and the argument for secrecy in the name of national security was compelling for most Americans.

After the war, two new developments broadened the scope of presidential secrecy: the National Security Act of 1947 and Harry Truman's executive order in 1951. The National Security Act created the Central Intelligence Agency which became the super-secret tool of the president. The director of Central Intelligence was specifically charged with the responsibility for "protecting intelligence sources and methods from unauthorized disclosure."[11] An agent of the president by statute, the director of CIA was directed to keep some things secret. Truman's order extended the secrecy system to nonmilitary bureaus and departments as it allowed any part of the executive branch of government to classify "official information the safeguarding of which is necessary in the interest of national security."[12]

Dwight Eisenhower issued another executive order in 1953 that changed Truman's term "national security" to "national defense" and reduced the number of agencies authorized to classify information. Eisenhower's order reduced the number of categories of information and redefined "Top Secret," "Secret," and "Confidential."[13] Although Eisenhower and John Kennedy would make minor changes later, Eisenhower's Executive Order 10501 served as the framework for presidential secrecy until Richard Nixon's executive directive in 1972. The central point to be made about the system of official secrecy, and David Wise makes the point better than anyone, is that the secrecy system is essentially a *presidential* system.[14] Congress passed no laws (except perhaps the NSA of 1947) to establish the secrecy system since the groundwork for presidential secrecy was set through executive fiat. It is important to note that Congress could have reversed or challenged presidents on this issue, but chose not to until the mid-1970s. When Eisenhower issued his original executive order on the classification system, he was presumably relying on his interpretation of the implied powers of the presidency and on previous statutes. But as Harold Relyea has shown, "a search of the statutes failed to reveal any specific provision sanctioning such a policy instrument."[15]

Evaluating the Present Presidential Secrecy System

Democratic political systems can be measured by the extent to which they maximize certain democratic values and civil liberties, such as freedom of speech, freedom of the press, right to petition government for redress of grievances,[16] but the "right to know" is not usually considered to be an explicit civil liberty in the same sense as are the rights enumerated within the First Amendment. The framers did not see fit to include the citizen's "right to know." Constitutionally, however, one might argue that one's "right to know" could be protected by the vague Ninth Amendment, which guarantees "The enumeration in the Constitution of certain rights shall not be construed to deny or disparage others retained by the people." More important, one's "right to know" is implied in the First Amendment since citizens are given the right to speak freely and the right to a free press. In any system of free expression, a right to access to information that is necessary for one to form a reasoned opinion is fundamental.[17] One of Robert Dahl's defining characteristics of polyarchal democracy is the requirement that "all individuals possess identical information about (policy) alternatives,"[18] and this principle should be viewed as the obverse of the citizen's "right to know."

What does a citizen have a right to know? Everything that the president does? Something? Nothing? Certainly a citizen has a right to know what action his or her government is taking on behalf of the citizen. But what if this revelation of the government's action seriously jeopardizes national security? Does the citizen still have the right to know? Who will decide what constitutes a threat to national security? Who will decide what information shall be released to citizens? Government secrecy per se might appear to be inherently undemocratic, but paradoxically a certain amount of government secrecy is necessary for the maintenance of the political system. The substantive nature of the policies, decisions, and actions that are kept secret by the president becomes the focal point in determining whether the process is consistent with democratic theory and whether it is justified.[19]

Although the idea of secret government action is typically inconsistent with most conceptions of normative democratic theory, presidential secrecy has had a long tradition within the American political experience as has already been noted. The need for executive flexibility has often outweighed the competing tension for open, accountable presidential action. As Thomas Cronin has observed, "Everybody believes in democracy until he gets into the White House."[20] When a person becomes the president and faces a new set of responsibilities and a new political environment, his attitudes about government secrecy often change. As an academician Woodrow Wilson could argue that "corruption thrives in secret places and avoids public places," and "secrecy means impropriety,"[21]

but as president Wilson defended the tactics of secret diplomacy. As a
senator, John Kennedy might complain about the continued "abuse of
executive privilege," but in his first press conference as president he spoke
with new insights when he answered a query on executive privilege by
saying, "But I must say that I do not hold the view that all matters and
all information which is available to the Executive should be made available at all times, and I don't think any member of the press does."[22]

What is it about the nature of secrecy that turns presumably sincere
men like Wilson and Kennedy into occasional defenders of secrecy? Perhaps in this dilemma, as in the bureaucratic politics paradigm, where a
player sits often determines his stand.[23] Even though most observers
agree that the questions posed by the tensions between secrecy and freedom
are important and have serious consequences for all, the exact nature of
the dilemma is still in question.

For some analysts this dilemma is viewed as a game with a zero sum
outcome. James Wiggins best represents this view as his use of a simplistic
relationship between secrecy and freedom indicates. Wiggins contends,
"Each added measure of secrecy measurably diminishes our freedom."[24]
In the same fashion Thomas Emerson maintains that "to the extent that
information is withheld from a citizen the basis for government control
over him becomes coercion, not persuasion."[25]

Other observers note that secrecy is a powerful narcotic. Edward Teller
felt that "secrecy, once adopted becomes an addiction,"[26] and Arthur
Schlesinger, Jr., concurs.[27] According to their view, secrecy becomes a
powerful intoxicant for the president as he experiences the incredible
satisfaction of knowing certain things that others do not. In this way,
secrecy becomes an obsessive religion that attracts presidents to the cult.

Still others view no inverse relationship between secrecy and freedom.
Francis Rourke stresses the need to balance the value of national security
with other values in the democratic community.[28] This view makes a
distinction between legitimate secrecy and excessive, illegitimate uses
of secrecy.

Finally, perhaps the most productive way to evaluate the present presidential secrecy system is to enumerate the benefits and costs of executive
secrecy. Secrecy can *benefit* society in the following ways:

1. Secrecy protects the development of diplomatic negotiations by
   giving flexibility to advisors in the negotiating stage.
2. Secrecy protects intelligence and covert intelligence gathering means.

3. Secrecy guards military plans, troop movements, strategy, and weapons research and development.
4. Secrecy protects treaties and agreements with other nations.
5. Secrecy guards information about other nations' defense plans, diplomatic negotiations, treaties, agreements, and intelligence reports and sources which if disclosed would compromise the other nation.
6. Secrecy guards the executive process by providing for a higher level of candor in the routine exchange of confidences, and it makes it easier for dissenters to attack policy from the inside without having their loyalty questioned.[29]

Presidential secrecy, on the other hand, may have great *costs* for society. Scholars who compute and speculate on the costs of secrecy to society often speak of the costs of *"excessive"* secrecy since most of them do accept some minimal levels of secrecy to maintain defense security. However, they do not recognize all of the enumerated *"benefits"* of secrecy in the preceding list. It is argued that excessive presidential secrecy creates the following *costs* to society (the arguments overlap in some instances):

1. Secrecy provides an internal threat to a stable balance of power by creating a class of people with a "need to know" in a system where "information is power."[30]
2. Presidential secrecy is undemocratic, unjust, and morally wrong. It enables leadership by coercion and not persuasion.[31]
3. Secrecy costs society by providing uncertainty in the arms race because it may allow the enemy to underestimate our real military strength.[32]
4. Presidential secrecy creates a loss of trust and a loss of support for government policy when a real or imagined "credibility gap" exists.[33]
5. Presidential secrecy fosters a climate that encourages the growth of undemocratic personality traits in leaders.[34]
6. Secrecy inhibits scientific exchange.[35]
7. Secrecy makes possible the corrupt conduct of foreign affairs.[36]
8. Presidential secrecy encourages presidential lying. For one to effectively keep a secret, he must be prepared to lie.[37]
9. Secrecy encourages the excessive leaking of confidential information which might possibly threaten the national security.[38]
10. Secrecy hinders free competition within the military-industrial complex and covers huge cost overruns from citizens.[39]

11. Presidential secrecy hides dissent with the executive and obscures the administrative history of most crucial decisions.[40]

12. Secrecy is politically unwise. The presidential secrecy system increases the chance that covert operations will be selected over other alternatives, reduces the effectiveness of such operations, hinders accurate intelligence evaluation, and distorts the executive decision-making process.[41]

The literature regarding the benefits and costs of secrecy tends to be rather heavily skewed toward the costs. Academicians have found it easier and more productive to focus on the troublesome consequences that a secrecy system poses for a democracy than to note the problems a democracy poses for a security system. The distrust of secret and arbitrary power has a long tradition in the United States, and it is little wonder that the arguments against secrecy are greater in number than the arguments for secrecy. If the problem of presidential secrecy could be resolved by merely counting arguments for or against presidential secrecy, the scope of presidential secrecy would have been fundamentally reduced long ago. However, the dilemma is more than just a simple quantitative problem. The arguments for presidential secrecy are weighted and they often carry more qualitative weight than the arguments against presidential secrecy.

At various times throughout the development of the presidential secrecy system when Congress, the press, and the public provided the pressure for disclosure, presidents *could* defend the system of presidential secrecy by citing one of three principles: "executive prerogative," "executive privilege," and "the right to lie." In carrying out his constitutionally specified role as commander-in-chief, the president may be confronted with an emergency situation. In responding to crises the president may interpret his role as commander-in-chief in a broad, expansive fashion.

John Locke in his *Second Treatise of Government* provided the philosophical arguments for the broad interpretation of executive power with his concept of "executive prerogative."[42] Legislatures cannot provide for all the possibilities that crisis situations pose for society in their laws and statutes, and legislatures cannot convene and deliberate promptly to avoid the perils of the crisis, according to Locke. Thus, it is up to the executive through "executive prerogative" to "act according to discretion for the public good, without the prescription of the law and sometimes even against it."[43] By this logic presidents could take secret and deceptive action or they could withhold information if they chose to do so in response to emergency situations.

Thomas Jefferson noted that "a strict observance of the written laws is doubtless *one* of the high duties of a good citizen, but it is not the *highest.* The laws of necessity, or self-preservation, of saving our country when in danger, are of a higher obligation."[44] Abraham Lincoln extended this tradition when he responded to the *Merryman* case, which held that presidential suspension of *habeas corpus* was unconstitutional, by asking, "Are all the laws but one to go unexecuted, and the Government itself go to pieces lest that one be violated?"[45]

In further interpreting a president's implied powers of his office, presidents could argue that "executive privilege" justifies withholding secrets from Congress. Combining the doctrine of separation of powers with a claim of inherent right to secrecy for the executive, presidents argued that they could withhold certain information from the Congress and the courts. This position of withholding information came to be labeled as "executive privilege" in the 1950s by Eisenhower's Attorney General William Rogers, although no firm constitutional basis for such a position existed.[46] In short, prior to recent legislation, the president could withhold national security information, secret executive agreements, secret executive orders, diplomatic strategy, executive advice, documents, and witnesses from the Congress, and there was not a whole lot Congress could do about it unless Congress wanted to cite the president for contempt or take the ultimate step of impeachment.

Finally, in trying to justify deceptive acts within the presidential secrecy system, a president could draw on the doctrine of the executive's "right to lie," *though no president has ever claimed such a right.* The right to lie in order to save the country can be justified by combining the implied powers of the presidency with executive prerogative, but of course no American president would want to make this underlying implicit assumption an explicit position. The classification system allows officials acting in the name of the president to engage in partial truths by withholding information. Truth, openness, complete candor, and disclosure are antithetical to the presidential secrecy system. If the president has been given the power not to tell the truth, then he has been given in effect the "right to lie" in order to save the country. As Arthur Sylvester, Kennedy's assistant secretary of defense for public affairs, first articulated the doctrine, "It's inherent in [the] government's right, if necessary, to lie to save itself

when it's going up into a nuclear war. That seems to me basic—basic."[47]
Moreover, as Daniel Ellsberg has observed:

Keeping secrets effectively does involve lying. It means that when you are
asked if you have certain information, you don't say "No Comment," because that is an answer. To protect that secret you have to lie and say,
"No, I don't know that." You learn the technique of lying in a way that
seems entirely legitimate and essential for national security.[48]

Some presidents seem to have assumed a "right to lie" in order to maintain an effective presidential secrecy system in the name of national
security.

The Courts and Presidential Secrecy

The courts have often been called upon to make decisions in the struggle between presidential secrecy and the competing call for disclosure as
advocated by Congress, the press, or citizens. Indeed the courts have often
found themselves in the precarious position of balancer between secrecy
and publicity. The courts have always been receptive to the idea that the
executive could keep certain information secret if it was in the national
interest. However, the government had to convince the courts that the
information withheld was indeed vital to the national security. In *Totten*
v. *United States* (1876) the Supreme Court held that a suit against the
government could not be entertained in a court of claims if it would inevitably result in the disclosure of a state secret.[49] In a series of federal
court decisions a defendent was acquitted of contempt for refusing to
divulge state secrets,[50] evidence was stricken from the record on the
grounds that it contained state secrets,[51] and an objection by a litigant
that production of documents requested would violate the Espionage
Act was sustained.[52] By 1944 the lower court had ruled that the right of
the Army to refuse to disclose confidential information, the secrecy of
which the Army deems necessary to national defense, was indisputable.[53]

The Supreme Court in the 1950s did not move against the institution
of presidential secrecy; in fact, in some instances the Court strengthened
the president's claim over certain information. The Court moved in a
piecemeal fashion on the constitutional questions posed by the Truman
and the Eisenhower loyalty programs. The loyalty programs were instru-

ments which allowed presidents to secure their secrets more efficiently within the secrecy system. If workers could be released on the basis that they *might* pose a security threat, then the system of presidential secrecy could be strengthened. The probability that secret information would leak out was presumably reduced under the presidential loyalty programs, but this did not necessarily provide constitutional justification for such programs.

Truman's loyalty program was established in 1947 by an executive order directing the Federal Bureau of Investigation to investigate all federal employees and to forward charges of disloyalty to loyalty review boards within the various bureaus. Hearings were conducted to determine whether accused workers were in fact disloyal, but the accused had no right to examine the FBI files or to learn the name of his accusers.[54] If an individual belonged or had belonged to any organizations that the Attorney General labeled as "subversive," the loyalty review boards considered this fact evidence of disloyalty. By 1953 the Attorney General labeled over 200 organizations as subversive,[55] and the loyalty review boards no longer had to prove disloyalty for discharge, but could remove employees if they could find "reasonable doubt" of the employee's loyalty.[56] Eisenhower established a wider security program by executive order in 1953 which expanded the disloyalty criteria to include "sexual immorality, perversion, drug addiction, conspiracy, sabotage, treason, unauthorized disclosure of classified information, and refusal to testify before authorized government bodies on grounds of possible self-incrimination."[57]

In *Bailey* v. *Richardson* (1953) the Supreme Court upheld a lower court decision that agreed to the constitutionality of the loyalty programs. The lower court had ruled that the loyalty programs did not constitute a bill of attainder, that there was no inherent right to federal employment, and that presidents had the power to remove workers for political reasons.[58] Later in the mid-1950s the Supreme Court would decide three loyalty program cases on narrow technical grounds rather than confront directly the constitutional questions.[59]

Another case, *United States* v. *Reynolds* (1953) armed the presidential secrecy system with more power. Three widows sued the United States in federal tort claims action after their husbands had been killed in a plane crash while testing secret equipment for the Air Force. The women and the court requested the Air Force accident report, but the Air Force refused the request on the grounds that the report contained military secrets. The lower court requested the report again to verify the claim of state secrets but the Air Force refused again. The case was decided in favor of the plaintiffs and later upheld by the court of appeals.[60] The Supreme Court reversed the decision in a six to three ruling and held that the judge is not warranted in insisting that he be given an opportunity to inspect documents to verify a claim of military secrets, but should determine whether there is a reasonable possibility that state secrets are within such records.[61]

After the Supreme Court had recognized the citizen's "right to know" for the first time in *Lamont* v. *Postmaster General* (1965),[62] the Court was asked in the 1970s to specify exactly what it was that citizens had the right to know. The presidential secrecy cases involved leaking of classified information, the Central Intelligence Agency, and applications of the 1966 Freedom of Information Act. In one case the lower court had ruled that the court did not need to inspect classified documents but should rely on the statement from the director of Central Intelligence that the documents were classified,[63] but this 1960s standard was soon challenged.

The 1970s ushered in the period of key confrontation over the presidential secrecy system and the citizen's "right to know" in the *Mink* case, the *Marchetti* case, the *Ellsberg* case, and the *Nixon* case.[64] In 1971 Congresswoman Patsy Mink of Hawaii and 32 other members of Congress requested nine documents on the environmental impact of nuclear detonations on Amchitka Island that had been presented to the president. When the executive branch refused to release the documents because they were classified under Eisenhower's Executive Order 10501 precedents, the members of Congress initiated court proceedings to secure the documents and to test the Freedom of Information Act. The district court agreed with the executive's position that the reports were exempt from disclosure under the Freedom of Information Act's enumerated exemptions.[65] The court of appeals reversed the decision on the contention that only the secret portions of the classified documents could be withheld; the nonsecret materials should be sorted out by district court *in camera.*[66] The Supreme Court resolved the matter in 1973 with a five to three decision (Justice William Rehnquist not participating) that Mink dubbed "the Waterloo of the Freedom of Information Act."[67] The majority held that Congress never desired the Freedom of Information Act to subject executive security classifications to judicial review. As Stanley

Futterman put it, the Court held that "once the District Court is told by the government that a document is classified and that it contains sensitive matters relating to national defense or foreign policy, it may go no further."[68]

Victor Marchetti, a former Central Intelligence Agency worker, wanted to write a book on the CIA and had signed a secrecy agreement with the CIA while still employed there. Fourth Circuit Court Judge Clement Haynsworth granted CIA an injunction that required Marchetti to submit to them for their approval all writings relating to the agency. Haynsworth denied judicial review of Marchetti's work since he felt "The question for decision is the enforceability of a secrecy agreement exacted by the government, in its capacity as employer, from an employee of the CIA."[69] The Supreme Court denied *certiorari* in 1973, which in effect acquiesced to the Haynsworth ruling that imposed prior restraint on Marchetti. Later Marchetti's publisher would challenge the CIA deletions in Haynsworth's court, again only to lose in *Knopf* v. *Colby* (1975).[70]

Countervailing the *Mink* and *Marchetti* cases, which backed the presidential secrecy system, were the *Ellsberg* and the *Nixon* cases. The *Ellsberg* case was the criminal litigation that grew out of the *New York Times Company* v. *United States* (1971), which centered on the question of publication of the Pentagon Papers.[71] After trying unsuccessfully to get members of the Senate and the House to publicize the Pentagon Papers, Ellsberg leaked copies of the study to various newspapers around the country. When the *New York Times* and the *Washington Post,* among others, began to publish the papers, the executive branch sought an injunction barring publication of classified material. In the New York Federal District Court, Judge Murray Gurfein issued a temporary restraining order, but in Washington Judge Gerhard Gesell refused to restrain the *Post.* Within seventeen days from original day of publication, the Supreme Court finally resolved the dispute over publication in a six to three decision. The majority agreed on only one point—that the government did not show justification to establish prior restraint.[72] The papers could be published, but the important questions of criminal liability were never resolved.

The Justice Department charged Ellsberg and Anthony Russo with violating three statutes in their handling of the Pentagon Papers and a federal grand jury returned an indictment. President Nixon wanted to settle the criminal questions as soon as possible and to discredit Ellsberg's actions. Accordingly, Ellsberg and Russo were charged with:

1. Conspiracy to defraud the United States of its lawful governmental function of controlling the dissemination of classified government studies, reports, memoranda, and communications.
2. Violation of the Espionage Laws which make it a crime to retain or transfer the unauthorized person's material relating to the national defense.
3. Stealing government property.[73]

The circuitous wording of the first charge, "conspiracy to defraud the United States of its lawful governmental function," was another way of saying that Ellsberg and Russo had challenged the discretionary powers of the presidential secrecy system. The second charge referred to "unauthorized persons," presumably the press and the American people. In the third charge, the Justice Department apparently wanted to establish that information is property.[74]

Unfortunately, these crucial questions were never resolved in a court of law. Because of Nixon's overzealous attempts to influence the outcome of the trial, Judge Matthew Byrne finally dismissed the case.[75] As Leonard Boudin noted, "So long as the law remains unclear in its defense of the individual's right to speak up, governments will likely be tempted to use concepts like 'theft of property' and 'espionage' to embrace communication of embarrassing information to the American people."[76]

Finally, in *United States* v. *Richard Nixon* (1974)[77] the Supreme Court ruled unanimously (Justice Rehnquist not participating) that the specific claim of executive privilege made by President Nixon to withhold evidence in a criminal proceeding was unjustified. In some circles the decision was hailed as a major victory over the presidential secrecy system, since the Court actually ordered a president to release information. Although the case contributed significantly to Nixon's ultimate resignation, in reality the decision explicitly recognized the doctrine of executive privilege. Furthermore, as Theodore Sorensen has explained, the decision gave implicit endorsement to an "unfettered presidential privilege of communication in the military and diplomatic area" and suggested that there may "even be unreviewability [of executive privilege] by the courts if the President invokes national security."[78] However, Nixon did not argue that his communications should be protected on the grounds that they were national secrets, therefore the case was decided on other merits and values that did not directly challenge the presidential secrecy system. As Chief Justice Warren Burger contended:

We are not concerned here with the balance between the President's generalized interest in confidentiality and the need for relevant evidence in civil litigation, nor with that between the confidentiality interest and congressional demands for information, nor with the President's interest in preserving state secrets. We address only the conflict between the President's assertion of a generalized privilege of confidentiality against the constitutional need for relevant evidence in a criminal trial.[79]

On the whole, with few exceptions, the courts have shown great reluctance to interfere with the presidential secrecy system. National security has been viewed as the responsibility of the president, and if the president or military agencies deem that certain information should be kept secret in the name of national security, then so be it. The courts have not felt obligated to settle matters that it views as being largely executive in nature. When the courts have acted, the decisions have left fundamental constitutional questions unresolved. Moreover, many court decisions have actually strengthened, condoned, or sanctioned the presidential secrecy system rather than moved to confront the president directly on precedents involving secrecy. More than ever in the mid-1970s, even after Vietnam and Watergate experiences, the presidential secrecy system remained firmly entrenched.

Recent Congressional Initiatives

Historically, Congress has recognized the fact that it is the major institution in American society that can contest the president's claim of executive privilege. Congress needs to be informed in order to pass legislation and to carry out its oversight function. Any doctrine which challenges the Congress' access to information directly challenges the legislative authority of Congress. This fundamental tension has been at the heart of the recurring contest between the executive and Congress over access to information that the executive claims is solely executive information.

This contest between Congress and the executive has been characterized by peaks and valleys in the intensity of the struggle. Certain factors promote greater oversight and congressional intensity in increasing the incidence of information demands on the executive. Joel Aberbach has enumerated the following factors promoting more oversight:

1. If different parties control the presidency and Congress, the majority in Congress has an incentive to harass and embarrass the executive for partisan gain.
2. If the bureaucracy is unresponsive to requests for assistance to the constituents of a strategically placed senator or representative, then oversight may be used as a means to set things aright.
3. Oversight increases when senators and congressmen wish to satisfy group interests.
4. Oversight increases when senators and congressmen want to protect favored agencies or to preempt opponents of the agency from entering into an uncontrolled investigation.
5. Decentralized committee structure promotes the opportunity for more oversight.
6. Increasing staff resources of a decentralized committee should lead to more oversight activity.
7. Corruption, crisis, and publicity: evidence of corruption, the breakdown of a program, or the subversion of accepted governmental processes as revealed by Watergate make oversight attractive because the overseer is almost sure to make a favorable public impression.[80]

Usually as oversight increases, Congress needs information from the executive. Congress tends to demand more information from the executive in the areas of domestic policy than of foreign policy. Thomas Franck and Edward Weisband have summarized Congress' operating principle in regard to important foreign policy and national security data by emphasizing the "voluntary reticence" of Congress. For them, Congress in effect has said to the executive:

We shall allow you to act as the judge of what may have to remain an executive secret in the field of foreign affairs, so long as we are convinced that you are keeping from us only those matters the withholding of which any reasonable Member would recognize to be absolutely essential to the national interest.[81]

Recently, this operating principle has failed because the executive has been unable to convince many congressmen (and reasonable ones) that particular executive secrets are in the national interest. After Vietnam, Watergate, the CIA-FBI revelations, and Nixon's much publicized abuse of the secrecy system, Congress has made new demands for information in the area of foreign affairs.

Many of the past abuses of the secrecy system have been revealed by the congressional investigative process, and Congress has moved to make clear its position on foreign policy information. The War Powers Act of 1973, passed over Nixon's veto by a Congress determined to regain some control, went a long way to prevent possible secret wars such as Laos and Cambodia, and it represented Congress' new demands for foreign policy information. According to the War Powers Resolution, the president can only send troops into combat in three situations: when Congress has declared war, pursuant to specific statutory authorization, or during a national emergency when the United States, its territories, possessions, or armed forces are attacked. By law, the president must consult with Congress if there is time before he sends troops. In any event, the president must report to Congress within forty-eight hours that he was in fact sent troops. If Congress does not declare war or specifically authorize the troop involvement within sixty days, the president must withdraw the troops. If the president certifies that the troops need more time to withdraw safely, the president and the troops get a thirty-day extension. At any time during the sixty-day period or the thirty-day safety period, the Congress could pass a concurrent resolution, not subject to the president's vote, that would require the immediate return of the troops.[82]

In 1973 the Senate Select Committee on Presidential Campaign Activities (Ervin-Watergate Hearings) and later the House Judiciary Committee in 1974 demonstrated the Congress' new interest in challenging the president over the nature of executive secrecy and executive privilege. In 1974 the Subcommittee on Intergovernmental Relations of the Committee on Government Operations of the United States Senate held hearings on government secrecy.[83] More important, oversight of all CIA covert operations was drastically changed by the *Hughes-Ryan Amendment* to the 1974 Foreign Assistance Act. The Hughes-Ryan Amendment mandated:

No funds appropriated under the authority of this or any other Act may be expended by or on behalf of the Central Intelligence Agency for operations in foreign countries, other than activities solely for obtaining necessary intelligence, unless and until the President finds that each such operation is important to the national security of the United States and

reports, in a timely fashion, a description and scope of such operation to
the appropriate committees of the Congress, including the Committee
on Foreign Relations of the United States Senate and the Committee on
Foreign Affairs of the United States House of Representatives.[84]

Thus, *by law the president must inform Congress of all covert operations
in a "timely fashion."* The importance of this fundamental change in the
presidential secrecy system cannot be overemphasized. For the first time
Congress recognized that presidents do have the power to engage in covert
operations in the name of national security *only* if Congress is informed
in an appropriate fashion by the president.

Moreover, in 1974 Congress amended the Freedom of Information Act
(FOIA) to require all agencies to release all documents except those involving national security, active criminal investigations, trade secrets, and
invasion of privacy. This put more power behind the original FOIA and
it made it clear that the bureaucracy had to comply with FOIA requests.

"The Year of Intelligence": Executive-Congressional Relations

Gerald Ford was called upon to respond to the most sensitive questions
regarding the role of the secret president when stories of alleged Central
Intelligence Agency wrongdoing broke during the early days of his administration. After the *New York Times* printed stories in September
1974 that the CIA was involved between 1970 to 1973 in an effort to
"destabilize" the Allende regime in Chile, Ford was asked whether the
United States had the right to attempt to destabilize the constitutionally
elected government of another country, at a news conference. The president replied:

I'm not going to pass judgment on whether it's permitted or authorized
under international law. It's a recognized fact that historically as well as
presently, such actions are taken in the best interests of the countries
involved.[85]

In this incredible exchange a United States president articulated for
the first time the underlying principle involved in the rationale for covert
operations. While other presidents would have issued "No comment" or
denied United States involvement in Chile while the intervention was still
at the "plausible denialability" stage, the "open" president responded in

a fashion that was shockingly frank. Ford admitted that the United States
was involved in covert operations and would continue to be as long as the
president deemed it to be in the national interest. It is difficult to understand how the overthrowing of Chile's constitutionally elected government
was in Chile's best interest, but this is the point that the "open" president
was arguing.

With that candid exchange, Ford kicked off a two-year period of managing the intelligence community crisis. Ford became involved in a complex situation that he had not created. He was being asked to account
for past wrongdoings by the intelligence community under various presidents at the same time that he was being pressured to maintain the covert
capabilities of the secret presidency. Certainly Ford did not want to
embarrass former presidents who were not around to defend themselves
and he did not want to limit his own options or curtail his powers within
the secret presidency, but the post-watergate morality and the pressures
for disclosure were mounting against the intelligence community—the
president's operational arm of the secret presidency. When Seymour
Hersh in his December 22, 1974, *New York Times* article charged that
the CIA had conducted a "massive, illegal domestic intelligence operation
during the Nixon Administration against the antiwar movement and other
dissident groups in the United States,"[86] Ford was forced to produce
some form of administrative response.

Ford instructed William Colby, the CIA director, to report on all published charges against the agency. Colby submitted his report, which was
in effect the in-house investigation of the CIA, to Ford on December 24,
1974. Rather than release the sensitive Colby report to the nation, Ford
decided to establish a "blue-ribbon" presidential commission to "ascertain and evaluate" the facts relating to CIA activities. In this way Ford
could not be charged with inaction on the issue, nor could he be charged
with just letting the CIA investigate itself. As the various investigations
into CIA activities developed, it became clear that investigators would
discover only what Colby was prepared to reveal about the agency and
had been revealed to the president on the in-house report. By establishing his own presidential commission by executive order, the president
beat Congress in the rush to investigate the intelligence community.

Ford's early strategy in managing the intelligence community investigation centered on two key assumptions. The first assumption was that a
"blue-ribbon" Rockefeller commission investigation could hold off congressional action in studying the matter, at least until the presidential

commission had finished. Other presidents had used this tactic before, for example, Lyndon Johnson's Warren Commission on the assassination of John Kennedy preempted congressional attempts to investigate the incident in 1964. The second assumption was that the Rockefeller commission would emphasize the domestic surveillance wrongdoing by the CIA, which was in clear violation of the original CIA charter, instead of other covert operations. Both of these early assumptions failed. The Senate established its own Select Committee to Study Government Operations with Respect to Intelligence Activities on January 27, 1975, with Senator Frank Church as chairman, and the House of Representatives created its own Select Committee on Intelligence in February. Evidently the Congress felt that the scope and magnitude of the allegations against the intelligence community demanded more of an accounting than what members of Congress thought a Rockefeller commission could deliver.

Ironically, the second assumption failed because the most explosive and sensational leak, that former presidents may have engaged in assassination plots, diverted national attention back to the covert operations side of the intelligence community. This top-secret leak came when President Ford held an informal luncheon with the top executives of the *New York Times* on January 16, 1975, and indicated "off the record" that he had discovered CIA involvement in assassination conspiracies which would "blacken the reputation of every President after Harry Truman."[87] Ford insisted in the name of the national interest that this information should not be revealed, but this was the first time that any of the publishing and edition executives of the *Times* had ever heard the story. Although the editors realized the significance of the sensational story, they did not publish it because they had been taken in by Ford's "off the record" confidences. After one month the story had filtered down to CBS television reporter Daniel Schorr, who searched in vain to establish the basic facts—who plotted, when, against whom, with what result? Schorr realized that he could not establish the facts since the details were in the 1973 in-house CIA investigation, which was for the president's eyes only. On February 28, 1975, Schorr finally broke the imposed silence on the story because he realized that the fact that the president knew of assassination plots in and of itself was an important story. Schorr reported: "President Ford has reportedly warned associates that if current investigations go too far they could uncover several assassinations of foreign officials involving the CIA."[88] Thus, the presidential bombshell about CIA assassinations was dropped and the "open" secret presidency was the source of the leak. President Ford's intentions in the incident are still not entirely clear since presumably Ford would realize that a story of such importance could not remain secret once he exposed it. Without Ford's leak it is conceivable that the congressional investigations and the Rockefeller commission would not have been forced to investigate this area.

After the assassination stories broke, Ford broadened the mandate of the Rockefeller commission and directed it to investigate the current assassination allegations. The life of the Rockefeller commission was extended until June 6, 1975, to enable the commission to look into the assassinations, but in the final report, released on June 10, 1975, the assassination issue was cleverly dodged. The assassination material had been omitted because the Rockefeller commission claimed they did not have enough time to do that investigation correctly and they turned their materials over to the Senate Select Committee to allow it to make the final determination. In short, it was risky business for President Ford's Rockefeller commission to be investigating allegations against former presidents, and Ford presumably decided that the Democrat-controlled Church committee could have the political "hot potato" of investigating assassination plots. Ford did not want to be in the position of "Monday-morning quarterbacking" over past presidential actions, and he asked Congress to handle the material with the "utmost prudence" so as to refrain from *ex post facto* judgments about honorable men.[89]

Considerable political friction developed for the president when his press secretary Ron Nessen announced the delay of the Rockefeller report release because President Ford wanted to read it and then "make a decision on the release, on whether to release it."[90] Although Ford aides claimed that the change of plans for the release indicated nothing more sinister than a desire by the president to read the report before making it public, Nessen's press announcement still drove home the point that the president had the final decision as to whether or not to release the commission report. Even in an "open" presidency it was the president who would decide how open that presidency would be. After the report was finally released, even critics of the Central Intelligence Agency were fairly amazed at the "full and fair" investigation carried on by the Republican-dominated Rockefeller commission. Seymour Hersh's original CIA stories were more than validated, and Hersh's original source reportedly pronounced the report as at least 90 percent complete.[91]

Nevertheless, the Senate Select Committee and the House Select Committee proceeded to investigate the intelligence community. The Church committee garnered most of the headlines with its interim reports and their various leaks of closed testimony throughout 1975. The president was forthcoming with the Rockefeller materials and, for the most part, Ford provided a model of cooperation in his dealings with the Church committee. Indeed, in the intelligence community's view, Ford's Director of Central Intelligence, William Colby, appeared to be too cooperative with the Church committee; Colby testified at great length about past CIA wrongdoings. Yet Colby succeeded by a brilliant public relations effort in minimizing the CIA's past misdeeds in a turbulent world. As David Wise noted, "His strategy was to minimize; the domestic spying was not massive, the shellfish poison was only two teaspoons, and so on."[92] In November 1975, Colby was unceremoniously dismissed as CIA director by President Ford, presumably because the president had deemed Colby to have been too open in his testimonies before the various investigating committees during 1975. Colby had gone too far in his managed disclosures and had violated a central principle within the presidential secrecy system; that is, Colby unilaterally decided what could be released to investigators without constantly seeking Ford's approval. Too much openness within the "open" presidency evidently can be a cause for dismissal.

It was the House Select Committee, however, that provided the fundamental challenges to the presidential secrecy system. After various internal struggles (Chairman Lucien Nedzi's alleged lack of oversight into intelligence abuses that he had been aware of during previous Congresses, and Congressman Michael Harrington's leaks of CIA involvement in the "destabilization" of the Allende regime, for example) destroyed the first House Select Committee on Intelligence by the summer of 1975, the second House Select Committee on Intelligence was created on July 17, 1975, with Otis Pike (D-N.Y.) as chairman and without congressmen Nedzi and Harrington. Pike clearly articulated the position that the Congress has as much right as the president to control secrets, and he set out early to test that proposition.

While Ford had nothing to fear from the Church committee investigation, which was essentially a Rockefeller-type investigation with headlines about past abuses, the Pike committee was asking hard questions: budgetary inquiries, performance evaluations, queries into intelligence accuracy in specific crisis, and comparative surveys of covert actions over a ten-year period. The hard questions were directly related to the presidential secrecy system, and they challenged Ford's control of that system. These questions led to the serious confrontation between Pike and Ford over the presidential secrecy system.

The final report of the Pike committee, as leaked by Daniel Schorr and published by the *Village Voice,* outlines eight ways in which the executive branch attempted to obstruct the Pike investigations. The president and people speaking in the name of the president adopted the tactics of "Delay," "Cut-off," "Silenced Witnesses," "Flank Attack," "Deletions," "Privileges," "Ongoing Diplomacy," and "The Right Question"[93] to impede the committee's work.

By adopting the "Delay" tactic the president refused to release necessary documents on intelligence budgets or intelligence evaluations of specific crises, such as the 1973 war in the Mideast, the 1974 Cyprus coup, the 1974 Portuguese coup, or the 1968 Tet Offensive, until after repeated formal requests and eventual subpoenas. The documents that were turned over were often "sanitized," which in the committee's view is "merely a euphemism for blank sheets of paper with a few scattered words left in, often illegible, sometimes misleading, and usually inconclusive."[94] The "Cut-off" came on September 12, 1975, when the president deprived the Pike committee of access to all classified information that was in the committee's possession. The president was retaliating for the committee's "unilateral" decision to release four words, *"and greater communication security,"* over the objections of the CIA, the State Department, and the head of Defense Intelligence Agency.[95] With the president decrying the committee's action as irresponsible, negotiations over the further access to classified information began again. In order to gain access to information, the committee had to agree that all future disputes over release would be referred directly to the president, and having little choice the committee agreed.

The tactic of "Silenced Witnesses" refers to the silencing of State Department officer Thomas Boyatt by Secretary of State Henry Kissinger. Boyatt was ordered not to disclose options "considered by or recommended to more senior officers in the Department,"[96] and this was the information that the committee was specifically seeking. The committee voted to subpoena Boyatt's critique of the Cyprus coup in 1974, but Kissinger denied that he was asserting a new "secretarial privilege," but since the president had not invoked executive privilege in the name of national security over the Boyatt issue, Kissinger's actions could only be described as "secretarial privilege."[97] The "Flank Attack" tactic describes

Kissinger's successful attempts to equate the committee's requests to 1950s McCarthyism although the implication was totally false.[98] In response to other subpoenaed documents concerning covert action, the executive adopted the tactic of "Deletions," whereby documents would be released to the committee with substantial deletions in the name of national security. On a second subpoena to Henry Kissinger to provide information on the kinds of covert activity the State Department had recommended since 1965, the Ford administration invoked executive privilege. The committee voted a contempt citation for Kissinger but before the full House could vote on the citation, Kissinger agreed to provide the committee with an oral briefing on covert activity and the committee relented.[99]

The committee encountered two other tactics that defended the presidential secrecy system and could not be counteracted by the Pike committee. A third Kissinger subpoena for the intelligence handling of the strategic arms limitation agreement would not be complied with because it would jeopardize the sensitive ongoing negotiations with the Soviets. The final tactic that was used throughout the investigation was the "Right Question." When members of the executive branch testified, they were forthcoming only if they were asked the correct question by members of the committee. Questions had to be exact and carefully worded or officials engaged in evasive answers according to the committee report.[100]

In late December 1975, while the committee was still at work, the "secrecy backlash"[101] began with CIA station chief Richard Welch's assassination in Athens. If the president's constant articulation of national security needs and Kissinger's charges of McCarthyism had not successfully challenged the committee's push toward disclosure, they had made initial dents into the public arena's discussion of secrecy versus disclosure. With Welch's assassination, which the CIA succeeded in blaming on the evils of disclosure, the tide of public support for investigations into the intelligence community began to decline.[102] The Ford administration increased its public relations campaign against the Pike committee's leaks and the president warned some members of Congress that "if Congress hopes to get secret information, it will have to set penalties, up to expulsion from Congress, for leaks on covert operations."[103] The "secrecy backlash" concluded on January 29, 1976, when by a vote of 246 to 124 the House of Representatives voted not to release the Pike committee report "until the report has been certified by the President as not containing information which would adversely affect the intelligence activities of the

CIA in foreign countries, or the intelligence activities in foreign countries of any other department or agency of the federal government."[104] Of course, Ford was not going to certify the report as suitable for release, so for all practical purposes the House was voting two to one to keep one of its own committee's reports secret. The president had managed the intelligence controversy successfully and kept the presidential secrecy system intact. Were it not for Daniel Schorr and the editors and publishers of the *Village Voice,* the Pike committee report would not be in the public record today.

Congress did not take this confrontation over executive secrecy as the last word. The Select Committee on Intelligence became a permanent committee in May 1976. The committee has the power to release classified information over the objection of the president if certain procedures are followed. If eight or more members of the fifteen-person committee want to make some CIA information public, they can bring the matter to the whole Senate for a vote in secret session. If the Senate votes to release the classified material, it will be released. If any person releases the classified information prior to a vote by the Senate, that person would be subject to disciplinary action according to Senate Resolution 400, which created the permanent committee. If the violator is a senator, that person could be subject to censure or expulsion, and if the violator is a member of the staff, that person would be subject to a citation for contempt or termination of employment.[105]

In 1977 Congress continued the trend toward requiring more information from the executive by strengthening the 1972 Case Act. The Case Act requires the Secretary of State to inform Congress within sixty days of any international agreement, other than a treaty, to which the president has committed the United States. The 1977 legislation mandated that "any department or agency of the United States government that enters into any international agreement on behalf of the United States"[106] must transmit to the State Department the text of the agreement within twenty days after its signing.

Thus, in the 1970s Congress made a concerted effort to regain access to presidential information. The lines for the struggle have been clearly drawn. The outcome of the confrontation will decide the future of the presidential secrecy system. Given the historical basis for the system, the judicial support, and the constitutional precedents, the sluggishness of Congress as an innovative institution, the inability of Congress to insure against security leaks, and the consensus that there are some things which must be kept secret (though few can specify exactly what they are), the president's continuing ability to dominate in the area of secrecy in national security can still not be underestimated. Keeping these factors in mind, this project will try to develop a system of accountability for the presidential secrecy system in the final chapter. But first it must be explained why presidents engage in secret and deceptive operations, and it is to this task that the investigation now turns.

Notes

1. In the Constitution's only use of the word "secrecy," the Congress, in Article I, Section 5, "shall keep a journal of its Proceedings, and from time to time publish the same, excepting such Parts as may in their Judgment require *Secrecy.*"

2. John Jay, "Federalist 64," *The Federalist Papers* (New York: New American Library, Mentor Books, 1961), p. 392.

3. Harold Relyea, "The Evolution of Government Security Classification Policy: A Brief Overview (1777-1973)," in *Government Secrecy,* hearings, p. 844. Hearings before the Subcommittee on Intergovernmental Relations of the Committee on Governmental Operations, United States Senate, 93rd Congress, Second Session, Thursday, May 23, 1974. Hereafter, *Government Secrecy. See also* Arthur M. Cox, *The Myths of National Security* (Boston: Beacon Press, 1975), pp. 32-34.

4. George Washington, in *A Compilation of the Messages and Papers of the Presidents 1789-1897,* Vol. 1, ed. James Richardson (Washington, D.C.: U.S. Government Printing Office, 1896), p. 194.

5. Arthur Schlesinger, Jr., *The Imperial Presidency* (New York: Popular Library, 1974), p. 319.

6. Ibid., p. 320.

7. Ibid., p. 321.

8. Cox, *The Myths of National Security,* p. 35.

9. Ibid., p. 36.

10. David Wise, *The Politics of Lying* (New York: Vintage Books, 1973), p. 89. The Office of War information defined the terms as "Secret information is information the disclosure of which might endanger national security, or cause serious injury to the Nation or any governmental activity thereof; Confidential information is information the disclosure of which although not endangering the national security would impair the effectiveness of government activity in the prosecution of the war; Restricted information is information the disclosure of which should be limited." In Cox, *The Myths of National Security,* p. 37.

11. The National Security Act of 1947, Public Law 80-253, Section 3, July 26, 1947.

12. Wise, *The Politics of Lying,* p. 90.

13. Cox, *The Myths of National Security,* p. 48.

14. Wise, *The Politics of Lying,* p. 91. Eisenhower's Executive Order 10501, Safeguarding Official Information, November 9, 1953 (24 F.R. 3779); Eisenhower

Executive Order 10816 (24 F.R. 3777); Eisenhower Executive Memorandum to Executive Order 10501 (24 F.R. 3777); Eisenhower Executive Order 10901 (26 F.R. 217); Eisenhower Executive Memorandum to Executive Order 10501 (25 F.R. 2073); Kennedy Executive Order 10964 (26 F.R. 8932); and Nixon Executive Order 11652, Classification and Declassification of National Security Information and Material, March 8, 1972.

15. Relyea, *Government Secrecy*, hearings, p. 857.

16. Robert A. Dahl, *Polyarchy* (New Haven, Conn.: Yale University Press, 1971), p. 3.

17. Thomas I. Emerson, "The Danger of State Secrecy," in *Watergate and the American Political Process*, ed. Ronald Pynn (New York: Praeger Publishers, 1975), p. 62; *and see* Robert A. Dahl, *A Preface to Democratic Theory* (Chicago: University of Chicago Press, 1956), p. 84; and James Wiggins, *Freedom or Secrecy* (New York: Oxford University Press, 1956), pp. 3-4.

18. Dahl, *Preface*, p. 84.

19. Some observers have specified categories of information which they argue that a democratic political system can legitimately keep secret. For example, see the nine exemptions of the Freedom of Information Act and Emerson's exemption to a publicity principle (advice privilege, national security, some aspects of foreign relations, bargaining positions, and some personal records) in his "The Danger of State Secrecy," pp. 66-68. Thomas Franck and Edward Weisband provide a taxonomy of principle foreign affairs secrets that includes eleven categories of secrets that in their view can be justified in carrying out foreign affairs. See their *Secrecy and Foreign Policy* (London: Oxford University Press, 1974), pp. 410-11.

20. Thomas Cronin, "Everybody Believes in Democracy Until He Gets to the White House," from symposium in *Law and Contemporary Problems*, 35, no. 3 (Summer 1970) published by Duke University School of Law; *and see* Cronin, *The State of the Presidency* (Boston: Little, Brown, 1975).

21. Woodrow Wilson, *The New Freedom* (Englewood Cliffs, N.J.: Prentice-Hall, 1961), p. 76.

22. Harold Chase and Allen Lerman, eds., *Kennedy and the Press* (New York: Thomas Y. Crowell, 1965), p. 8.

23. Graham Allison and Morton Halperin, "Bureaucratic Politics: A Paradigm and Some Policy Implications," *World Politics*, 24 (Spring 1972 supplement): 40-79.

24. Wiggins, *Freedom or Secrecy*, p. x.

25. Emerson, "The Danger of State Secrecy," p. 60.

26. Edward Teller, quoted in Schlesinger, The Imperial Presidency, p. 345.

27. Schlesinger, ibid., Chap. 10. *See also* Halperin testimony on secrecy as a disease when he stated, "I think this is a disease that spreads," in *Government Secrecy*, hearings, p. 69.

28. Francis Rourke, *Secrecy and Publicity* (Baltimore, Md.: Johns Hopkins University Press, 1961), p. 225.

29. For listings of possible societal benefits from secrecy, see Franck and Weisband, eds., *Secrecy and Foreign Policy*, pp. 6 and 410-11; Schlesinger, *The Imperial Presidency*, pp. 325-26; McGeorge Bundy, *Government Secrecy*, hearings, p. 53. Franck and Weisband are the only ones who specifically cite the sixth enumerated benefit of secrecy.

30. Franck and Weisband, *Secrecy and Foreign Policy*, pp. 8-9.

31. Emerson, "The Danger of State Secrecy," pp. 59-60.

32. See Martin McGuire, *Secrecy and the Arms Race* (Cambridge, Mass.: Harvard University Press, 1965), p. 214; Rourke, *Secrecy and Publicity*, p. 223; and Wiggins, *Freedom or Secrecy*, p. 113.

33. Emerson, "The Danger of State Secrecy," p. 60; Wiggins, *Freedom or Secrecy*, p. 113; and Schlesinger, *The Imperial Presidency*, p. 342.

34. Schlesinger, *The Imperial Presidency*, p. 342.

35. Cox, *The Myths of National Security*, p. 84; Wiggins, *Freedom or Secrecy*, p. 113; *and see* Edward Teller, *Government Secrecy*, hearings, p. 253, and in *Congressional Record*, May 23, 1972, E5675-E5678.

36. Schlesinger, *The Imperial Presidency*, p. 342.

37. Wise, *The Politics of Lying*; Daniel Ellsberg, *Papers On the War* (New York: Pocket Books, 1972), and Schlesinger, *The Imperial Presidency*, pp. 340-41.

38. Franck and Weisband, *Secrecy and Foreign Policy*, p. 9.

39. Cox, *The Myths of National Security*, p. 83.

40. Franck and Weisband, *Secrecy and Foreign Policy*, pp. 8-9.

41. Emerson noted that secrecy was politically unwise in his "The Danger of State Secrecy," p. 60. For decision-making costs of secrecy, see Morton Halperin and Jeremy Stone, "Secrecy and Covert Intelligence Collection and Operations," in *None of Your Business*, ed. Norman Dorsen and Stephen Gillers (New York: Penguin, 1975), pp. 110-11; *and see* Halperin *Government Secrecy*, hearings, pp. 54-55.

42. John Locke, *The Second Treatise of Civil Government* (New York: Hafner, 1947).

43. Locke, quoted in Edward S. Corwin, *The President: Office and Powers* (New York: New York University Press, 1957), p. 8.

44. Thomas Jefferson, cited in Stephan Boyan, "The Prerogative, The Constitution and the Presidency after Watergate," paper delivered at the 1976 Annual Meeting of the American Political Science Association, Chicago, September 1976, pp. 15-16.

45. Abraham Lincoln, cited in Corwin, *The President: Office and Powers*, p. 230. Clinton Rossiter noted that Theodore Roosevelt's "Stewardships Theory" assumed a "mighty reservoir of crisis authority," in Rossiter, *Constitutional Dictatorship* (Princeton, N.J.: Princeton University Press, 1948), p. 219; and, of course, Wilson and Franklin Roosevelt both assumed broad executive prerogative in World War I and II.

46. Schlesinger, *The Imperial Presidency*, p. 159. The executive privilege literature is broad. See, for example, Norman Dorsen and John Shattuck, "Executive Privilege: The President Won't Tell," in Dorsen and Gillers, eds., *None of Your Business*, pp. 27-60; Charles Mathias, "Executive Privilege and Congressional Responsibility in Foreign Affairs," in Franck and Weisband, eds., *Secrecy and Foreign Policy*, pp. 69-86; Raoul Berger, *Executive Privilege: A Constitutional Myth* (Cambridge, Mass.: Harvard University Press, 1974); and Relyea, *Government Secrecy*, hearings, p. 846.

47. Wise, *The Politics of Lying*, p. 56.

48. Daniel Ellsberg, "The Ellsberg Perspective," in Dorsen and Gillers, eds., *None of Your Business*, p. 284. *See also* Schlesinger, *The Imperial Presidency*, p. 340, on the "right to lie," and Chap. 7.

49. *Totten* v. *United States* (1876) 92 U.S. 105.

50. *In re Grove* (1910) 180 F. 62.

51. *Firth Sterling Steele Co.* v. *Bethlehem Co.* (1912) 199 F. 353.

52. *Pollen* v. *Ford Instrument Co.* (1939) 26 F. Supp. 583.

53. *United States* v. *Haugen* (1944) 58 F. Supp. 436 at 438.

54. During the period 1947 to 1953 Truman's loyalty program investigated 4,750,000 employees and found 26,000 of these to require further action. Then 16,000 of these were cleared, and 7,000 withdrew or resigned while under investigation. Only 560 people were removed or denied employment on loyalty charges. See Alfred Kelly and Winfred Harbison, *The American Constitution: Its Origins and Development* (New York: W. W. Norton, 1970), pp. 894-95.

55. Presumably this could be viewed as an early forerunner to Nixon's "enemies list." In *Joint Anti-Fascist Committee* v. *McGrath* (1951) the Court allowed the group to remove their name from the Attorney General's list since Truman's loyalty program had not authorized any subversive lists. Justices Black, Douglas, Frankfurter, and Jackson all attacked the constitutionality of such lists.

56. Truman Executive Order 10241, April 1951.

57. Eisenhower Executive Order 10450, April 1953; see Kelly and Harbison, *The American Constitution*, p. 895.

58. *Bailey* v. *Richardson* 341 U.S. 918 (1951).

59. *Peters* v. *Hobby* 349 U.S. 331 (1955); *Cole* v. *Young* 351 U.S. 536 (1956); and *Service* v. *Dulles* 354 U.S. 363 (1957).

60. *Reynolds* v. *U.S.* (1950) 10 F.R.D. 468; and *Reynolds* v. *U.S.* (1951) 192 F. 2d 987.

61. *United States* v. *Reynolds* (1953) 345 U.S. 1.

62. *Lamont* v. *Postmaster General* (1965) 381 U.S. 301.

63. *Heine* v. *Raus* (1966) 399 F. 2d 785.

64. *Environmental Protection Agency* v. *Patsy Mink* (1973) 410 U.S. 73; *U.S.* v. *Marchetti* (1972) 466 F 2d 1309; *New York Times* v. *United States* (1971) 403 U.S. 713; and *U.S.* v. *Nixon* (1974) 42 U.S. L.W. 5237.

65. Patsy Mink, "The Mink Case: Restoring the Freedom of Information Act," *Pepperdine Law Review*, 2, August 1974, 15; *and see* Mink, "The Cannikin Papers: A Case Study in Freedom of Information," in Franck and Weisband, *Secrecy and Foreign Policy*, pp. 114-31.

66. *Mink* v. *Environmental Protection Agency* (1972) 464 F 2d 792.

67. *Environmental Protection Agency* v. *Mink* (1973) 410 U.S. 73; *and see* Mink, "The Mink Case," *Pepperdine Law Review*, p. 10.

68. Stanley Futterman, "What Is the Problem with Classification," in Dorsen and Gillers, eds., *None of Your Business*, pp. 100-1. *See also Epstein* v. *Resor* (1970) 421 F 2d 930 at 931 where Judge Merrill ruled "The function of determining whether secrecy is required in the national interest is expressly assigned to the Executive . . . it is not the sort of question that courts are designed to deal with."

Justice Douglas's dissent in *Environmental Protection Agency* v. *Mink* (1973) 410 U.S. at 145 was particularly biting. Douglas said, "The Executive Branch now has carte blanche to insulate information from public scrutiny whether or not that information bears any discernible relation to the interests sought to be protected by subsection (b) (1) . . . the Executive will hold complete sway and by ipse dixit make even the time of day 'Top SECRET.' "

69. *United States* v. *Marchetti* (1972) 466 F 2d 1309 at 1311.

70. *Knopf* v. *Colby* (1975) 509 F 2d 1362. Haynsworth failed to note that the Freedom of Information Act had been amended by Congress to encourage judicial examination of classified evidence, and Haynsworth evidently decided to ignore *U.S.* v. *Welch* (1953) 345 U.S. at 10, that held "judicial control over the evidence in a case cannot be abdicated to the caprice of executive officials."

71. *New York Times* v. *United States* (1971) 403 U.S. 713. The *Pentagon Papers* or *United States-Vietnam Relations 1945-1967* were compiled by many top scholars, including Morton Halperin, Leslie Gelb, and Daniel Ellsberg.

72. *New York Times* v. *United States* at 714.

73. Leonard Boudin, "The Ellsberg Case: Citizen Disclosure," in Franck and Weisband, eds., *Secrecy and Foreign Policy*, p. 292.

74. Ibid., pp. 303-7.

75. Schlesinger, *The Imperial Presidency*, p. 332.

76. Boudin, "The Ellsberg Case," p. 311.

77. *United States* v. *Nixon* (1974) 42 U.S.L.W. 5237.

78. Theodore Sorensen, *Watchmen in the Night* (Cambridge, Mass.: The MIT Press, 1976), pp. 120-21.

79. *United States* v. *Nixon* (1974) published in Pynn, ed., *Watergate and the American Political Process*, p. 243.

80. Joel D. Aberbach, "The Development of Oversight in the United States Congress: Concepts and Analysis," paper delivered at the 1977 Annual Meeting of the American Political Science Association, Washington, D.C., Sept. 1-4, 1977, pp. 4-8. *See also* Robert Hammel, "Congressional Responses to Executive Privilege," 1977 American Political Science Association Annual Meeting, Washington, D.C., Sept. 1-4, 1977; Seymour Scher, "Conditions for Legislative Control," *Journal of Politics*, August 1963, pp. 526-51; Morris Ogul *Congress Oversees the Bureaucracy* (Pittsburgh: University of Pittsburgh Press, 1976); John F. Bibby, "Oversight—Congress' Neglected Function: Will Watergate Make a Difference," paper delivered at the 1974 Meeting of the Western Political Science Association; *and see* Joseph Harris, *Congressional Control of Administration* (Washington, D.C.: The Brookings Institution, 1964).

81. Franck and Weisband, eds., *Secrecy and Foreign Policy*, p. 427.

82. William Mullen, *Presidential Power and Politics* (New York: St. Martin's Press, 1976), pp. 101-5.

83. *Government Secrecy*, hearings.

84. 22 USC 2422, Sec. 662. Limitation on Intelligence Activities.

85. Transcript of News Conference, *New York Times*, Sept. 17, 1974, p. 22.

86. Seymour Hersh, "Huge CIA Operation Reported in U.S. Against Anti-War Forces, and Other Dissidents in Nixon Years," *New York Times,* December 22, 1974.

87. See David Wise, *The American Police State* (New York: Random House, 1976), p. 211, and Daniel Schorr, "My 17 Months on the CIA Watch: A Backstage Journal," *Rolling Stone,* April 8, 1976, p. 35. Among those attending the historic luncheon were Clifton Daniel, James Reston, Arthur Sulzberger, Abe Rosenthal, Max Frankel, John Oakes, Tom Wicker, Ron Nessen, Alan Greenspan, Robert Goldwin, and the president.

88. Schorr, "CIA Watch," p. 35. For his efforts in breaking the CIA assassination story, Schorr was labeled by former CIA Director Richard Helms as "Killer Schorr."

89. "The Cloak Comes Off," *Newsweek,* June 23, 1975, p. 18.

90. "Some Ford Aides Report Friction over CIA Study," AP Wire Story, Louisville, *The Courier-Journal,* June 11, 1975, p. 2.

91. "The Cloak Comes Off," *Newsweek,* p. 18.

92. Wise, *The American Police State,* p. 256. Colby's masterful public relations job drew protest from Nelson Rockefeller who thought Colby gave "too much" information to his committee, and Kissinger felt Colby had gone too far. See Schorr, "CIA Watch," p. 38.

93. "The Select Committee's Oversight Experience," *The Village Voice,* February 23, 1976, pp. 60-68.

94. Ibid., p. 61.

95. Ibid., p. 61, *and see* Schorr, "CIA Watch," p. 85. The text of the paragraph in which the four words appear reads: "Egypt—The [deleted] large scale mobilization exercise may be an effort to soothe internal problems as much as to improve military capabilities. Mobilization of some personnel, increased readiness of isolated units, *and greater communication security* are all assessed as part of the exercise routine. . . . there are still no military or political indicators of Egyptian intentions or preparations to resume hostilities with Israel."

96. "Oversight," *The Village Voice,* p. 62. *See also* Leslie Gelb and Anthony Lake, "A Tale of Two Compromises," *Foreign Policy* (Spring 1976) pp. 224-37.

97. "Oversight," *The Village Voice,* p. 63. Indeed, Kissinger's position on the secretary's duty to keep secrets is not far removed from the medieval Latin definition of the word *secretarius,* from which secretary is derived. Secretarius means "one entrusted with secrets."

98. *See* the *Washington Post* editorial of October 6, 1975, called "Mr. Pike's Committee," in which the text claims that "the analogy with McCarthyism evoked by the State Department is a relevant one"; *and see* The *New York Times* editorial labeled "Neo-McCarthyism?" which claimed "the Intelligence Committee's insistence that it has the right to reach into the interior of the State Department to subpoena the dissenting memoranda of junior and middle-rank officials—and to summon them to testify on policy issues—is clearly contrary to the national interest. . . ."

99. Gelb and Lake, "A Tale of Two Compromises."

100. *The Village Voice,* "Oversight," p. 66.

101. This is Daniel Schorr's concept in "CIA Watch," *Rolling Stone.*

102. Morton Halperin, "A Welch Affair Footnote: CIA Didn't Tell Whole Truth," Louisville, *The Courier-Journal,* January 23, 1977, p. d-3.

103. Schorr, "CIA Watch," p. 95.

104. Language voted upon as Amendment to House Resolution 982, January 29, 1976.

105. Senate Resolution 400, *Congressional Research Service* Update, 1/12/77 IB75037.

106. P.L. 95-45, 91 Stat. 224, sec. 5.

3. SETTING THE NEW PARAMETERS FOR THE SECRET PRESIDENCY: JOHN F. KENNEDY AND COVERT LEADERSHIP

John F. Kennedy's presidency remains a source of inspiration for his admirers. Kennedy possessed the qualities that are needed to build a strong presidential myth, and of course his untimely assassination secured a position for Kennedy in the memories of most Americans. Most presidential scholars of the 1960s tended to idealize Kennedy and his administration. Unfortunately for the Kennedy myth, however, new evidence and new interpretations of Kennedy's leadership surfaced in the 1970s that challenged the older images. If Theodore Sorensen, Arthur Schlesinger, Jr., Roger Hilsman, and William Manchester helped build the myth in the 1960s, then Richard Walton, Victor Navasky, Henry Fairlie, and Bruce Miroff supplied the critiques by establishing a revisionist school in the 1970s.[1] As Lewis Paper has noted, "Virtually all of the books about Kennedy's presidency can be categorized in one of two classes: those written by the 'mythologists' and those written by the 'revisionists.' "[2] My approach will attempt to avoid both the "mythologist" and the "revisionist" labels.

Kennedy and the "Free Flow of Information"

Kennedy placed high value on the concept of the open presidency and felt that the free flow of information in a democracy was absolutely essential. The free flow of information was crucial for an informed citizenry according to Kennedy's traditional notion of democracy, but, more important, a free press and active news media provided Kennedy with opportunities to promote his policies and to gauge reactions by the media

to his programs. In practice, however, Kennedy offered two exceptions
to the ideal of free flow of information: managed news and national
security.

Not surprisingly, like most presidents Kennedy wished to publicize
his accomplishments and underplay his failures. To achieve these goals,
Kennedy adopted strategies that some observers labeled as attempts to
manage the news. Kennedy had developed close relationships with certain
members of the press during his senatorial days and his presidential campaign. As president, Kennedy maintained these close personal friendships
and worked the press in virtuoso performances. Kennedy's performances
at live press conferences are legendary. Indeed, his behavior set the
standard by which following presidents would be judged. If a president
performed well during the live news conference, and if he appeared "cool"
under pressure while maintaining a sense of humor, then his performance
more than likely would be labeled "Kennedyesque." As James Reston
observed about Kennedy, "He either overwhelmed you with decimal
points or disarmed you with a smile and a wisecrack."[3]

Kennedy became, in David Halberstam's words, the "first television
President."[4] Kennedy was well suited for the medium. He institutionalized
presidential uses of television as he established the basic precedents. When
Kennedy traveled throughout the nation or around the globe, television
picked up the drama. When Kennedy wanted to stress his family image,
he talked CBS television into televising a tour of the White House with
Jacqueline Kennedy.[5] He granted special televised interviews with the
major network correspondents. He demanded network time during periods
of crisis to educate and comfort the public. He allowed a new genre of
televised programs to develop, which might be labeled "a day in the life
of President Kennedy." Finally, Kennedy was the first president to conduct live television news conferences.

Specifically, the charges against Kennedy for news management concern
Kennedy's "overly" sensitive reactions to adverse criticisms in the media
and his desire for favorable publicity for his presidency. He timed news
releases and took great precautions in scheduling live presidential news
events to get maximum exposure. He often called friends in the press
corps to congratulate them on stories favoring the administration and
criticized those members of the media who produced unfavorable stories.
These qualities are *hardly* the stuff of a presidential "manager of news,"
but rather they represent the normal range of president-press relations.

At worst, Kennedy might be chastised for planting some questions at his "spontaneous" news conferences, but other presidents have used this tactic as well. As Sorensen noted, Kennedy was "amused by a poll of newsmen declaring (1) that his administration worked harder than all others at 'managing the news' and (2) offered more accessibility than all others to news sources."[6]

In short, Kennedy should not be singled out as a presidential "manager of news" because all presidents in some way control information about their activities. Timing of press releases has always been a political consideration that the modern president must deal with. The president attempts to control information within his domain that helps his political programs, and one crucial form of information control is "publicity."[7] By publicity, I mean the opposite of complete secrecy. The president selectively releases some information at certain times and selectively *chooses* to withhold certain information or not to *publicize* a matter. All presidents are likely to have a broad array of presidential information at their disposal and *all presidents* engage in information control of one form or another.

The second exception to an ideal free flow of information in a democracy, the "national security" exception, raises more crucial questions about the control of information. Kennedy, like other presidents, strongly believed that the requirements of a free press had to be balanced with the need for national security. After the Bay of Pigs defeat Kennedy addressed the American Society of Newspaper Editors to give them his views on the free press-national security dilemma. He maintained that government should not cover up its mistakes or suppress dissent. The government had an obligation, according to Kennedy, "to provide you [the press] with the fullest possible information outside the narrowest limits of national security," and not "withhold from the press and the public facts they deserve to know."[8] Kennedy then changed the focus of his speech and criticized the press for its judgment in publishing pre-Bay of Pigs stories about the operation. Kennedy pleaded:

I do ask every publisher, every editor, and every newsman in the nation to re-examine his own standards, and to recognize the nature of our country's peril. . . . It requires a change in outlook, a change in tactics, a change in missions—by the government, by the people, by every businessman or labor leader, and by every newspaper. For we are opposed the world around by a *monolithic* and *ruthless conspiracy* that relies primarily on *covert means* for expanding its sphere of influence.[9] (emphasis added)

Kennedy noted that the enemies of the United States could acquire information through American newspapers that they "would otherwise hire agents to acquire through theft, bribery or espionage."[10] He called on the news editors to take voluntary steps to reexamine their national security judgments with respect to publications during the Cold War.

During the Cuban missile crisis and in its aftermath, the Kennedy administration had to practice control of information for national security reasons that conflicted with the needs of a free press and an informed public. On October 24, 1962, the White House released a list of twelve categories of information vital to national security that the Department of Defense would cease to release. The memorandum requested restraint from the media in publishing such information that might be gained through sources other than the Department of Defense.[11] Arthur Sylvester, assistant secretary for public affairs, articulated two "rights" that the president has during times of genuine national security crises which had been heretofore implicit assumptions. According to Sylvester, the president had the duty to "manage the news" during national security crises such as the Cuban missile crisis, and, moreover, the government had "the right, if necessary, to lie to save itself from nuclear war."[12] This statement should not have caused the uproar that it did since it contained no basic change in presidential assumptions about national security. Indeed, Kennedy had lied (that is, issued statements intended to deceive targeted individuals or groups) on at least two occasions before Sylvester's pronouncement. About one week before the Bay of Pigs invasion, the following exchange occurred at a Kennedy press conference:

Question: Mr. President, has a decision been reached on how far this country will go in helping anti-Castro uprising or invasion of Cuba?

President
Kennedy: First, I want to say that there will not be, *under any conditions,* an intervention in Cuba by the United States Armed Forces. This government will do everything it possibly can, I think it can meet its responsibilities, to make sure that

there are no Americans involved in any actions inside Cuba.
. . . The basic issue in Cuba is not one between the United
States and Cuba. *It is between the Cubans themselves. I intend to see that we adhere to that principle* and as I understand it this administration's attitude is so understood by
anti-Castro exiles from Cuba in this country.[13] (emphasis
added)

Kennedy also lied when he abruptly cancelled a speech in Chicago due
to a "cold" in order to quickly fly back to Washington to manage the
Cuban missile crisis. The press remembered these incidents and labeled
Kennedy's behavior as within the acceptable boundaries of presidential
cover stories for national security reasons. Kennedy was perceived by
many to have "manufactured cover stories" and not really to have lied
in any sense. Thus, Sylvester's right to lie statement appeared controversial
because it made implicit assumptions explicit.

In summary, Kennedy's rhetoric about the needs for a free press and
an informed citizenry to have a free flow of information from the president was commendable, if one values open discussion within a democratic
polity. Also, his performance in supplying the media and the public with
information about his presidency was adequate when considered along
with the requirements for national security. But there is another category
of information that Kennedy did not reveal to Congress, the media, or the
public because there were no pressures for its disclosure. This information
concerns the details of Kennedy's covert actions in foreign policy, which
apparently went undetected. Obviously there were no pressures for disclosure or publicity on these presidential actions because only a select
few within the Kennedy administration even knew of the existence of
these *secret* programs of covert intervention. It is to two such programs
that the investigation now turns.

The Programs to Undermine Systematically the Castro Regime

Between 1961 and November 1963 Kennedy entered into two specific
covert programs designed to systematically undermine Fidel Castro's regime
in Cuba: the Bay of Pigs operation and Operation Mongoose. Moreover,
Kennedy *may* have been involved in the Central Intelligence Agency's related assassination plots against Castro during that same period. Thus, to

say that Kennedy was a "Cold Warrior" is to understate the case. It would imply that Kennedy used Cold War rhetoric in his speeches and believed in monolithic Communism and the "domino theory," as most other politicians of his day. But what set Kennedy apart from other rhetorical Cold Warriors was the fact that he believed in *action*. More important, Kennedy was in a position to take covert action if he believed it was necessary.

Covert action dramatically increased during the Kennedy administration. Whereas in the late 1940s and during the 1950s under Truman and Eisenhower, covert action was used more as a last resort, Kennedy used covert action as a routine part of secret activities in American foreign policy. The Church committee made a rough determination of covert program approval by the 40 Committee (or its predecessors) from 1949 to 1967.[14] Their assumption was that if the 40 Committee had approved of a covert operation, then the president had approved or had knowledge of the covert plan. Eighty-one covert operations gained high-level approval during the Truman administration, and 170 during the Eisenhower administration. During the Kennedy administration 163 operations gained the 40-Committeelike approval, and the Johnson administration (through 1967) had approved 142 operations through the 40-Committeelike approval system. However, if one breaks down the Church committee's statistics according to the length of administration, a more accurate picture of the frequency of covert program adoption emerges. (see Table 1). The point of Table 1 is the dramatic increase in the number of covert programs adopted by a 40-Committeelike system during the Kennedy administration between 1961 and 1963. The Church committee's estimates do not include the number of covert programs that each president entered into without the knowledge or written approval of the 40 Committee.[15]

TABLE 1: Covert Operations Approval 1949-1967 as Tabulated by the Church Committee

Administration	Length (Yrs.)	No. of Programs	Average/Yr.
Truman	4	81	20.2
Eisenhower	8	170	21.2
Kennedy	2.8	163	58.2
Johnson	3.3	142	43.0

Source: Computed from data in the Final Report of the Select Committee to Study Governmental Operations with Respect to Intelligence Activities, United States Senate (the Church committee), April 26, 1976, Book I, p. 56.

Covert action can be defined as "clandestine activity designed to influence foreign governments, events, organizations or persons in support of U.S. Government [i.e., the president] is not apparent."[16] Covert action may take the following forms:

1. political advice and counsel;
2. subsidies to an individual;
3. financial support and "technical assistance" to political parties;
4. support of private organizations, including labor unions, business firms, cooperatives;
5. covert propaganda;
6. "private" training of individuals and exchange of persons;
7. economic operations;
8. "paramilitary" operations designed to overthrow or to support a regime;
9. covert political actions, including coups and assassinations designed to overthrow or support a regime.[17]

In the early 1960s the Kennedy administration ran the gamut of these responses in an effort to undermine the Castro regime.

The program to systematically sabotage the Castro regime had its genesis during the Eisenhower administration. Ironically it was Vice-President Richard Nixon who first suggested that the United States train Cuban exiles for an attack on Cuba.[18] In March of 1960 at a National Security Council (NSC) meeting, President Eisenhower directed the Central Intelligence Agency to follow through on Nixon's suggestion and to organize Cuban exiles in the United States into a strong anti-Castro army. At the NSC meeting of March 10, 1960, the assassinations of Castro, his brother Raul, and Che Guevara were discussed as possible responses to the "Cuban problem."[19] Eisenhower abandoned the guerrilla operations and the assassination talk by November 1960, but Allen Dulles and the Joint Chiefs of Staff repeatedly urged paramilitary operations against Castro. Two days after his inauguration, Kennedy was delivered a detailed proposal for the invasion of Cuba from Dulles and General Lyman Lemnitzer, chairman of the Joint Chiefs of Staff. In April 1961, after many deliberations over the CIA plan, the key Kennedy advisors gave their approval for the invasion plan.[20] On April 17, 1961, the "Bay of Pigs" invasion began and turned into a perfect foreign policy fiasco.

The accounts of what went wrong with the Bay of Pigs invasion are voluminous.[21] Janis has summarized the false assumptions that Kennedy made during the decision-making process, as revealed by Sorensen and Schlesinger's accounts. Kennedy and his advisors *wrongly assumed:*

1. No one will know that the United States was responsible for the invasion of Cuba. Most people will believe the CIA cover story, and skeptics can easily be refuted.
2. The Cuban air force is so inefficient that it can be knocked out completely just before the invasion begins.
3. The fourteen hundred men in the brigade of Cuban exiles have high morale and are willing to carry out invasion without support from United States ground troops.
4. Castro's army is so weak that the small Cuban brigade will be able to establish a well-protected beachhead.
5. The invasion by the exile brigade will touch off sabotage by the Cuban underground and armed uprisings behind the lines that will effectively support the invaders and probably lead to the toppling of the Castro regime.
6. If the Cuban brigade does not succeed in its prime military objective, the men can retreat to the Escambray Mountains and reinforce the guerrilla units holding out against the Castro regime.[22]

The reasons for the failure in the Bay of Pigs invasion are almost as numerous as the false assumptions the operation was based on. Kennedy loyalists argued that the CIA used a strong political appeal to trap Kennedy into approving the plan to demonstrate that he was as willing as Eisenhower and Nixon to regain Cuba. Kennedy found himself in the position of a "new administration bottled in an old bureaucracy."[23] Kennedy did not want to appear soft on communism and this crucial option arrived on his desk before he had time to develop his national security decision-making process adequately, the Kennedy loyalists argued. Schlesinger argued that the secrecy of the operation caused the failure, because "The same men both planned the operation and judged its chances of success. . . . The 'need-to-know' standard, i.e., that no one should be told about the project unless it becomes operationally necessary—thus had the idiotic effect of excluding much of the expertise of government at a time when every alert newspaper man knew something was afoot."[24] Finally, Janis argued that the Bay of Pigs failure was a perfect example of "groupthink."[25]

For whatever reasons one attributes the Bay of Pigs failure to, most accounts stress the tremendous growth and development that Kennedy supposedly made in his managerial style to handle foreign policy decision making. Sorensen noted that "The lessons of the Bay of Pigs altered Kennedy's entire approach."[26] Stephen Hess stressed Kennedy's attempts to regain "control of the intelligence community by reactivating the Foreign Intelligence Advisory Board to watch CIA, and by charging his brother, Robert Kennedy and close advisor Sorensen with new responsibilities overlooking CIA."[27] Richard Johnson has shown how Kennedy's Bay of Pigs failure helped him to develop his "collegial" approach to managing the White House in that Kennedy sought out advisors of diverse opinions and encouraged them to speak out on issues.[28] Even Janis succumbed to the notion that somehow after the Bay of Pigs failure, Kennedy became a new crises manager with innovative approaches to foreign policy crisis decision making. Janis outlined and maintained that "Many of Kennedy's innovations avoided the usual drawbacks of traditional bureaucratic practices such as maintaining such strict secrecy that the flow of information to the decision-making body is restricted." Moreover, Janis held that the "President's procedural changes also set up the conditions that promote independent thinking by curtailing the adverse influence of groupthink tendencies."[29] The pragmatic Kennedy was portrayed as the president who learned from experience and made the necessary changes in his bureaucratic environment to gain control of an intelligence community that was presumably out of control.

However, Kennedy did not behave like a president who recognized that the failure of a covert operation was his responsibility. Although Kennedy accepted "full responsibility" for the failure, (much as Nixon who took the responsibility but not the blame for Watergate), it was never really clear whether Kennedy learned anything from the failure. Within eight months of the Bay of Pigs, Kennedy approved of another covert operation of sabotage and economic warfare against Castro called Operation Mongoose, which will be discussed shortly. Immediately after the Bay of Pigs, Kennedy wanted to "shatter the CIA into bits,"[30] and felt that something "had to be done about the State Department."[31] Even though publicly Kennedy maintained he was responsible, the Joint Chiefs of Staff received a large measure of the blame from within the Kennedy administration.

Kennedy began to make personnel changes designed to correct the "problems" that the Bay of Pigs failure highlighted. In November 1961

John McCone replaced Allen Dulles as director of Central Intelligence
and later Richard Helms replaced Richard Bissell as deputy director of
plans (the Clandestine Services) in CIA. Maxwell Taylor, Kennedy's
special military advisor, was ordered by Kennedy to conduct a complete
investigation of the United States intelligence community. Soon after his
report, General Taylor became the chairman of the Joint Chiefs of Staff,
replacing Bay of Pigs proponent General Lemnitzer. James Killian, chairman of the President's Advisory Board, used his committee to investigate
the CIA and the intelligence community as Kennedy requested. Arthur
Schlesinger, Jr., on the White House staff, conducted an investigation into
the fiasco and made new broad proposals for an intelligence reorganization
that never came to pass.

Perhaps the most revealing indicator of Kennedy's inability to accept
responsibility for the Bay of Pigs can be seen in his attack on the press.
Kennedy lashed out against the press for their coverage of pre-Bay of
Pigs activity, which he felt could harm the national security in the future
if the press continued the practice of writing about covert operations
before they occurred. In short, Kennedy never acted as though he realized
the failure of the Bay of Pigs was his fault.

During the investigations within the White House, no one ever challenged
the basic premise of the whole operation. Only Arthur Schlesinger, Jr.,
argued that "secret activities are permissible so long as they do not affect
the principles and practices of our society, and that they cease to be permissible when their effect is to corrupt these principles and practices."[32]
As Marchetti and Marks have noted, Taylor's report was basically a criticism of "tactics" used in the Bay of Pigs operation and not an indictment
of the "goals" of the operation.[33] Miroff writes perceptively on this point:

At first, however, we must dispose of the argument that Kennedy and his
associates learned their lesson with the Bay of Pigs. It is true that they
learned something useful—not to trust so completely in the CIA and its
vaunted enterprise. *But this hardly constituted an admission that unrelent-
ing hostility to the Cuban Revolution and an attempt to undo it by force
were wrong in themselves.* Kennedy and his men were quick to acknowledge that their plans had been mistaken; *for their intentions, they never*
apologized.[34] (emphasis added)

Indeed, from 1961 to 1963 the Kennedy administration never gave up
the idea of using force to eliminate the Castro regime. The new personnel

and organization changes had no effect on the basic goal—the removal of Fidel Castro from power in Cuba.

The Assassination Plots

During the investigations into the intelligence community from 1974 to 1976, the possible existence of presidential ties into "alleged assassination plots involving foreign leaders" became the most explosive and controversial tidbit of the intelligence revelations. Using hindsight and the benefit of much calmer political climates, many Americans were shocked and outraged at the thought that former presidents may have plotted to assassinate foreign leaders. President Ford announced that he was "totally opposed to political assassination"[35] and issued Executive Order 11905, which concluded with the statement that "No employee of the United States Government shall engage in, or conspire to engage in, political assassination." Attorney General Edward Levi said no president had the legal authority to order assassinations, even though the matter had never been tested in the courts. CBS and Bill Moyers called the plots "morally repugnant."[36] Indeed, for most Americans even the idea that Dwight Eisenhower or John Kennedy might have plotted to assassinate foreign leaders was "un-American" and "immoral." But as Ray Cline noted, "Whether President Eisenhower or Dulles or President Kennedy had actually intended to authorize Castro's murder is simply not clear from the records."[37]

The specially appointed Rockefeller commission reviewed the available data on assassination plots but refused to write specifically on the potential assassinations and forwarded this political "football" to the Democrat-controlled Church committee in the Senate.[38] Senator Frank Church of Idaho developed his famous "rogue elephant" theory about the CIA wrongdoing, which proclaimed that at times the agency acted on its own without responsible officials and the president being aware of what was going on. Among the wide variety of respectable evidence of such a situation, Church cited the fact that President Nixon had ordered the destruction of the CIA's toxic agents, and a low-level chemist who had been working on the project for his professional career refused to destroy his shellfish toxin. But the CIA assassination plots were the clearest example of the agency operating out of control in Church's estimation.[39] The Church committee findings on assassination plots did not blame former presidents for past deeds. In short, the Church committee found that:

1. Officials of the United States government initiated plots to assassinate Fidel Castro and Patrice Lumumba.
2. *No foreign leaders were killed as a result of assassination plots initiated by officials of the United States.*
3. American officials encouraged or were privy to coup plots that resulted in the deaths of Rafael Trujillo of the Dominican Republic, Ngo Dinh Diem of South Vietnam, and General Rene Schneider of Chile.
4. The plots occurred in a Cold War atmosphere perceived to be of crisis proportions.
5. American officials had exaggerated notions about their ability to control the actions of coup leaders.
6. CIA officials made use of known underworld figures in assassination efforts.

Moreover, the committee recommended the following:

1. The United States should not engage in assassination.
2. The United States should not make use of underworld figures for their criminal talents.
3. The apparent lack of accountability in the command and control system was such that the assassination plots *could have been undertaken* without express authorization. (emphasis added)
4. CIA officials involved in the assassination operations perceived assassination to have been a permissible course of action.
5. The failure in communications between agency officials in charge of assassination operations and their superiors in the agency and in the administration was due to: (A) the failure of subordinates to disclose their plans and operations to their superiors; and (B) the failure of superiors in the climate of violence and aggressive covert actions sanctioned by the administrations to rule out assassinations as a tool of foreign policy; to make clear to their subordinates that assassination was impermissible; or to inquire further after receiving indications that it was being considered.
6. Practices current at the time in which the assassination plots occurred were revealed by the record to create the risk of confusion, rashness and irresponsibility in the very areas where clarity and sober judgment were most necessary.

Finally, in its epilogue the Church committee concluded:

The Committee does not believe that the acts which it has examined represent the real American character. They do not reflect the ideals which have given the people of this country and of the world hope for a better, fuller, fairer life. We regard the assassination plots as aberrations.[40]

Kennedy himself, were he still alive, could not have written a more favorable absolution. Though the Church committee was given an almost impossible task of tracing the assassination plots, they carried out their duties in a most responsible fashion. According to the Church Report there were eight CIA plots to assassinate Fidel Castro between August 1960 and November 1963. The plots called for poison pens, a contaminated diving suit with disease-bearing fungus, exploding exotic seashells, poison pills, thallium salts to depilate Castro's beard, and Mafia hit men.[41] The plots raise serious questions about the CIA's effectiveness and ability to initiate and carry out a program of action once adopted. More important, the plots raise crucial questions about the accountability of presidents and control of the CIA.

The central plot against Castro was conceived during the Eisenhower administration when Deputy Director for Plans in CIA Richard Bissell *thought* he had been authorized to plan Castro's assassination. Bissell then asked Security Director Sheffield Edwards to find someone to eliminate Castro.[42] The National Security Council in March 1960 had theoretically discussed in euphemistic terms the elimination of Castro, Raul Castro, and Che Guevara, so Bissell had not come by the idea of assassinating Castro out of the blue.[43] Edwards, in search of an assassin, contacted Howard Hughes's aide, Robert Maheu to ask him to recruit Mafia mobster John Rosselli for the job. Rosselli was offered $150,000 by the CIA for Castro's assassination.[44] Rosselli and the Mafia had vested interests in the elimination of Castro. Before Castro's revolution in Cuba, the Mafia, particularly Santos Trafficante, ran a profitable gambling, dope, and prostitution circle in Havana. With Castro eliminated, the Mafia hoped to move back into control in Havana.[45]

Rosselli recruited two friends to help organize the assassination of Castro: Sam Giancana and Santos Trafficante. While the planning continued, the Eisenhower administration left office and the Kennedy administration came to power in January 1961, with neither president apparently knowing of the plots at this time. The first CIA-Mafia plot against Castro failed in April 1961 after the CIA had provided the poison pills and

Rosselli had made arrangements for their delivery to Castro's meal.[46]
By most accounts Kennedy did not know that this plot was taking place
around the time of the Bay of Pigs invasion.

After the dismal failure of covert action against Cuba in the Bay of
Pigs invasion, Kennedy worked to gain more control over the intelligence
community and placed his brother Robert Kennedy, the Attorney General
of the United States, in charge of the White House's effort to control the
CIA. President Kennedy did not abandon the idea of covert action. He
approved in writing a program of intelligence gathering missions, propaganda activities, paramilitary operations, and sabotage raids against Castro
called Operation Mongoose.[47] A mongoose is a ferretlike, flesh-eating
animal known for its ability to kill rats and poisonous snakes, and some
members of the administration clearly put Castro in the same league as
poisonous snakes. It is not clear from the written record whether Kennedy
at first realized that one component of Operation Mongoose contained
a special group to engage in "Executive Action" (the CIA euphemism for
assassination) headed by William Harvey, a CIA covert operator. The goal
of Operation Mongoose was to overthrow Castro by October 1962, but
the accepted program did not specifically mention the assassination
planning.

Harvey reorganized the CIA-Castro assassination planning by dropping
Giancana and Trafficante from assassination discussions and retaining
only John Roselli for his expertise on assassinations. In April 1962 Harvey
had more poison pills delivered to Rosselli, who in turn had them delivered
to Cuba. The poison pill plot failed once again and it was finally dismissed
as a viable means to eliminate Castro by February 1963.[48] In the extremely loose chain of command, the CIA officers found it difficult to trace
what was happening to the pills once they were delivered to Rosselli.[49]
Rosselli had the pills delivered to Cuba through Mafia connections, but
they never reached Castro. The Cuban intelligence community became
aware of these strange attempts to eliminate Castro, thus the "covertness" of the CIA-Mafia relationship remained effective only in the United
States. In the 1970s, after the Church committee revealed the existence
of eight plots against him, Castro claimed that his security police had
foiled about three times that many plots that he knew were directed by
the CIA.[50] In September 1963, Castro told the Associated Press, "We are
prepared to fight them and answer in kind. United States leaders should
think that if they are aiding terrorist plans to eliminate Cuban leaders,

they themselves will not be safe."[51] Ironically the last recorded plot against Castro that the Church committee uncovered was proceeding on schedule when a high official of the Castro government was delivered a poison pen for use against Castro by a CIA case officer in Paris on November 22, 1963. As a once-secret CIA assassination report revealed, according to the Church committee report, "It is likely that at the very moment President Kennedy was shot, a CIA officer was meeting with a Cuban agent and giving him an assassination device for use against Castro."[52]

Presidential Responsibility

Besides the obvious questions the plots raise about the CIA's efficiency and effectiveness in carrying out covert missions, the plots direct one to question presidential responsibility. Did Kennedy know about the assassination plots against Castro? Did he order them? Did he try to terminate them if he ever found out about them? Did he condone assassination attempts against Castro? In short, what was the president's role in the assassination plots?

When the activities against Castro became public knowledge in the United States in 1975, many Kennedy loyalists were enraged at what they perceived to be attempts to tie Kennedy in with the assassinations. Adam Walinsky and Frank Mankiewicz suggested that the Kennedy assassination gossip was nothing more than Republican attempts to smear the Kennedy family and to embarrass indirectly Senator Ted Kennedy. Both claimed that the Kennedy brothers were not involved in the assassination plots in any way.[53] Frank Church examined the evidence and claimed that Kennedy did not know what the "rogue elephant" CIA was doing about assassination plots. The Church committee report, which relied on testimony and the written record, came to the conclusion that no written evidence exists to demonstrate that John Kennedy knew about the assassination plots against Castro or that he had ordered them.

Clearly, Kennedy loyalists were in a no-win position when they argued that Kennedy did not know about the assassination plots. If he did not know, then, much like Nixon who claimed that he did not know the Watergate break-in was going to occur, Kennedy would be guilty of gross neglect as an administrator who did not know that questionable acts were being committed by his subordinates in his name. If Kennedy was ignorant of the CIA plots against Castro, he must be rated also as an extremely

inept manager of the intelligence community, especially since after the
Bay of Pigs he moved swiftly to try to gain control of the intelligence community. Shortly after Lyndon Johnson took office in 1963 he was able
to discover what Kennedy supporters claim Kennedy could not—that the
CIA was involved in assassination plots. As Johnson told Leo Janos, he
had discovered in late November 1963 that "we had been operating a
damned Murder, Inc. in the Carribean."[54] Johnson was referring to the
discovery of CIA assassination plots against Castro and specifically to a
CIA-backed assassination team that had been caught in Havana in 1962.
Evidently Johnson was more adept at securing intelligence information
from the CIA than Kennedy was.

Some evidence does exist that suggests Kennedy knew about the assas-
sination plots. In May 1961 J. Edgar Hoover, the director of the Federal
Bureau of Investigation, informed Robert Kennedy by memo that the
CIA was using Sam Giancana and John Rosselli in some "dirty business."[55]
The memo did not mention assassination plots, but it bore a handwritten
note, "Have this followed up vigorously," and it was initialed "R.F.K."
No evidence exists indicating that Robert Kennedy pursued the matter
or discovered the nature of the dirty business immediately thereafter. In
November 1961, John Kennedy had a private conversation with reporter
Tad Szulc (the only other person present was presidential assistant Richard
Goodwin) in the Oval Office and asked Szulc, "What would you think if
I ordered Castro to be assassinated?"[56] Szulc responded that he was
against assassination as a matter of principle and that it would not solve
the Cuban problem. Szulc reported:

Kennedy leaned back in his chair, smiled, and said that he had been testing me because he was under great pressure from advisors in the Intelligence Community (whom he did not name) to have Castro killed, but he
himself violently opposed it on the grounds that for moral reasons the
United States should never be party to political assassinations. "I'm glad
you feel the same way," he said.[57]

Early in 1962 Kennedy tested the idea of Castro's assassination on his
friend Senator George Smathers of Florida. Smathers recalled the conversation in 1964 and wrote the following about it:

We had further conversation of assassination of Fidel Castro, what would
be the reaction, how would people react, would the people be gratified.
I'm sure he [Kennedy] had his own ideas about it, but he was picking my

brain. . . . As I recollect he was just throwing out a barrage of questions—he was certain it could be accomplished. . . . But the question was whether or not it would accomplish that which he wanted it to, whether or not the reaction throughout South America would be good or bad. And I talked with him about it and, frankly, at this particular time I felt, and later learned that he did, that I wasn't so much for the idea of assassination, *particularly when it could be pinned on the United States.*[58] (emphasis added)

Later in the year (May 1962) Robert Kennedy received another memo from CIA officials that for the first time formally informed Robert Kennedy that the CIA had plotted with Rosselli and Giancana in 1960-61 to assassinate Castro. CIA officials met with Robert Kennedy and personally assured him that the plots had ended. Robert Kennedy met with Hoover to relay the information and, according to Hoover's memo of the meeting, Robert Kennedy had expressed concern that the CIA could not afford the prosecution of Giancana or other Mafia leaders because it might reveal the CIA plot to eliminate Castro.[59]

In Kennedy's defense one could respond to the preceding four items of evidence of presidential awareness in the following fashion. The Hoover memo to Robert Kennedy and the briefing of Robert Kennedy by CIA officials establishes only the fact that Robert Kennedy knew about the plots, and only after the plots had ended. It does not establish the fact that President Kennedy knew about the plots. No written evidence exists to establish that fact. The conversations with Szulc and Smathers were just trial balloons in conversation among friends and apparently nothing more. Besides, we only have Szulc's and Smathers's testimonies, while John Kennedy's version will never be available. In both conversations Kennedy clearly rejected the use of the assassination of Castro on pragmatic as well as moral grounds.

Alternatively, the evidence suggests that Kennedy knew about the assassination plots. Why would he discuss the possibility of the assassination of Castro with two friends if such a possibility did not in fact exist? Defending Kennedy, one cannot use the Szulc testimony to show that Kennedy morally rejected the CIA's assassination attempts in 1961 and use the same conversation to maintain Kennedy never knew about the plots at all. Trial balloons can often be sent up after the fact. The other argument, that it cannot be proved that John Kennedy knew about the plots just because Robert Kennedy knew about them, is extremely bold.

Without written documents showing the president knew about the plots, it is impossible, so it is claimed, to infer that he was knowledgeable. This argument fails on two grounds.

First, by all accounts the Kennedy brothers were extremely close and had the highest level of trust and mutual confidentiality. Without making any daring leaps in logic, violating common sense, or jumping to unsupported inferences, on all other working levels (except assassination plots), Kennedy defenders generally agree that if Robert Kennedy knew about a major and important policy decision then John Kennedy also knew of it. Certainly it is unlikely that either held from the other major secrets about his political life or government activity. Yet many observers have required written proof to verify that John Kennedy had the same knowledge as his brother about assassination plots.

Second, the insistence upon written orders to verify Kennedy's complicity is unrealistic. Historians who rely only on the written record can overlook historical facts of great significance. For example, revisionist historian David Irving claims that Adolf Hitler did not order the extermination of the Jews in Nazi Germany and that Hitler did not even know about it until late 1943,[60] since no written instructions from Hitler exist on the subject. Albert Speer, Hitler's armaments minister, claims that Hitler knew all along about the extermination of the Jewish community and that historian Irving is completely wrong in his analysis that defends Hitler. Speer commented on Hitler's complicity in an interview:

Question: But how is it that—as Irving states—there is no written trace of his (Hitler's) instructions concerning the "final solution"?

Speer: Why should there be? Must all decisions taken by a country at the topmost level always be promulgated in the form of signed notes from the Head of State? . . . What happened was that Hitler gave a series of daily verbal orders and there was no written confirmation needed, bearing Hitler's signature to implement these orders. . . . And for all concerned, an order signed by Bormann, Himmler, Goering or Speer was tantamount to an order from Adolph Hitler himself.

Question: Do you believe that written orders cannot be found because Hitler's subordinates did not want him to bear the responsibility himself?

Speer: You know, Hitler was not the kind of man to make speeches over a period of years, announcing what he would do to the

Jews, and then ask his subordinates to remove all traces of his decisions concerning them. That was not his way. The truth is that under the Third Reich, no one would have taken the risk of carrying out any policy without Hitler's earlier agreement. . . . And if anyone had acted in such a way as to circumvent Hitler, the news would very quickly have got back to Hitler, and that person would . . . have found himself in very bad trouble indeed.[61]

The point of this important historical analogy is not that John Kennedy was Adolph Hitler, but rather that there exists a certain level of state secrecy which is higher even than "for your eyes only." The ultimate level of state secrecy does not rely on written orders for instructions on how to proceed with policy, but instead uses verbal agreements, informal discussions, and policy assumptions by subordinates as to what the leader really wants done. As Senator Charles Mathias realized while questioning former CIA Director Richard Helms during the Church committee investigation, the whole process of accountability was similar to the assassination of Thomas Becket, killed by knights who had heard Henry II's plea of "Will no one rid me of this turbulent priest?" Mathias asked Helms if the King Henry II-Becket problem spanned the generations and the centuries, and Helms replied, "I think it does, sir."[62] Senator Walter Mondale described the process of ascertaining accountability in the assassination plots as "trying to nail jello to the wall." He noted that "the system was intended to work that way: namely that things would be ordered to be done that should it be made public, no one could be held accountable."[63]

Explanation of Kennedy's Covert Response: Applying the Framework

Kennedy's reliance on the covert response to deal with the perceived national security threat that Castro posed for the United States can be partly explained by applying the framework outlined in Chapter 1.

Pragmatic Calculations Component

As should be clear from this discussion, Kennedy was the consummate pragmatist, a man of action. Kennedy as the rational, national actor selected the Bay of Pigs covert operation and Operation Mongoose as his covert presidential policy with respect to a set of objectives. Kennedy *appeared* to choose among alternative courses of action and selected the covert response after using a crude cost-benefit calculation to determine whether the program should be public or covert. Elements in the crude calculus include the need to promote national security, the strategic advantages gained from secrecy, ongoing foreign policy commitments, the domestic political environment, and the need to conceal incompetence, inefficiency, wrongdoing, personal embarrassment, national embarrassment, or administrative error.

Kennedy viewed the Soviet Union and the "communist menace" with great concern. Always sensitive to the criticisms of the conservative element in American politics, Kennedy never wanted to project an image of being "soft on communists." In the 1960 presidential debates, it was Kennedy who implied that Nixon was not taking a hard line on the communists in Cuba.[64] On one campaign stop Kennedy presumably got carried away in trying to label Nixon as weak in the face of communist aggression. Forgetting that the president heads the National Security Council and not the vice-president, Kennedy said:

During the past eight years that he [Nixon] has presided over the National Security Council, never in all that time in our nation's history has our strength declined more rapidly than it has during the comparable period, in terms of our alliances, in terms of our scientific effort, and our national reputation.[65]

Kennedy charged that the Eisenhower administration had let the United States falter seriously in its strategic position. Indeed, according to Kennedy, the United States trailed the Soviet Union in offensive missile capabilities—the infamous "missile gap."[66] Most important for the purposes of this analysis, Kennedy charged Nixon with being part of the administration that lost Cuba to the communists.

These campaign statements and Cold War rhetoric by Kennedy might easily be discounted by some as not revealing his "true" convictions and world view toward "monolithic" communism. Since the statements were articulated during a presidential campaign, some observers did not blame Kennedy for raising the level of Cold War tensions and reviving the bogey of falling dominoes. However, as Richard Walton has demonstrated, Kennedy conducted aspects of his foreign policy not as "conciliator" but as "Cold Warrior" once he was elected to the presidency.[67]

After his inaugural address, which presented a positive and optimistic view of possible peaceful relations with the Soviet Union, Kennedy lapsed into a bellicose state of the union address some ten days later. Kennedy warned, "Each day the crises multiply. Each day their solution grows more difficult. Each day we draw nearer the *hour of maximum danger,* as weapons spread and hostile forces grow stronger" (emphasis added).[68] Even though Kennedy had learned that there was no "missile gap" during his first ten days in office and that indeed the United States had a strong strategic advantage over the Soviet Union in ballistic missiles, Kennedy continued to view the world in terms of the strong Soviet offensive.

The major assumptions in his foreign policy, as I understand them, were (1) that Moscow directed worldwide revolutionary uprisings, (2) that the Soviets were expansionists, (3) that the "domino theory" was valid, and (4) that it was the duty of the United States to defend and protect freedom around the globe.[69] His world outlook and his interpretations of the available data allowed Kennedy to live in a world of perpetual international crisis.

Kennedy was an exciting president who challenged those around him to action. The Kennedy men, the "Best and the Brightest" in David Halberstam's phrase,[70] were often measured by their capacity to get involved on the international level. Kennedy described the struggle in these terms:

We dare not fail to see the insidious nature of this new and deeper struggle. We dare not fail to grasp the *new concepts,* the *new tools,* the *new sense of urgency* we will need to combat it, whether in Cuba or South Vietnam. And we dare not fail to realize that this struggle is taking place every day, without fanfare, in thousands of villages and markets, day and night, and in classrooms all over the globe.

The message of Cuba, of Laos, of the rising din of Communist voices in Asia and Latin America—these messages are all the same. The complacent, the self-indulgent, the soft societies are about to be swept away with the debris of history. Only the strong, only the industrious, only the determined, only the courageous, only the visionary who determine the real nature of our struggle can possible survive. (emphasis added)[71]

Perhaps the concepts and the new tools that Kennedy was referring to included covert action. If the Soviets engaged in secret manipulation and deceit to control the destinies of other nations, then the United States must be prepared to play by the same set of international rules. A secret CIA report developed in 1954 by a blue-ribbon panel of American citizens stated, *"If the United States is to survive, long-standing American concepts of 'fair play' must be reconsidered. We must learn to subvert, sabotage and destroy our enemies by more clever, more sophisticated and more effective methods than those used against us"*[72] (emphasis added). Evidently, Kennedy had reached the same conclusion.

Always the pragmatist, Kennedy supported covert action within his administration as a flexible response to fight communism. The Kennedy men appeared to believe that they could control events in an uncertain world. Moreover, as Bruce Miroff has shown, Kennedy's "nonideological," "rational" decision-making approach, the pragmatic approach, soon became an ideology unto itself.[73]

Indeed, the ideology of pragmatism pervaded the Kennedy administration's approach to covert action. The pragmatic liberal president has been characterized by Miroff as being "tough-minded."[74] Pragmatic liberals believe that they are nonideological and they abhor ideologues. They value "facts" over theories and "realities" over values. If a strategy works, then it is considered acceptable. The president is viewed as one who must make the "tough" decisions and the "hard" choices in a "hostile" world.

One tough decision that faced the Kennedy administration was what to do about the Castro regime. The Kennedy advisors recognized the need to protect national security in taking actions against Castro. The spectacle of a communist dictatorship some ninety miles off the coast of Florida was sufficiently threatening to arouse national security interests in a pragmatic Kennedy administration. The secrecy of the operations was necessary because the "covertness" provided strategic advantages. The Kennedy administration never seriously challenged the goals and the general principles of the covert operations against Cuba, but they measured the operations in terms of their success and their ability to retain plausible deniability. Ongoing foreign policy commitments to the general idea that the United States was bound to defend the western hemisphere against any outside intervention played an important role in the Kennedy administration's calculations. The domestic political environment was such that Kennedy could not appear soft in the face of Castro in Cuba. The conservative element in American politics demanded action on this issue.

Covert action allowed Kennedy to get involved without being held accountable. If the practical actions against Castro failed, the secrecy of the operation was supposed to conceal incompetence, wrongdoing, and national embarrassment. In short, the benefits derived from covert operations against Castro outweighed the cost of such actions in Kennedy's estimation. Of course, Kennedy could have chosen "no-action" as a response or he could have selected direct, open, publicized military action against Cuba, but this would have been tantamount to a unilateral declaration of war against Cuba. Both choices were viewed as unacceptable and the covert response was selected by the Kennedy administration to bridge the gap between "no-action" and the open, belligerent policy.

Personality-Private Motives

The personality perspective plays an important role in ultimately helping one to understand the decision by the Kennedy administration to undermine Castro. By most accounts, Kennedy had an extreme dislike for the Cuban leader. James David Barber described it as an "almost personal animosity" toward Castro, and Kennedy loyalist Sorensen described the situation as Kennedy's "deep feeling against Castro (unusual for him)."[75] Though this feeling could hardly be described as *compulsive* hatred, Kennedy's strong dislike of Castro was potent enough to pervade throughout the upper echelon of his administration. As Kennedy's secretary of defense, Robert McNamara testified to the Church committee, "We were hysterical about Castro at the time of the Bay of Pigs and thereafter."[76]

Castro may have emerged as a particularly threatening figure to Kennedy after Kennedy's humiliating Bay of Pigs bungling. Castro even had developed into an appealing figure to some members of the American intellectual community, a community where the Kennedy myth also was competing. Castro was often portrayed in the world press as a young, macho revolutionary. Kennedy, who also cultivated a young, macho image, may have personalized the conflict between Cuba and the United States beyond ideological conflict to the point of personal competition between Castro and himself.[77]

Yet, given the fact that Kennedy had personal animosity toward Castro, it is difficult to demonstrate how this personality factor related to the decision to resort to *secret* and *deceptive* programs against Castro. After all, Kennedy could have selected an *open* response against Castro, given his personal feelings, just as well as the covert response. There are few indicators that Kennedy was particularly psychologically comfortable using secrecy and deception as stylistic modes of interpersonal communication within the White House staff. Thus, when he resorted to secrecy and deception, it was usually because of pragmatic concerns to engage in these forms of information control, and not because of any personality traits that compelled the use of secrecy and deception as routine modes of behavior.

Bureaucratic Politics

When Kennedy's pragmatic concerns and his personal feelings toward Castro are considered within the bureaucratic politics explanation, it becomes easier to understand the covert response to Castro. Kennedy helped create the "Henry II-Becket problem" within the bureaucracy with his personal feelings. In testifying before the Church committee, Richard Helms noted that "some spark had been transmitted" from the White House indicating that if Castro "disappeared from the scene they would not have been unhappy."[78]

The bureaucratic component of the framework views the Kennedy administration's response to Castro as the outcome of the national security bargaining process where presidential interests are only part of the reality in the bargaining environment. As Morton Halperin has observed about national security decision making:

We can see that most governmental actions, which look to the casual observer as if they resulted from specific presidential decisions, are more often an amalgam of a number of coincidental occurrences: actions brought about by presidential decisions (not always those intended), actions that are really maneuvers to influence presidential decisions, actions resulting from decisions in unrelated areas, and actions taken at lower levels by junior participants without informing their superiors or the President.[79]

Thus, presidential interests are *not* the determining factor in governmental action, according to the bureaucratic politics component, but they can be important contributing factors. Many national security bureaucrats can be persuaded at times to view national security from the narrow perspective of presidential interests. According to Halperin, "Even many of those who are not necessarily sympathetic to the President's perspective on national security . . . still do take such factors into account in arriving at their own stands on national security issues or in planning strategies for getting the desired decisions."[80]

The bureaucratic perspective, in explaining the Kennedy administration's Cuban response, maintains that the secret and deceptive policy emerged out of the bargaining process between the deputy director of plans (CIA), his staff, the CIA director, the president's top Cuban policy advisor (in this case Robert F. Kennedy), and the president. The CIA is viewed as an organization that pushed for a particular covert response because of its own organizational interests. After all, that is what the covert branch of the CIA does—it creates and proposes covert responses.

One year after the Kennedy-approved Operation Mongoose had been in effect, Robert Kennedy expressed the "general dissatisfaction of the President" with Mongoose. The Special Group, headed by CIA agent William Harvey was a direct link between the White House and the Cuban covert activity that bypassed the National Security Council. The Special Group gained John Kennedy's disapproval not because of the covert goals of Mongoose, but because, as Robert Kennedy stated, "Mongoose had been under way for a year . . . [and] that there had been no acts of sabotage and that even the one which had been attempted against a copper mine had failed twice."[81] The president clearly wanted more action, though he did not specify what kind. ("Will no one rid me of this turbulent priest?")

In an interview with Ray S. Cline (former deputy director of intelligence for CIA, from 1962 to 1966 and now director of studies at the Georgetown University Center for Strategic and International Studies), this writer asked about the climate of the 1960s within CIA. Cline stated that he had not been involved in any assassination planning but that he was in a position to be aware of the broad outlines of what was going on. During the early 1960s most Americans believed that we were engaged in an undeclared war with Cuba, according to Cline. He said that "the CIA assassination plots were aberrations" committed in a difficult political climate.[82] Moreover, Cline maintained that it was unfortunate that contemporary critics of the agency were willing to dismantle the CIA because of some wild schemes developed by the senior deputy director of plans in the early 1960s.[83] Cline felt that if Bissell erred, he "made the mistake of being too logical."[84] If the president approves of a plan to secretly invade Cuba, which requires 1,400 soldiers to overthrow Castro, logically the president would be willing to see Castro assassinated—an act that might make the whole invasion unnecessary, according to Cline.

Bissell in some ways agrees with Cline's analysis. On the CBS Documentary "The CIA's Secret Army," aired June 10, 1977, Bill Moyers asked Bissell if he was willing to concede now that the assassination plots were morally wrong. Bissell replied that he was unwilling to rule out assassination as a possible covert response in the name of national security and that the only drawback of the Castro plots was that they could not maintain their "covertness."[85] In other words, if the United States could assassinate an enemy of their foreign policy for "legitimate" national security interests and maintain plausible denialability, then Bissell apparently would still approve of such a plot.

Institutional Component

The institutional perspective adds a new dimension to our understanding of the Kennedy administration's behavior. Covert action in this respect is viewed as a learned response inherited from the Eisenhower administration and regarded as necessary by Kennedy to fulfill his institutional responsibilities as commander-in-chief and top national security manager. The programs to eliminate the Castro regime were developed originally during the Eisenhower administration, and Kennedy first learned about this covert warfare against Cuba during the early Bay of Pigs briefing. The only preparation for the president as national security manager is on-the-job training, and Kennedy may have been socialized to believe that covert responses were acceptable and expected presidential behavior.

Summary

Though all four perspectives help to illuminate different aspects of why the Kennedy administration supported covert operations against Cuba, some perspectives appear to be more helpful than others. The pragmatic component best explains the resort to secrecy and deception by the Kennedy administration in the attempt to the elimination of the Castro regime. However, I would argue that the bureaucratic politics explanations for the secrecy and deception of the operations ranks a close second. The institutional explanation that offers some evidence to suggest that Kennedy was just acting like Eisenhower as national security manager against Castro fails because it overlooks the dramatic increase in the use of covert action that took place during the Kennedy administration. In short, Kennedy selected the covert response for reasons other than the fact that Eisenhower had engaged in this kind of action. Although Kennedy's personality may ultimately have played an important role in the decision to "get Castro," Kennedy's personality-private motives do not help us predict whether Kennedy would select a secret and deceptive response against Castro. The pragmatic perspective and the bureaucratic politics explanation offer the most plausible view of why Kennedy opted for a secret and deceptive response.

Notes

1. See Theodore Sorensen, *Kennedy* (New York: Bantam Books, 1966); Arthur Schlesinger, Jr., *A Thousand Days: John F. Kennedy in the White House* (Greenwich, Conn.: Fawcett, 1967); Roger Hilsman, *To Move a Nation* (New York: Dell, 1967); and William Manchester, *Portrait of a President* (New York: Manor Books, 1967): *and then see* revisionists such as Richard Walton, *Cold War and Counterrevolution* (New York: Viking Press, 1972); Victor Navasky, *Kennedy Justice* (New York: Atheneum, 1977); Henry Fairlie, *The Kennedy Promise* (Garden City, N.Y.: Doubleday, 1973); and Bruce Miroff, *Pragmatic Illusions: The Presidential Politics of John F. Kennedy* (New York: David McKay, 1976).

2. Lewis Paper, *The Promise and the Performance* (New York: Crown Publishing, 1975), p. 3.

3. Quoted in Fairlie, *The Kennedy Promise*, p. 214.

4. David Halberstam, "The Power and the Profits," Part II, *Atlantic Monthly*, February 1976, p. 63.

5. Ibid., p. 65.

6. Sorensen, *Kennedy*, p. 361.

7. Francis Rourke, *Secrecy and Publicity* (Baltimore, Md.: Johns Hopkins University Press, 1961).

8. Quoted in Walton, *Cold War and Counterrevolution*, p. 54.

9. John Kennedy, *Public Papers*, 1961, p. 334.

10. Ibid., p. 334.

11. Harold Chase and Allen H. Lerman, eds., *Kennedy and the Press* (New York: Thomas Y. Crowell, 1965), p. 336.

12. Sorensen, *Kennedy*, p. 359.

13. Quoted in Walton, *Cold War and Counterrevolution*, p. 46.

14. Final Report of the Select Committee to Study Governmental Operations with Respect to Intelligence Activities, United States Senate, (the Church Committee) April 26, 1976, Book I, p. 56. The 40 Committee was established by Nixon with NSDM 40 on February 17, 1970. It refers to the high level committee within the

national security bureaucracy that approves covert actions. The Truman administration's covert actions had to be approved by the 10/2 or the 10/5 panels. Eisenhower administration approval had to come from Operations Coordination Board or the Psychological Strategy Board. Later in the Eisenhower administration the committee came to be known as the Special Group. The Kennedy administration operated with the Special Group and the Johnson administration used the 303 Committee. All of the groups were similar to the 40 Committee. On February 17, 1976, President Ford reorganized the covert operation process by disbanding the 40 Committee to form a committee known as Operations Advisory Group. The Operations Advisory Group has the same functions as the 40 Committee had: to approve covert operations for the president. The new group consists of the assistant to the president for national security affairs, the secretary of state, the secretary of defense, the director of Central Intelligence, the chairman of the Joint Chiefs, the attorney general (observer) and the director of Office of Management and Budget (observer).

15. Another interpretation from the data is that the Kennedy administration may have been more honest in its reporting of covert operations than previous administrations.

16. The Church Committee Report, Final Volume, Book I, p. 131. President Ford in his reorganization of the national security bureaucracy in 1976 defined special activities (or covert operations) as those activities "designed to further official United States programs and policies abroad which are planned and executed so that the role of the United States Government is not apparent or publicly acknowledged." Executive Order No. 11905, 2/18/76.

17. Richard Bissell, in 1968 Meeting with Council on Foreign Relations, Secret Minutes published as an appendix to Victor Marchetti and John Marks, *The CIA and the Cult of Intelligence* (New York: Dell, 1975), p. 364. *See also* Harry Rositzke, *The CIA's Secret Operations* (New York: Reader's Digest Press, 1977), Chaps. 9-11; and Miles Copeland, *Beyond Cloak and Dagger: Inside the CIA* (New York: Pinnacle Books, 1975), pp. 202-3.

18. Irving Janis, *Victims of Groupthink* (Boston: Houghton Mifflin, 1972), p. 14.

19. The Church committee interim report, "Alleged Assassination Plots Involving Foreign Leaders—An Interim Report," November 20, 1975, pp. 92-93.

20. By most accounts no Kennedy advisor opposed the plan. Among those who did not express disapproval were Dean Rusk, Robert McNamara, Paul Nitze, Lyman Lemnitzer, William Fulbright (of the Senate Foreign Relations Committee) and Arthur Schlesinger, Jr. See Janis, *Victims of Groupthink*, Chap. 2, and Ray S. Cline, *Secrets, Spies and Scholars* (Washington, D.C.: Acropolis Books, 1976), p. 188.

21. See Hilsman, *To Move a Nation*, Chap. 3; Sorensen, *Kennedy*, Chap. 11; Schlesinger, *A Thousand Days*; Janis, *Victims of Groupthink*, Chap. 2; James Barber, *The Presidential Character* (Englewood Cliffs, N.J.: Prentice-Hall, 1972), pp. 319-25; David Wise and Thomas Ross, *The Invisible Government* (New York: Random House, 1964), Chaps. 2-4; Tad Szulc and Karl Meyer, *The Cuban Invasion: The Chronicle of a Disaster* (New York: Ballantine, 1962); and Haynes Johnson, et al., *The Bay of Pigs* (New York: W. W. Norton, 1964).

22. Janis, *Victims of Groupthink*, pp. 19-26.

23. Ibid., p. 32.

24. Schlesinger, *A Thousand Days*, p. 248.

25. Janis, *Victims of Groupthink*, pp. 197-98. The eight symptoms of Group-think include an illusion of invulnerability, collective efforts to rationalize, a sense of inherent morality, stereotyping, pressure on dissenters, self-censorship and mind guards, a shared illusion of unanimity, and emergence of members who protect the group from adverse information.

26. Sorensen, *Kennedy*, p. 710.

27. Stephen Hess, *Organizing the Presidency* (Washington, D.C.: The Brookings Institution, 1976), pp. 84-88.

28. Richard Johnson, *Managing the White House* (New York: Harper & Row, 1974) p. 127. After the Bay of Pigs, Kennedy required "generalists" instead of spokesmen from the respective agencies. See p. 138.

29. Janis, *Victims of Groupthink*, p. 147.

30. Cline, *Secrets, Spies and Scholars*, p. 191.

31. Hilsman, *To Move a Nation*, p. 34.

32. Ibid., p. 79.

33. Marchetti and Marks, *Cult of Intelligence*, p. 53.

34. Miroff, *Pragmatic Illusions*, p. 114.

35. Rositzke, *The CIA's Secret Operations*, p. 199.

36. CBS Documentary, Bill Moyers host, "The CIA's Secret Army, aired June 10, 1977.

37. Cline, *Secrets, Spies and Scholars*, p. 187.

38. See Report to the President by the Commission on CIA Activities within the United States (The Rockefeller commission) (New York: Manor Books, 1975). On NBC "Meet the Press" Rockefeller said that there was "White House knowledge and/or approval of all major undertakings." See Daniel Schorr, "The Assassins," *The New York Review*, October 13, 1977, p. 14.

39. On July 18, 1975, Senator Frank Church at a posthearing briefing said that "The agency [CIA] may have been behaving like a rogue elephant on a rampage." For a more academic approach to the problem of an uncontrollable bureaucracy, see Graham Allison, *Essence of Decision* (Boston: Little, Brown, 1971), his Model II, pp. 67-143. Yet Rositzke disputed this notion of an uncontrolled CIA when he wrote, "If there is one clear fact that emerges from the reports of his [Church's] committee, as well as the Rockefeller Commission, it is that the CIA has operated since 1947 under the direct control of the President and his national security advisor." See Rositzke, *The CIA's Secret Operations*, p. 238.

40. See "Alleged Assassination Plots Involving Foreign Leaders." *See also* condensed findings of the Senate Select Committee's interim report in Congressional Research Service, UpDATE, 1/12/77, pp. 92-93.

41. "Alleged Assassination Plots," pp. 92-93; *and see* Schorr, "The Assassins."

42. "Alleged Assassination Plots," pp. 92-93.

43. Ibid., pp. 92-93. *See also* Cline, *Secrets, Spies and Scholars*, p. 186.

44. Ibid., pp. 92-93. *See also* Schorr, "The Assassins," p. 16.

45. Ibid., pp. 80-81. "Trafficante and other racketeers [were] interested in

securing 'gambling, prostitution, and dope monopolies' in Cuba after the overthrow of Castro."

46. Ibid., pp. 140-42. See Schorr, "The Assassins," p. 16.

47. Ibid., pp. 196-201. *See also* Rositzke, *The CIA's Secret Operations*, p. 179; Cline, *Secrets, Spies and Scholars*, p. 195; and Wise, *The American Police State* (New York: Random House, 1976), p. 216.

48. "Alleged Assassination Plots," pp. 196-201. *See also* Rositzke, *The CIA's Secret Operations*, p. 198.

49. Ibid., pp. 196-201. *See also* Schorr, "The Assassins," p. 16.

50. Senator George McGovern revealed this information from Castro after a visit. On July 30, 1975, McGovern said Castro felt that there had been 24 CIA plots against his life from 1960 to 1971. See Schorr, "The Assassins," p. 14.

51. Associated Press Interview, September 9, 1963. See Schorr, "The Assassins," p. 20.

52. "Alleged Assassination Plots," pp. 72, 89, and 174.

53. Moreover, on September 22, 1975, Senator Edward Kennedy appeared before the Church committee to testify that he was "morally certain" that neither of his brothers had a role in assassination plots against Castro. See Schorr, "The Assassins," p. 15.

54. Leo Janos, "Johnson Interview," in "The Last Days of the President," *Atlantic Monthly*, July 1973, p. 39, in Peter Dale Scott, Paul Hoch, and Russell Stetler, eds., *The Assassinations: Dallas and Beyond* (New York: Vintage Books, 1976), pp. 302-3.

55. Nicholas M. Horrock, "Memo Says RFK Knew in 1961 of CIA Dealings with Mafia," *New York Times* News Service, Louisville, *The Courier-Journal*, May 30, 1975, p. A-2.

56. Tad Szulc, "Cuba on Our Mind," *The Assassinations*, ed. Scott, Hoch, Stetler, pp. 382-83.

57. Ibid., p. 383.

58. George Smathers, interview recorded March 31, 1964, in the Oral History Interviews, Kennedy Library, cited in Walton, *Cold War and Counterrevolution*, pp. 47-48.

59. Lawrence Houston, former CIA general counsel, said that in 1962 he had briefed Attorney General Kennedy on the CIA-Mafia plots to eliminate Castro and Robert Kennedy's *only* reaction according to Houston, was, "If we were going to get involved with the Mafia again, please come to him first because our involvement with the Mafia might impede his drive against the Mafia in general crimebusting." See Schorr, "The Assassins," p. 14; and Wise, *The American Police State*, p. 217.

60. David Irving, *Hitler's War* (New York: Viking Press, 1977).

61. "Speer's Comments," *Newsweek*, September 19, 1977, p. 56.

62. "Alleged Assassination Plots," p. 149.

63. Wise, *The American Police State*, p. 214.

64. See Sidney Kraus, ed., *The Great Debates* (Bloomington, Ind. and London: Indiana University Press, 1962 and 1977).

65. Kennedy made the speech at Alexandria, Virginia on August 24, 1960. Cited in Walton, *Cold War and Counterrevolution*, p. 9.

66. Miroff, *Pragmatic Illusions*, pp. 36-37 and 45-48.

67. Walton, *Cold War and Counterrevolution*, p. 6. *See also* Fairlie, *The Kennedy Promise*, and Miroff, *Pragmatic Illusions*, for more arguments on Kennedy as Cold Warrior.

68. Kennedy, *Public Papers*, 1961 (Washington, D.C.: U.S. Government Printing Office, 1962), pp. 22-23.

69. These are not unique assumptions on Kennedy's part. These images were heavily shared at the top of the national security bureaucracy. See John Donovan, *The Cold Warriors* (Lexington, Mass.: D. C. Heath, 1974); Graham Allison, "Cool It: Foreign Policy of Young America," *Foreign Policy*, no. 1 (Winter 1970-1971): pp. 144-60; Morton Halperin, "Shared Images," *Bureaucratic Politics and Foreign Policy* (Washington, D.C.: The Brookings Institution, 1974), pp. 11-12.

70. David Halberstam, *The Best and the Brightest* (Greenwich, Conn.: Fawcett Crest, 1972).

71. John Kennedy, "Address to the American Society of Newspaper Editors," April 20, 1961, in John Kennedy, *To Turn The Tide: John Kennedy's Public Statements* (New York: Harper & Row, 1962), p. 47. *See also* pp. 49-50 for a continuation of the theme on "Urgent National Needs."

72. Cited on CBS News Documentary, Bill Moyers host, "The CIA's Secret Army," aired June 10, 1977.

73. Miroff, *Pragmatic Illusions*.

74. Ibid., pp. 283-88.

75. James David Barber, *The Presidential Character* (Englewood Cliffs, N.J.: Prentice-Hall, 1972), p. 324; *and see* Sorensen, *Kennedy*, p. 343, along with Miroff, *Pragmatic Illusions*, p. 133.

76. "Alleged Assassination Plots," p. 142, note 1. *See also* Schorr, "The Assassins," p. 16.

77. John Lovell suggested this speculative point to me. *See also* John Orman, "The Macho Presidential Style," *Indiana Social Studies Quarterly*, 29, no. 3, (Winter 1976-1977): 51-60; Richard Barnet, *Roots of War* (Baltimore, Md.: Pelican Books, 1973), p. 109, on "bureaucratic machismo."

78. "Alleged Assassination Plots," p. 149.

79. Halperin, *Bureaucratic Politics and Foreign Policy*, p. 293.

80. Ibid., p. 83.

81. David Martin, "Master Spy Harvey Was a Legend Upon Return to States," *Washington Post* Service, *Indianapolis Star*, October 18, 1976, p. 1 and p. 5.

82. Personal interview with Ray S. Cline on Friday, August 12, 1977, in Washington, D.C.

83. Ibid.

84. Cline, *Secrets, Spies and Scholars*, p. 188.

85. CBS Documentary, "The CIA's Secret Army." William F. Buckley, Jr., takes a similar pragmatic approach to assassination of foreign leaders. See his *Firing Line* PBS interview with former CIA official Vernon Walters, aired June 18, 1978.

4. BUREAUCRATIC SECRECY: LYNDON JOHNSON

Lyndon Johnson did not invent presidential deception, but he seems to have been remembered by many as if he did. After all, Dwight Eisenhower was the first president in this period to acknowledge publicly the fact that he had lied in statements involving the U-2 flight over the Soviet Union, after Gary Powers was shot down in May 1960.[1] Later Kennedy was involved in covert actions that required elaborate cover stories. But to most observers, Johnson is remembered as the president who had the most serious "credibility gap," which was a euphemistic way of saying he did not always communicate the truth of his actions to Congress, the press, and the public. Perhaps because Johnson's apparent deception about aspects of the war in Vietnam was systematic and persisted over a five-year period, he is remembered by many as the preeminent example (along with Nixon) of a misleading president.

One should always be cautious when speaking about the "lessons of the Pentagon Papers" since experts have disagreed over their actual meaning, but one lesson that seems to have emerged from the Pentagon Papers is that presidents often did not tell the whole truth about U.S. involvement in Indochina.[2] Specifically with Johnson, the Pentagon Papers reveal that at the time he was making dovish statements on the campaign trail in 1964 and hinting that challenger Barry Goldwater desired a land war in Southeast Asia, the Pentagon and the National Security Council had already considered the option of escalating the war in Vietnam. On the campaign trail in 1964 Johnson talked like a "dove":

Some others are eager to enlarge the conflict. They call upon us to supply American boys to do the job that Asian boys should do. They ask

us to take reckless action which might risk the lives of millions and en-
gulf much of Asia and certainly threaten the peace of the entire world.
Moreover, such action would offer no solution at all to the real problem
of Vietnam. (New York City, August 12, 1964)

There are those that say you ought to go North and drop bombs, to try
to wipe out supply lines, and they think that would escalate the war.
We don't want our American boys to do the fighting for Asian boys. We
don't want to get involved in a nation with 700 million people and get
tied down in a land war in Asia. (Eufaula, Oklahoma, Sept. 25, 1964)

In Asia we face an ambitious and aggressive China, but we have the will
and we have the strength to help our Asian friends resist that ambition.
Sometimes our folks get a little impatient. Sometimes they rattle their
rockets some, and they bluff about their bombs. But we are not about to
send American boys nine and ten thousand miles away from home to do
what Asian boys ought to be doing for themselves. (Akron, Ohio, October 21, 1964)[3]

However, these prudent sentiments spoken by Johnson-the-candidate
did not correspond with the action of Johnson-the-president, as revealed
in the Pentagon Papers. Johnson had approved the use of covert actions
against North Vietnam and Laos during 1964; he had also approved options as of September 10, 1964, that gave presidential consent to widen
the war in Indochina by resuming covert air and naval operations against
North Vietnam, and by preparing for the resumption of the bombing of
Indochina along with ground troop escalation.[4]

Some might excuse Johnson for his duplicitous campaign statements
since the logic involved in running for office is not the same logic as that
required for acting as commander-in-chief. Johnson, as David Wise has
noted, rationalized the inconsistencies of the 1964 presidential campaign
by saying, "I did not mean that we were not going to do any fighting, for
we had already lost many good men in Vietnam."[5] Nevertheless, his deceptive actions were not limited to campaign statements about the Indochina War. One of his most deceptive acts while president involves his
efforts to obtain a congressional resolution that would support any actions the president deemed necessary to handle the crisis in Vietnam.
William Bundy had presented him with a scenario on May 23, 1964, for
immediate escalation in Indochina, part four of which called for a joint
congressional resolution "approving past actions and authorizing what-

ever is necessary with respect to Vietnam."[6] Later that summer, Johnson secured congressional support through the Gulf of Tonkin Resolution.

The events surrounding the Gulf of Tonkin incident were unclear and remain murky today. The first attack on the United States destroyer Maddox on August 2, 1964, was not unprovoked because the North Vietnamese had just been bombarded by eight coastal patrol craft supplied by the United States to South Vietnam.[7] By some accounts, the Maddox fired the first shots and was struck only once by a machine gun bullet.[8] On August 4, the Maddox and the destroyer Turner Joy reported that they were under constant torpedo attack by North Vietnam. Johnson convened the National Security Council and ordered air retaliatory strikes as new information began to filter in. One cable sent by Commodore John Herrick of the Maddox discounted the earlier "attacks." This crucial cable was not made public in 1964 and did not become known to the public until 1968 when the Senate Foreign Relations Committee secured the cable. Herrick's message read:

Review of action makes recorded contacts and torpedoes fired appear doubtful. Freak weather effects and overeager sonarman may have accounted for many reports. No actual visual sightings by Maddox. Suggest complete evaluation before any further action.[9]

However, this evidence was discounted and the Johnson administration continued in its policy of retaliation against the North for an attack which more than likely did not occur. The rest of Johnson's deception surrounding the handling of the war in Vietnam has been well documented in David Halberstam's *The Best and the Brightest,* Daniel Ellsberg's *Papers on the War, The Pentagon Papers,* David Wise's *The Politics of Lying,* and others.[10] Unfortunately for the public, this record of deception was not made explicit until the early 1970s when Johnson was no longer in a position to be held accountable for his actions.

The Secret War in Laos

Perhaps the most instructive use of secret and deceptive presidential policy during the Johnson administration involved the so-called secret war in Laos from 1964 to 1968. The covert war spanned three presidents from Kennedy to Nixon as the United States was involved in Laos essen-

tially between 1962 and 1972. Labels "the secret bombing" of Cambodia
or "the secret war" in Laos are probably misnomers. Certainly, the Laotian
people knew about the United States' involvement when the CIA's forces
grew so large that they could no longer be plausibly denied, and they
realized the extent of U.S. involvement when tons of bombs were dropped
on them throughout the period. Moreover, the Soviet Union, the People's
Republic of China, and most of the U.S. foreign policy allies knew about
the covert involvement in Laos and Cambodia. About the only people who
were not *explicitly* told about U.S. involvement in neutral Laos were Congress and much of the American public. In this limited sense, then, the
United States' covert action in Laos can be called "the secret war" in Laos.

It is sometimes difficult to remember that in the early 1960s Laos rather
than Vietnam was considered the important domino in the Indochina
situation. President Eisenhower had warned incoming President Kennedy
not to lose Laos to the communists.[11] Eisenhower felt that if Laos fell to
the communists, the rest of the area would turn in that direction.

During the first three months of his administration, Kennedy sought an
open diplomatic solution in Laos that would guarantee a truly neutral
government, but he kept alive the option of using U.S. overt military intervention if necessary. Then Great Britain and the Soviet Union called for
an end to the fighting in Laos and a resumption of the Geneva Conference
in late April 1961. This diplomatic call, along with the international embarrassment that the Kennedy administration suffered over the Bay of
Pigs invasion, helped Kennedy to discard the option of overt military
intervention in Laos. As Theodore Sorensen quoted the president, "Thank
God the Bay of Pigs happened when it did. Otherwise we'd be in Laos by
now—and that would be a hundred times worse."[12] However, Kennedy
never discarded the option of covert intervention. Indeed, as Walt Haney
observed, Kennedy approved plans at an April 29, 1961, National Security
Council meeting to "dispatch agents" to Laos and North Vietnam for
purposes of harassment and sabotage under the direction of General
Edward G. Lansdale.[13] This approval of covert intervention in Laos came
two weeks before the opening of the second Geneva Conference.

Under the Kennedy administration's direction, Lansdale administered
the early CIA covert intervention that took the form of organizing the
Meo tribesmen into a paramilitary group. By September 1961 some
11,000 Meos had been organized into guerrilla forces to challenge com-
munist-controlled areas of Laos,[14] and they were operating under the
orders of the CIA in Vientiane, Laos. This covert intervention continued

throughout 1961 and the first half of 1962 as the conflict in Laos continued. Finally, in July 1962, the fourteen nations at the second Geneva Conference agreed to a diplomatic settlement. Prince Souvanna Phouma was given seven seats on the coalition cabinet to represent the neutralist factions, the Pathet Lao communist faction received four seats, and four seats went to the right-wing faction led by Prince Boun Oum and Phoumi Nosavan. Unfortunately, the Geneva Agreements on Laos broke down before the year was over. The North Vietnamese continued supplying covert support to the Pathet Lao and the Kennedy administration continued covert support to the CIA-trained Meo tribesmen.

After the Geneva Agreements in 1962, Kennedy made an important decision to continue U.S. covert intervention in Laos, but, most important, as Fred Branfman has outlined, Kennedy set up a bureaucratic structure to turn the conduct of the secret war in Laos over to the Central Intelligence Agency.[15] Besides giving the CIA control of the conduct of the secret war in Laos, the Kennedy administration made three other structural changes, according to Branfman:

1. The CIA would fund directly an irregular ground force of hill tribes people and others; this force would, in turn be on the front lines and be expected to bear the brunt of the fighting.
2. The CIA would be given direct control over a number of key organizations, allowing it to provide air transport (Air America, later Continental Airlines also) bombing, and other air services.
3. Above all, the CIA would be in operational control of Army and Air Attache offices established in Laos.[16]

These bureaucratic arrangements remained throughout the Kennedy administration as the covert war in Laos continued. When Johnson was thrust into the presidency in November 1963, he was faced with the ongoing covert war in Laos and a bureaucratic agreement that provided support for the ongoing intervention.

The first record of Johnson's approval of the covert intervention in Laos against the Pathet Lao and the National Liberation Front came on January 16, 1964. The program of covert military intervention and operations against North Vietnam called for increased activities in South Vietnam and Laos. The program was developed in the Kennedy administration in May 1963 and approved by the Joint Chiefs on September 9, 1963.[17] Kennedy was assassinated before he could give approval, but the new president, Johnson, gave the go-ahead to the new bureaucratic maneuvers within the first two months of his administration. Thus, Eisenhower's determination not to lose Laos to the communists, which was passed on to Kennedy, had been adopted by the Johnson administration.

The pressure on Johnson to approve the covert intervention does not appear to have been as intense as the bureaucratic pressures on Kennedy during his first two months of office to continue the Bay of Pigs operation. Johnson was merely asked to ratify a CIA-controlled program that was already operating, and not to initiate a new program. However, there may have been subtle, informal pressure on Johnson to manage national security as "Kennedy would have done." New presidents suddenly thrown into office by the death of their former bosses usually do not make radical changes in the management of national security policy. For example, Harry Truman was asked to ratify ongoing bureaucratic projects like the Manhattan Project when he suddenly became the president in 1945, not whether he wanted to continue or discontinue the projects. Likewise, Johnson apparently acquiesced to the CIA-controlled program of covert military operation at first.

The Pentagon Papers do not provide a clear record of the "secret war" in Laos during 1964-68, but they do provide some evidence of the American effort within Laos when it relates to attempts by the United States to stop the DRV (North Vietnam) troop movement within Laos. They also indicate that Johnson expanded the secret war in Laos into an air war in northern and southern Laos while the CIA continued the secret ground war with their makeshift group of Meo tribesmen, other Lao minorities, and Thai recruits.[18] Johnson viewed Laos in the context of "considerations for American interests in Vietnam."[19] In the internal struggles for power within Laos, the United States backed the faction that would allow the United States to continue to violate Laos' neutrality in the fight against North Vietnam. This faction most consistently was the faction led by Prince Souvanna Phouma.

By the mid-1960s the CIA in Laos had grown to immense proportions. No longer did the CIA just organize a small army of Meo tribesmen numbering 11,000, but the CIA found itself commanding an army numbering more than 100,000.[20] The CIA station in Laos had created an organization of huge numbers of Meo, Lao, and Thai peasants, U.S. military advisors, mercenaries, diplomats from the U.S. Mission in Vientiane, Army and Air Force attaches, members of the International Voluntary Services, people from the United States Information Service, some Americans in the Agency for International Development, and pilots from the Navy, Air Force and Marines to form a paramilitary group to conduct the ground and air war in Laos.

The CIA bureaucratic charade required elaborate bookwork to hide the extent of the U.S. commitment in Laos from Congress and the American people. The General Accounting Office was not allowed to monitor the CIA's bookkeeping on the conduct of the war in the 1960s.[21] None of the appropriate committees of Congress were notified about the full extent of U.S. involvement in Laos. Johnson elected to classify the important documents concerning Laos in the name of national security. When information was released by the executive branch, it was often misleading as to the real actions of the CIA's secret force in Laos. For example, Senator Stuart Symington's Subcommittee on Security Agreements and Commitments Abroad released the following item in December 1970:

By classifying the number of daily missions flown by United States aircraft over Northern Laos since 1964—as distinguished from those missions flown over the Ho Chi Minh Trail and thus directly connected to the Vietnam war—the Executive Branch hid from Congress as well as the people that additional commitment, in men and dollars, undertaken to support the Royal Government of Laos.[22]

While giving the CIA the latitude to conduct the covert ground war in Laos during 1964-68, Johnson maintained control over the bombing decisions that would affect Laos during his administration. The neutrality of Laos was consistently violated by the Johnson administration's bombing policies in the Indochina war, and in Johnson's determination, the bombing raids had to remain covert operations because of the complex agreement with Prince Souvanna Phouma. Souvanna Phouma did not want the world to know that the United States was playing a major military role in Laos, since Laos wanted to maintain its neutrality in the eyes of world opinion. Yet, Souvanna needed U.S. backing in order to hold off his competing faction, the Pathet Lao, and Johnson needed his permission to secretly bomb North Vietnam troops that were operating in southern Laos. Johnson and Souvanna reached agreement in principle on the complex secret pact that would maintain Laos' neutrality by denying existence of the U.S. military position in Laos and, at the same time, grant the United States permission to disregard the neutral status of Laos.

This secret agreement between Johnson and Souvanna Phouma often led to absurd consequences. For example, in August 1964 the U.S. position on a Geneva-like peace conference to settle Laos was remarkable in that the United States moved against the peace conference because it would harm interests of the United States, which was trying to bring peace to Indochina. A negotiated settlement in Laos would have ended the CIA's secret ground war in Laos and eliminated the secret bombing option against North Vietnam troops in the panhandle of southern Laos. In short, peace in Laos would have hindered the war-making effort against North Vietnam. In a memo of August 11, 1964, William Bundy clearly stated the U.S. position:

1. We would wish to slow down any progress toward a conference and to hold Souvanna to the firmest possible position. . . .
2. If, despite our best efforts, Souvanna on his own, or in response to third-country pressures, started to move rapidly toward a conference, we would have a difficult problem. . . .[23]

Later Johnson and the National Security Council would consider the problem of how to keep U.S. involvement in Laos a secret while publicizing the American effort in Laos to the South Vietnamese troops to bolster their spirits. On November 29, 1964, a final draft called "Draft Position Paper on Southeast Asia" (principal author William Bundy) outlined Johnson's early policy:

In the case of Laos, we will obtain RLG [Royal Laotian Government] approval of an intensified program of [U.S. armed] reconnaissance strikes both in the Panhandle area of Laos and along the key infiltration routes in central Laos. These actions will not be publicized except to the degree approved by the RLG. It is important however, for the purposes of morale in SV, that their existence be generally known.[24]

However, it was still important for the executive branch that the bombing operation in Laos be kept secret, at least from Congress and the public, in order to minimize opposition and honor Laotian neutrality. At a meeting of the National Security Council on December 12, 1964, that adopted a new bombing proposal created by the Joint Chiefs to expand the bombing war in Laos to the central and northern areas, the NSC agreed that no public statements would be made about the bombing in Laos "unless a plane were lost."[25] Then the United States "would con-

tinue to insist that we were merely escorting reconnaissance flights as requested by the Laotian government"[26] if any nation protested after the
discovery.

The U.S. bombing continued throughout the Johnson administration;
each year saw increasing bomb tonnage dropped on Laos. The U.S. Congress was not informed about the extent of the bombing, and the appropriate committees of Congress did not press the executive on these matters.
The few members of Congress who were selectively informed about the
administration's Laotian bombing were led to believe that the bombing
was minimal and that it was related "solely to operations around the Ho
Chi Minh Trail and the war in Vietnam."[27]

As Walt Haney has observed, Johnson engaged in substantial deceptions
about the bombing war in Laos even during times that were usually considered his "dove" moments.[28] For example, when Johnson announced
on March 31, 1968, that he would not seek reelection and that he had
called a partial halt to the bombing of North Vietnam, the U.S. planes
were actually sent to bomb Laos. Likewise, when Johnson announced a
total bombing halt over North Vietnam on October 31, 1968, to make a
complete gesture for peace, the U.S. planes that had been participating
in the limited bombing of North Vietnam moved over to join in the total
bombing of Laos.[29] Note in Table 2 the tonnage dropped over Laos in
November and December 1968 during Johnson's peace efforts.

TABLE 2: U.S. Bombing in Laos, 1965-1968

Year	Fighter Bomber Tonnage	B-52 Tonnage	B-52 % of Total	Total Tonnage
1965	12,599 (est.)	469	3.6	13,068
1966	60,552	13,068	17.8	73,620
1967	82,911	45,114	35.2	128,025
1968				
(Jan.-Oct.)	88,975	58,811	39.8	147,786
(Nov.-Dec.)	56,059	35,772	39.0	91,831
1968 Total	145,034	94,583	39.5	239.617
TOTALS	301,096	153,234	32.0	454,330

Source: Inset by Senator Stuart Symington, *Congressional Record,* July 18,
1973, S. 13848.

The remarkable thing about the Johnson administration's conduct of the air war in Laos during 1965 through 1968 was the degree to which it kept U.S. participation hidden from most of Congress and the public. Johnson's successor, Richard Nixon, would have trouble keeping from Congress and the public the fact that he had secretly bombed the neutral country of Cambodia for fourteen months, but Johnson was able to effectively engage in secret bombings for *four years*. The Nixon administration continued the Johnson administration's policy of bombing Laos, but Nixon had difficulty in keeping the bombing covert, especially since Nixon, prone to excesses, increased the tonnage dropped on Laos to four times what the Johnson administration had dropped. (See Table 3.)

TABLE 3: U.S. Bombing in Laos, 1969-1973

Year	Fighter Bomber Tonnage	B-52 Tonnage	B-52 % of Total	Total Tonnage
1969	356,551	159,491	30.9	516,042
1970	235,080	232,025	49.7	467,105
1971	216,987	230,016	51.5	447,003
1972	77,406	61,392	44.2	138,798
1973 (Jan.-March)	33,935	42,790	55.8	76,725
TOTALS	919,959	725,714	44.0	1,645,673

Source: Inset by Senator Stuart Symington, *Congressional Record*, July 18, 1973, S. 13848.

Within Nixon's first year in office, his administration had caused more tonnage to be dropped on Laos than the Johnson administration had dropped in the entire four-year air war in Laos. By March 1970, it had become ludicrous for the Nixon administration to deny that the United States was engaged in such a massive air war in Laos, therefore Nixon became the first U.S. president to admit the presence of U.S. military personnel in Laos when he admitted that the United States was flying "combat support missions for Laotian forces when requested to do so by the Royal Laotian Government."[30]

Explanation of the Johnson Administration's Covert Response: Applying the Framework

Personality-Private Motives

Many students of the presidency, including myself, have a tendency to personalize presidential decision making. This can become a scholarly sin when one overemphasizes presidential responsibility in the decision at the cost of neglecting other inputs from presidential advisors—the National Security Council, the Pentagon, the CIA and the State Department, for example. Thus, when presidential decision making is overpersonalized, the conduct of the Korean War becomes "Truman's policy" rather than the "Truman administration's policy"; or the federal intervention in the Little Rock schools in 1957 becomes "Eisenhower's decision" rather than the "Eisenhower administration's decision." Yet, sometimes a presidential personality so dominates a specific decision that the decision is more accurately labeled *his* decision than his *administration's* decision.

Johnson had such a forceful personality, which was at times capable of compelling submission from subordinates. On issues that were important to Johnson, he sometimes used techniques to gain consensus within his inner circle of advisors that went beyond presidential persuasion. The techniques included berating, humiliating, ignoring, and seeking sympathy from aides. These techniques to gain consensus were not unique to Johnson, of course. It is just that he did them so well, as the vast literature on the Johnson administration suggests.

There are four aspects of Johnson's personality that may be important in understanding the covert war in Laos: his passion for secrecy, his inability to take personal criticism, his symptoms of classic paranoia, and his machismo.

By most accounts, Johnson had a "passion for secrecy."[31] As Chester Cooper has noted about Johnson's secrecy, "This compulsive secrecy was not so much a conscious conspiracy as it was a reflection of the President's personal style—a style that favored a 'closed' rather than an 'open' system of policymaking."[32] Johnson had a tendency to regard secrecy as an end in itself rather than a means. On a number of occasions, Johnson was known to have changed his policy decision after it had "leaked" to the press in order to embarrass the press for their "mistake." John Franklin Campbell reported:

When the *Wall Street Journal* published speculation that the United States might bomb oil depots near Hanoi, Johnson, who had already ordered such an attack, cancelled it and launched an investigation of the bureaucracy to determine the source of the "leak." In a pattern that had been repeated before and would be repeated again, FBI agents descended on the State Department to interview all officials who were privy to the secret information.[33]

When Johnson used secrecy as a means, he often used it as an instrument of control. Johnson once told several reporters on his plane in 1964, "If you play along with me, I'll play along with you. . . . If you want to play it the other way, I know how to play it both ways, too, and I know how to cut off the flow of news."[34] David Halberstam described Johnson's passion for secrecy and its decision-making consequences in the following passage:

His was a far more structured government; decisions were made at the very top, in part because of his almost *neurotic desire for secrecy.* The more men who participate, the more gossip there is going to be, the more rumor that maybe Lyndon Johnson himself didn't make those decisions, that he needed people to make them for him, or worse, that there was disagreement at the top level of government, thus perhaps an inkling, an impression, that the decision was not perfect. *So the way to control secrecy was to control decision making,* to keep it in as few hands as possible and make sure those hands were loyal, more committed to working with the President than anything else.[35] (emphasis added)

Apparently, Johnson had a compulsion to control most aspects of presidential decision making. George Reedy wrote that Johnson insisted upon "maintaining tight control" over every minor detail, and James David Barber described Johnson's personal involvement in the bombing decision, "At least from 1966 on, it was the war in Vietnam that consumed these immense energies, as Johnson pored over detailed maps to choose bombing targets and had himself awakened at three in the morning to get reports on air strikes."[36]

Closely related to Johnson's passion for secrecy and his compulsion to control most aspects of presidential decision making is Johnson's inability to take criticism. As Erwin Hargrove has observed, "He [Johnson] wanted *no criticism at all.* . . . Johnson's general style of policy decision and executive rule was to seek unanimity in government and absolute submission to his wishes"[37] (emphasis added). Johnson could not distinguish very well between criticisms of his policies and personal criticism. If someone opposed the Johnson admininstration's policy in Indochina, then Johnson interpreted this as personal criticism of Lyndon Baines Johnson. Moreover, *Johnson tended to personalize his own decisions.* Within the inner circle of advisors he often spoke of "my boys in Vietnam," "my planes," and "my ships," and how he was going to slip "his hand up Ho Chi Minh's leg before Ho even knew about it."[38]

This inability to take what he interpreted as personal criticism often manifested itself in his exhibition of symptoms of classic paranoia. To be sure, there is not enough evidence available to be able to precisely label Johnson's personality as "paranoid" in the clinical sense. The level of sophistication and the systematic effort that is needed to exactly classify a person as paranoid is beyond the scope of this research. However, Johnson did exhibit a few symptoms of paranoia in the popular psychological sense of the word. As antiwar criticism mounted, Johnson began to see enemies everywhere. He told an aide, "I can't trust anybody! What are they trying to do to me. Everybody is trying to cut me down, destroy me!"[39] As Halberstam described the situation, "he [Johnson] was immobilized, surrounded, seeing critics everywhere. Critics became enemies; enemies became traitors; and the press, which a year earlier had been so friendly, was now filled with enemies baying at his heels."[40] Johnson once commented about the press that, "They warp everything I do, they lie about me and what I do, they don't know the meaning of truth. They are liars and cheats."[41]

Yet even "paranoids" have real opposition. When most modern presidents look out from the isolated White House, they seem to view only the restraints on their power. As Roger Hilsman has noted, "They see obstacles and opposition, whether actual or potential, in mass publics, in the press, in Congress, in the departments and agencies of the Executive Branch, in the embassies overseas, and in the foreign governments."[42] However, the problem comes about when presidents move beyond this institutionalized state of perpetual opposition that characterizes some democracies to a condition that equates legitimate, systemic opposition to challenges by one's *enemies.* At times, Johnson appeared to make that jump in logic. Richard Hofstader in *The Paranoid Style in American Politics* noted that "the central preconception of the paranoid style is the existence of a vast, insidious, preternaturally effective international conspiratorial network designed to perpetuate acts of the most fiendish character."[43] Johnson wanted to believe that the "international conspiratorial network" that was behind the domestic opposition to his Indochina policies was communism. Since he was the president and he believed that presidents should have united, bipartisan support in foreign affairs, opposition to his foreign policy could have only come about because of some conspiracy to "get him," or so Johnson seemed to believe, and not because of any legitimate policy differences.

Finally, another aspect of Johnson's personality that might relate to his covert response in Laos was his machismo. Johnson seemed to want to be viewed as a tough, macho president who would not back down from a challenge by the communists. A real "man" would not have doubts about the president's Vietnam policy, he seemed to believe, therefore, opponents of the war were less than real "men." When Johnson was informed that one member of his administration had suddenly become a "dove" on Indochina, Johnson reportedly said, "Hell, he has to squat to piss."[44]

A personality-focused explanation of the Johnson administration's covert response in Laos would combine the four previously discussed aspects of Johnson's personality—his passion for secrecy, his inability to take criticism, his paranoia, or more accurately his inability to separate legitimate opponents from enemies, and his macho posturing—to argue that within Johnson's psychological make-up there existed a self-defeating tendency toward secrecy and deception. Barber described Johnson's presidential character as the classic "active-negative," a president who expends an enormous amount of energy on the job without reaping any psychological rewards that can follow from a competent exercise of presidential power.[45] Like other "active-negatives," Johnson had a tendency to rigidify around an important (to him) policy issue which he had personalized in the face of substantial opposition and in the face of counterarguments and counterevidence. Johnson's character and psychological make-up was such that it may have led him to select deceptive behavior over overt presidential policy actions when faced with a choice, or so the personality explanation of Johnson's covert behavior would contend. As Barber observed:

President Johnson's *manipulative* maneuvering, his penchant for *secrecy,* his *lying,* his avid interest in himself, his sense of being *surrounded by hostile forces,* and his immense anger all indicate, I think, a profound insecurity—not so much about his "intelligence and ability" (he knew he had those), but precisely about his "heart" and "guts." His heart symbolizes his conscience-bound need to be loving and generous, to "do unto others as you would have others do unto you." His gut symbolizes toughness, the press for power, the *need to do it to the other guy before he can do it to you.* Caught between those forces, Johnson thrashed about for some ground in the middle, loosing the tremendous tension he felt in a flood of talk.[46] (emphasis added)

Although the personality perspective perhaps helps us to understand the psychological context in which Johnson processed information and made decisions, it does not specifically tell us why, in the particular case of Laos, Johnson selected covert action in the ground and air war while selecting more overt actions in Vietnam.

Pragmatic Calculations Component

The pragmatic calculations approach helps one distinguish between more or less covert actions in Laos and more or less publicized actions in Vietnam. One may fault Johnson's specific calculations and computations in the cost-benefit analysis of whether one ought to bomb a neutral country secretly, or one may argue that another president would have decided differently. But the pragmatic component argues that Johnson appeared to choose covert action in Laos by using a pragmatic approach.

As noted earlier, the elements of the calculus include the need to promote national security, the strategic advantages gained from secrecy, ongoing foreign policy commitments, the domestic political environment, and the need to conceal incompetence, inefficiency, wrongdoing, personal embarrassment, national embarrassment, or administrative error. In the bombing of Laos, the most crucial component in Johnson's calculation was the fact that Laos was a neutral country and that Souvanna Phouma had specifically requested covert intervention. The request by the Royal Laotian government to intervene on its behalf while keeping the operation secret provided Johnson with a particular reason for keeping the specific bombing of Laos covert. Johnson had no similar hesitations about publicizing bombing in Indochina, particularly in North Vietnam. Indeed, for Johnson, the bombing was all part of his political game plan. Publicizing the scope and intensity of U.S. bombing efforts in Southeast

Asia was a means for Johnson to demonstrate his toughness and resolve in meeting the communist threat. As Johnson confided to Doris Kearns:

> I saw our bombs as my political resources for negotiating a peace. On the one hand, our planes and our bombs could be used as carrots for the South, strengthening the morale of the South Vietnamese and pushing them to clean up their corrupt house, by demonstrating the depth of our commitment to the war. On the other hand, our bombs could be used as sticks against the North, pressuring North Vietnam to stop its aggression against the South.[47]

By keeping part of his Indochina bombing secret, as in the case of Laos, Johnson specifically went against the grain of his desire to publicize the bombing as a diplomatic tool. Clearly, then, the main reason Johnson secretly bombed Laos was because Souvanna Phouma had requested that it remain secret so he would not be accused of violating his neutral stance. If the Royal Laotian government had requested that Johnson publicize the bombing in Laos, then Johnson would probably have done so, since he had shown no great reluctance to publicize previous escalations in the war in Indochina.

Thus, Johnson engaged in the secret bombing of Laos not because publicity of the operation would hurt the United States in the eyes of world opinion for violating a neutral country and not because publicity would have further aroused public opinion at home against the war (which it might have done), but because Johnson wanted to protect Souvanna's position. As a rational, pragmatic actor, Johnson governed his Indochina policy by three sets of decision rules, according to Ellsberg:

> Rule 1. *Do not* lose South Vietnam to Communist control or appear likely to do so, before the next election.
> Rule 2. *Do not,* unless essential to satisfy Rule 1 in the immediate crisis or an earlier one:
> a. bomb South Vietnam or Laos;
> b. bomb North Vietnam;
> c. commit U.S. combat troops to Vietnam;
> d. commit U.S. combat troops in Laos or Cambodia;
> e. institute wartime domestic controls;
> f. destroy Hanoi or Haiphong or the dike system, or mine Haiphong harbor;
> g. mobilize reserves;

h. assume full, overt administrative authority and military command in South Vietnam;
i. invade North Vietnam;
j. use nuclear weapons.

Rule 3. Do choose actions that will:

a. minimize the risk of loss—or public expectation of eventual loss—within the next six months, so far as possible without violating Rule 2.
b. if this risk is significant without certain actions so far "prohibited" by Rule 2, break constraints to use the types of actions minimally necessary (as judged by President) to reduce the risk to a very low level.
c. so far as is consistent with Rule 1, and using fully any action no longer prohibited, maximize the probability of an eventual "win," in the sense of eliminating the Communist party in South Vietnam and assuring indefinitely a non-Communist regime.
d. so far as is consistent with Rule 1, do not take actions that might *appear* to preclude or indefinitely forgo an eventual "win," i.e., a "no-win strategy."[48]

Johnson did not want to be the first president to lose a war, and he particularly did not want to lose South Vietnam to the communists.[49] By secretly bombing Laos, Johnson could continue fighting the North Vietnamese *who had also violated the neutrality of Laos,* and at the same time he could support Souvanna Phouma against the Pathet Lao.

Bureaucratic Politics Component

Though Richard Neustadt's book *Presidential Power,* with its Machiavellian maxims, guided Kennedy in his effort to gain control of presidential decision making, Johnson used no such manual. However, Johnson tried to actively structure those decisions that were important to him in an effort to not waste valuable presidential time. The conduct of the ground war in Laos was not an issue that demanded a lot of Johnson's presidential time. Making foreign policy with regard to Laos was just a sideshow compared to the amount of presidential energy that Johnson expended in formulating a Vietnam policy. As Dean Rusk noted about the lack of importance of the Laotian crisis, "After 1963 Laos was only the wart on the hog of Vietnam."[50] Warts do not demand constant presidential attention. Rather, they allow the president to delegate some of his decision-making powers to the appropriate bureaucratic structures.

In the conduct of the war in Laos, Johnson delegated the control of the secret ground confrontation to the CIA. Kennedy had left him with the bureaucratic structure and the covert intervention heritage in Laos. Johnson retained the informal agreement that delegated the command power of running a clandestine war to the U.S.'s top clandestine bureaucratic organization—the operations and plans section of the Central Intelligence Agency. The decision to engage in covert intervention in Laos can partly be explained by the bureaucratic politics perspective, which focuses on the process by which the decision emerged. Johnson can be viewed as just one player in the bargaining environment in late 1963 and early 1964 when his initial commitment was made. The other players included the State Department, the National Security Council, leftover Kennedy national security advisors, and, most important, the CIA.

One of the CIA's main organizational interests was the need to maintain autonomy in conducting covert interventions. The CIA competed for a role and a mission during the Kennedy administration's Laotian crisis during 1961-62. As William Colby, head of the CIA Laotian operations in 1962, described the competition:

My arguments [for covert intervention] became more forceful, reflecting the intense cables I was receiving from the two CIA officers who were still up in the hills observing and reporting on what was happening. . . . During some of our weekly sessions he [Averell Harriman] would ostentatiously turn off his hearing aid in the middle of my arguments, or bait me mercilessly until we engaged in a shouting match, to test how firmly I believed in the proposals I was advancing . . . he knew that CIA offered a unique capability to do what needed to be done quickly, effectively, and under discipline, without the bureaucratic and institutional problems other agencies, military and civilian, presented.[51]

After Colby's arguments eventually won out in the bureaucratic struggle within the Kennedy administration, Colby directed the early ground war in Laos.[52] When Johnson was suddenly thrown into the White House in November 1963, the CIA had no desire to give up their clandestine operations in Laos. Moreover, Johnson showed no inclination to reevaluate the bureaucratic arrangements that allowed the CIA to run a large-scale paramilitary operation in Laos. Even if he had wanted to terminate the intervention, that goal would have been very difficult to accomplish. As Cyrus Vance told the Church committee:

Paramilitary operations are perhaps unique in that it is more difficult to withdraw from them, once started, than covert operations. This is well illustrated by the case of the Congo, where a decision was taken to withdraw in early 1966, and it took about a year and a half before the operation was terminated. Once a paramilitary operation is commenced, the recipient of the paramilitary aid tends to become dependent upon it and inevitably advances the argument that to cut back or terminate the aid would do the recipient great damage. This makes it especially difficult to disengage.[53]

Although the bureaucratic politics component is helpful in understanding some aspects of the Johnson administration's covert ground war in Laos, the component does not have as much success in explaining the Johnson administration's covert bombing in Laos. Johnson certainly did not engage in the practice of covert bombing because the Kennedy administration had left such a heritage; Kennedy left no such legacy. The bombing policy came clearly from the Johnson administration.

Much of the work that has been done on the decision to escalate the war in Indochina and on the decision to bomb stresses the cohesiveness of Johnson's small decision-making group within the White House. The bombing decision (and, thus, indirectly the decision to bomb Laos) was made in a piecemeal, incremental fashion without the knowledge or awareness of the "quicksand" in Vietnam, according to some accounts.[54] Johnson is portrayed as a president who, through faulty advice, commits the United States to the never-ending quagmire of Vietnam. Johnson is relieved of direct responsibility by some accounts because he was unaware of the consequences of actions that he took under the cohesive national security advice that came his way. Johnson is viewed as the one who led the United States as a stumbling, bumbling giant into the morass of Indochina. Johnson's personality and private motives do not play a crucial role in explaining the decision to escalate in these quagmire accounts, as Ellsberg has noted.[55] For example, Townsend Hoopes maintained about the pattern of escalation:

It was, then this somewhat amorphous set of arrangements for foreign policy formulation, coordination, and control that President Johnson inherited. While it is speculative, to say the least, whether a man of his galvanic temperament, irregular administrative habits, and *passion for secretiveness* could or would have used a more formal structure to good advantage, the fact is that he was bequeathed a rather fragile apparatus tailored to John F. Kennedy's specifications and heavily dependent upon the kind of affinity for foreign affairs that Kennedy possessed and Johnson did not. This seemed another of those incongrous inheritances, with which our recent history is liberally sprinkled, that produce an unfortunate, even a tragic effect, *but are traceable to no villain.*[56] (emphasis added)

However, as Ellsberg and, particularly, Doris Kearns have observed, Johnson was not "the prisoner of a bureaucratic structure that coerced or deceived him into escalation."[57] Although compelling arguments can be made that Johnson was the victim of an inadequate advisory system,[58] or the victim of "groupthink" in escalation in Vietnam,[59] Kearns's counter-argument is even more compelling. As Kearns explains:

If Johnson had wanted different advice, or a wider range of opinion at the top, he could have changed his group of advisors. He could have dismissed Dean Rusk and elevated George Ball to Secretary of State. He could have replaced McGeorge Bundy with Bill Moyers. He could have promoted Westmoreland out of Vietnam and appointed a new commander more congenial to withdrawal. Moreover, many of those advocating escalation had taken that position as it became clearer that escalation would be the President's own decision. If he had shifted, most of them would have shifted. . . . The point is that Lyndon Johnson never tried.[60]

Institutional Component

An institutional approach to understanding the Johnson administration's covert response in Laos would be to examine the interaction between the president's role enactment as commander-in-chief and the institutional responsibilities of Congress to engage in oversight. Johnson had seen other presidents such as Eisenhower and Kennedy make major commitments in Indochina to prevent the area from falling to communist aggression, but as Hilsman has observed, "It is clear that President Johnson felt more strongly than Kennedy that American security was affected by the struggle in Vietnam."[61] In Johnson's conception of his commander-in-chief duties, he expected bipartisan support from Congress for his foreign policy. After all, he was the "leader of the free world," and the "only president that we had," as he liked to believe.

The CIA covert ground war had begun to develop standard operating procedures and routines by the time Johnson replaced Kennedy as the top national security manager, but the air war grew out of Johnson's own peculiar conception of his commander-in-chief responsibilities. Congress was not totally excluded from these covert operations. Rather it was asked to give its unqualified support for the operations in the few limited oversight encounters that occurred during 1964-68.

The idea that the president of the United States was engaged in a unilateral, covert, unconstitutional, and undeclared war within Laos would have been an absurd notion to Johnson. He had informed Congress, in his view, and if Congress did not agree with his administration's policy, then it was free to challenge the president. As former CIA Director Richard Helms later told the Senate Intelligence Committee, "I don't know of any director, at least during my time, who fiddle-faddled with Congress. We presented a budget every year that had all the details. *There were no secret wars in Laos and all that nonsense.* That's part of the mythology of Washington"[62] (emphasis added).

Was Congress informed about the covert war in Laos? The answer to this is still very much in dispute. Former chairman of the CIA subcommittee of the Senate Appropriations Committee, Senator Allen J. Ellender, added to the confusion in the following exchange with Senator William Fulbright:

Fulbright: It has been stated that the CIA has 36,000 there [in Laos]. It is no secret. Would the Senator say that before the creation of the army in Laos they came before the committee and the committee knew of it and approved it?
Ellender: *Probably so.*
Fulbright: Did the Senator approve it?
Ellender: I was not—*I did not know anything about it. . . .* I never asked, to begin with, whether or not there were any funds to carry on the war in this sum the CIA asked for. It never dawned on me to ask about it.[63] (emphasis added)

Ellender went on to say, "I did see it published in the newspapers some time ago."[64] Ellender's testimony is confusing because first he claimed that the CIA came before his commitee with the budget details of the Laotian operation and then he claimed he did not know anything about it.

William Colby has long maintained that the so-called secret war in Laos was not really a secret war. Colby told Senator Stuart Symington, "The appropriate committees of the Congress and a number of individual senators and congressmen were briefed on CIA activities in Laos during the period covered."[65] Most recently in his book *Honorable Men,* Colby argued that the so-called secret war controversy led to such things as "Ellender saying on the Senate floor that he did not know whether CIA funds were being used to conduct the war in Laos, a statement that was simply not true, and another Senator publicly attacked CIA's 'secret war' when he had been fully briefed on it and had actually visited the area."[66] Given Colby's record of straightforward and relatively honest testimony with the Rockefeller commission and the Church committee, it becomes more difficult to doubt the veracity of Colby's statements on Laos. However, Colby has been known to make misleading statements about the Laotian operation in the past. In 1974 Colby told a group of scholars that CIA had lost only eight officers during the entire period, but in 1978 Colby said that "CIA casualties during this long war [were limited] to only about five killed."[67]

Regardless of Colby's claims to honesty, Senator Symington also has a claim to sincerity. Symington told Colby in 1973 that "I learned most of my information about Laos from the newspapers."[68] In 1970 Symington's Subcommittee on Security Agreements and Commitments Abroad submitted their final report, which indicted the executive branch for its secrecy over the covert ground war and the covert air war in Laos. The subcommittee concluded, *"The Congress did not inquire into, nor was it kept informed of,* United States military activities in and over Laos."[69]

It is probably fair to conclude that the executive, particularly various CIA directors, did not go out of the way to keep the full Congress informed of CIA activities in Laos during the Johnson administration. Nor did the Johnson administration provide the complete story of its covert bombing of Laos. However, Congress made no effort to become informed as it relied on the minimal "oversight" of the appropriate committees. The various committees engaged in collective intelligence "overlook" rather than oversight during the period of the "secret war" in Laos.

Summary

Again, by applying the four components of the framework to explain covert presidential actions, different aspects of the problem of secrecy and deception are highlighted. For the secret CIA ground war in Laos during the Johnson administration from 1963 to 1968, the bureaucratic politics component seems to best fit the case study, with the pragmatic component supplying a strong second best explanation for secrecy and deception. However, for the secret bombing of Laos from 1964 to 1968, the pragmatic component best explains Johnson's secret and deceptive actions. But the personality approach provides a moderately strong second explanation for this case study.

During the period 1964-68, Johnson continually communicated two false impressions to the public, as Barber has noted:

1. that the major emphasis of effort in his government was on making peace through negotiations. (Johnson knew this to be false—in fact, he kept the top brainpower in his administration constantly working on warmaking.)
2. that he was not altering the character of the war as he escalated it. (Johnson knew this to be false—in fact, he transformed a minor military advisory mission into a full-scale war.)[70]

The consequences of this kind of secretive and deceptive behavior will be evaluated in Chapter 7.

Notes

1. David Wise, *The Politics of Lying* (New York: Vintage, 1973), pp. 48-51.

2. Daniel Ellsberg, *Papers on the War* (New York: Simon & Schuster, Pocket Books, 1972), pp. 139-40; Wise, *The Politics of Lying*; Richard J. Barnet, *Roots of War* (New York: Pelican Book, Penguin, 1973), p. 126; *The Pentagon Papers* (The Senator Gravel ed.) Vol. 5, Critical Essays. ed. Noam Chomsky and Howard Zinn (Boston: Beacon Press, 1972); and *The Pentagon Papers* (New York: New York Times-Bantam Books, 1971).

3. Quotes from Jack Sheperd and Christopher S. Wren, eds., *Quotations from Chairman LBJ* (New York: Simon & Schuster, 1968), pp. 64-70.

4. Document no. 81, *The Pentagon Papers* (New York: New York Times-Bantam), pp. 359-60.

5. Lyndon Johnson, *The Vantage Point,* cited in Wise, *The Politics of Lying,* p. 66.

6. *See* Charles M. Hardin, *Presidential Power and Accountability: Toward a New Constitution* (Chicago: University of Chicago Press, 1974), p. 100; *The Pentagon Papers* (New York: New York Times-Bantam), p. 247.

7. Hardin, *Presidential Power and Accountability,* p. 101; Wise, *The Politics of Lying,* pp. 62-66; Joseph C. Goulden, *Truth Is the First Casualty* (New York: Rand McNally, 1969), contains an excellent account of the deception surrounding the Tonkin Gulf "incident,"; *see also The Gulf of Tonkin, The 1964 Incidents, Hearings* (Senate Foreign Relations Committee, February 20, 1968).

8. Wise, *The Politics of Lying,* p. 62.

9. Hardin, *Presidential Power and Accountability*, p. 103; Wise, *The Politics of Lying*, pp. 62-63; *and see* in general Eugene G. Windchy, *A Documentary of the Incidents in the Tonkin Gulf* (Garden City, N.Y.: Doubleday, 1971); Anthony Austin, *The President's War* (New York: A New York Times Book, 1971); and *The Pentagon Papers* (New York: New York Times-Bantam, 1971), Chap. 5, "The Covert War and Tonkin Gulf—February to August, 1964."

10. David Halberstam, *The Best and the Brightest* (New York: Fawcett Crest, 1973); Ellsberg, *Papers on the War; The Pentagon Papers* (Gravel ed.); *The Pentagon Papers* (New York: New York Times-Bantam); Wise, *The Politics of Lying;* Barnet, *Roots of War;* and Ben Bagdikian, "LBJ and the Press: or the Commander-in-Chief Thought He Was Editor-in-Chief," in Bagdikian, *The Effete Conspiracy* (New York: Harper & Row, 1974).

11. *The Pentagon Papers* (Gravel ed.) 2, pp. 636-37.

12. Theodore Sorensen, *Kennedy* (New York: Harper & Row, 1965), p. 64.

13. *The Pentagon Papers* (Gravel ed.) 2, pp. 640-41; *and see* Walt Haney, "The Pentagon Papers and the United States Involvement in Laos," in *The Pentagon Papers* (Gravel ed.) 5, p. 262.

14. Ibid., 2, p. 647; 5, p. 263; *and see The Pentagon Papers* (United States Government ed.) edition 11, pp. 247-48.

15. Fred Branfman, "The President's Secret Army: A Case Study of CIA in Laos, 1962-1972," in *The CIA File*, ed. Robert Borosage and John Marks (New York: Grossman, 1976), p. 54.

16. Ibid., p. 54; Haney, "The Pentagon Papers and the United States Involvement in Laos," p. 267; Charles Stevenson, *The End of Nowhere: American Policy in Laos Since 1954* (Boston: Beacon Press, 1972), p. 186; *see also* Fred Branfman, "Presidential War in Laos 1964-1970," in *Laos: War and Revolution*, ed. Nina Adams and Alfred McCoy (New York: Harper & Row, 1970), pp. 223-64.

17. Noam Chomsky, "The Pentagon Papers as Propaganda and History, in *The Pentagon Papers* (Gravel ed.) 5, p. 191.

18. Haney, "The Pentagon Papers and the United States Involvement in Laos," p. 273.

19. Ibid., p. 279.

20. Branfman, "The President's Secret Army," p. 71.

21. Ibid., p. 71.

22. Report to the Committee on Foreign Relations, U.S. Senate by Subcommittee on Security Agreements and Commitments Abroad (Senator Stuart Symington, Chairman), December 21, 1970, 91st Cong., 2nd sess., p. 17.

23. *The Pentagon Papers* (Gravel ed.), 3, pp. 528-29.

24. *The Pentagon Papers* (New York: New York Times-Bantam), p. 376.

25. Haney, "The Pentagon Papers and the United States Involvement in Laos," p. 271.

26. *The Pentagon Papers* (Gravel ed.), 3, pp. 253-54.

27. Subcommittee on Security Agreements and Commitments Abroad (Senator Symington, Chairman), p. 5.

28. Haney, "The Pentagon Papers and the United States Involvement in Laos," p. 275; *and see The Pentagon Papers* (Gravel ed.) 4, p. 595.

29. Haney, ibid., p. 275; *and see* Raphael Littauer and Norman Uphoff, eds. *The Air War in Indochina* (Boston: Beacon Press, 1972) p. 78.

30. *New York Times,* text of Nixon's Speech, March 7, 1970.

31. Townsend Hoopes, *The Limits of Intervention* (New York: David McKay, 1970), p. 5. *See also* James David Barber, *The Presidential Character* (Englewood Cliffs, N.J.: Prentice-Hall, 1972), p. 94; and Erwin C. Hargrove, *The Power of the Modern Presidency* (New York: Alfred Knopf, 1974), p. 38.

32. Chester Cooper, *The Last Crusade: America in Vietnam* (New York: Dodd Mead, 1970), p. 416.

33. John Franklin Campbell, *The Foreign Affairs Fudge Factory* (New York: Basic Books, 1971), p. 155. *See also* Cooper, *The Last Crusade,* p. 416.

34. Chalmers Roberts, *First Rough Draft* (New York: 1973), p. 229.

35. Halberstam, *The Best and the Brightest,* p. 556.

36. George Reedy, *The Twilight of the Presidency* (New York: New American Library, 1970), p. 31; *and see* Barber, *The Presidential Character,* pp. 52-53.

37. Hargrove, *The Power of the Modern Presidency,* p. 38.

38. Halberstam, *The Best and the Brightest,* p. 721.

39. Barber, *The Presidential Character,* p. 53.

40. Halberstam, *The Best and the Brightest,* p. 757.

41. Barber, *The Presidential Character,* p. 54.

42. Roger Hilsman, *The Politics of Policy Making in Defense and Foreign Affairs* (New York: Harper & Row, 1971), p. 22. *See also* Richard Neustadt, *Presidential Power* (New York: John Wiley & Sons, 1960 and 1964).

43. Quoted in Howard Zinn, "Munich, Dominoes, and Containment," in *Trends and Tragedies in American Foreign Policy,* ed. Michael Parenti (Boston: Little, Brown, 1971), p. 180.

44. Halberstam, *The Best and the Brightest,* p. 645. *See also* Richard Barnet, *Roots of War,* and John Orman, "The Macho Presidential Style," *Indiana Social Studies Quarterly* February 1977, pp. 51-60.

45. Barber, *The Presidential Character.*

46. Ibid., p. 94.

47. Doris Kearns, *Lyndon Johnson and the American Dream* (New York: Harper & Row, 1976), p. 264.

48. Ellsberg, *Papers on the War,* pp. 137-38. The consequences of these decision-making rules in regard to communications from the president to Congress and the public are that the president expresses optimism on both the short- and the long-term prospects of the actual programs. Moreover, the president, according to Ellsberg, conceals indications of possible inadequacy of current programs. Finally, the president conceals the full extent of programs actually decided upon, instead giving the impression that fully scheduled buildups are resulting from sequential, marginal, contingent *ad hoc* decisions. Ellsberg, *Papers on the War,* pp. 139-40.

49. Kearns, *Lyndon Johnson,* pp. 258-59, and Barnet, *Roots of War,* p. 87.

50. Dean Rusk, quoted in Stevenson, *The End of Nowhere,* p. 180.

51. William Colby, *Honorable Men: My Life in the CIA* (New York: Simon & Schuster, 1978), pp. 193-94.

52. Ibid., pp. 191-202. *See also* Victor Marchetti and John Marks, *The CIA and*

the Cult of Intelligence (New York: Dell, 1975), pp. 235-37.

53. Cyrus Vance testimony, 12/5/75, Hearings, Vol. 7, p. 85 footnote; *and see Foreign and Military Intelligence, Final Report,* Book I, of the Select Committee to Study Governmental Operations with Respect to Intelligence Activities, U.S. Senate (Senator Frank Church, Chairman), April 26, 1976, pp. 155-56.

54. The "quagmire" views include Arthur Schlesinger, Jr., *The Bitter Heritage: Vietnam and American Democracy 1941-1966,* rev. ed. (New York: Fawcett World, 1968); Halberstam, *The Best and the Brightest;* Irving Janis, *Victims of Groupthink* (Boston: Houghton Mifflin, 1972), Chap. 5; and Hoopes, *The Limits of Intervention.*

55. Ellsberg, *Papers on the War,* in "The Quagmire Myth and the Stalemate Machine"; *and see* Ellsberg, "Escalating in a Quagmire," *Public Policy* (Spring 1971), pp. 217-74.

56. Hoopes, *The Limits of Intervention,* p. 5.

57. Kearns, *Lyndon Johnson,* pp. 262-63; *and see* Ellsberg, *Papers on the War,* for his theory of presidential responsibility in Vietnam decision making.

58. See, for example, I. M. Destler, "National Security Advice to U.S. Presidents: Some Lessons from Thirty Years," *World Politics* (January 1977), pp. 143-76; Stephen Hess, *Organizing the Presidency* (Washington, D.C.: The Brookings Institution, 1976); Hoopes, *The Limits of Intervention,* pp. 2-4; I. M. Destler, *Presidents, Bureaucrats and Foreign Policy* (Princeton, N.J.: Princeton University Press, 1972); Alexander George, "The Case for Multiple Advocacy in Making Foreign Policy," *American Political Science Review,* 66 (September 1972): 751-85; Halberstam, *The Best and the Brightest;* Thomas Cronin and Sanford Greenberg, eds., *The Presidential Advisory System* (New York: Harper & Row, 1969); and Richard Johnson, "Managing the White House," and his "Presidential Style," in *Perspectives on the Presidency,* ed. Aaron Wildavsky (Boston: Little, Brown, 1975), pp. 262-300.

59. Janis, *Victims of Groupthink; and see* James Thomson, "How Could Vietnam Happen; An Autopsy," *The Atlantic Monthly,* April 1968.

60. Kearns, *Lyndon Johnson,* p. 263.

61. Hilsman, *The Politics of Policy Making,* p. 29. *See also* Hilsman, *To Move a Nation* (Garden City, N.Y.: Doubleday, 1967), Chap. 34 and note on p. 537.

62. Richard Helms, "Ex-Chief Denies CIA Held Back," (AP) Louisville, *The Courier-Journal,* May 17, 1978, p. A-6.

63. Wise, *The Politics of Lying,* p. 167.

64. Branfman, "The President's Secret Army," p. 73.

65. Colby, in Borosage and Marks, eds. *The CIA File,* p. 185.

66. Colby, *Honorable Men,* p. 202.

67. Colby, in Boroage and Marks, eds. *The CIA File,* p. 185; *and see* Colby, *Honorable Men,* p. 198.

68. Symington, in *CIA File,* p. 73.

69. Symington Subcommittee on Security Agreements (*see* note 22), p. 5.

70. Barber, *The Presidential Character,* p. 54.

5. THE SECRET PRESIDENCY OUT OF CONTROL: RICHARD NIXON

Richard Nixon's conduct of the presidency from 1969 to 1974, with all of its associated abuses of power, has been well documented.[1] Much of the work on Nixon tries, at least in some fashion, to address itself to delineating the "lessons of Watergate." No doubt the codeword "Watergate," which has grown more generally to mean abuses of power within the Nixon administration, is central to a tutorial on the limits of presidential power, but there has not been universal agreement on just exactly what the lessons of Watergate were. Watergate demonstrated to some people the importance of personality within the White House and the danger that a psychologically unbalanced president can cause for the nation.[2] Watergate taught other people the dangers of the strong presidency and reaffirmed their fears about Lord Acton's aphorism and Machiavelli's maxims about political power.[3] For others Watergate showed that the system worked. At various times the maintenance of the constitutional order was credited to the collective efforts of Judge John Sirica, Senator Sam Ervin, Archibald Cox, Congressman Peter Rodino, Leon Jaworski, the press, the House Judiciary Committee, the Ervin committee, the Supreme Court, and the American people.[4]

Among the many other "lessons" of Watergate that one can discern from the events of 1969 to 1974 are:

1. It can happen here or, alternately, it cannot happen here.[5]
2. The system needs more restraints on presidential power or the system needs fewer restraints on presidential power, since Nixon's failure was the failure of a weak presidency.[6]

3. Nixon's failure can best be understood as staff failures and problems of organizing the presidency.[7]
4. It already happened here before Nixon, or Nixon just "got caught."[8]
5. Finally, it cannot happen again.[9]

Of course, this list is by no means inclusive, but it does indicate the wide range of commentary that has evolved from Nixon's performance. Two other important lessons of Watergate that have gained more currency than most others are: (1) that Watergate posed the most dangerous challenge to the constitutional order since the Civil War,[10] and (2) that Watergate clearly demonstrates the consequences of excessive secrecy within the presidential secrecy system.[11]

Indeed Nixon's performance in the White House suggested that the secret presidency had gone to extremes. Most of the so-called attendant abuses of power involved unilateral *secret* and *deceptive* action on the part of the Nixon administration. Among those secret and deceptive actions, Nixon bombed Cambodia for 14 months from March 1969 to May 1970.[12] Nixon promised President Thieu of South Vietnam that the United States would respond with "full force" to any violations of the January, 1973 cease-fire in Vietnam.[13] Nixon entered into a program designed to "get" Daniel Ellsberg because he had leaked the *Pentagon Papers.*[14] Nixon engaged in policies and programs designed to obstruct the investigation into Watergate.[15] As noted previously, Nixon bombed Laos until the cover of the operation was blown. Nixon taped his presidential activities and the activities of others within the White House. He tried to use the CIA for his own partisan political concerns. He condoned and approved the counseling of witnesses to give false and misleading statements in order to obstruct justice.[16] He used the Internal Revenue Service to obtain potentially embarrassing information on his political opposition. He used the FBI in a program of electronic surveillance against certain citizens in direct violation of their constitutional rights.[17] Subordinates acting in his name engaged in an illegal program to gather domestic political intelligence on his opposition and then destroyed crucial evidence of such a plan. In short, Nixon participated in a wide range of covert and deceptive activities, many of which were highly questionable and illegal.

With respect to presidential deception, Nixon took Johnson's "credibility gap" and expanded it beyond recognition. From 1972 to 1974, presidential deception was no longer euphemistically called a "credibility gap" but rather clear-cut examples of presidential lying. Nixon's statements in the public record about the associated abuses of power during the Watergate constitutional crisis were clearly at odds with his secret record of behavior within the White House. When Nixon selected the option of limited publicity for some of his covert programs, his statements of "fact" were false and misleading. As Theodore White has noted, Nixon's downfall came because he chose to explode the presidential myth that presidents are always honest.[18]

As the White House transcripts revealed, Nixon consciously engaged in presidential deception. In a conversation in the oval office with Bob Haldeman and John Dean on March 21, 1973, Nixon stumbled into national security as a possible defense for Watergate.

President: What is the answer on this? How can you keep it out I don't know. You can't keep it out if Hunt talks. You see the point is irrelevant. It has gotten to this point . . .

Dean: You might put it on a national security grounds basis. . . .

President: With the bombing thing coming out and everything coming out, the whole thing was national security.

Dean: I think we could get by on that. . . .

President: Bud [Krogh] should just say it was a question of national security, and I was not in a position to divulge it. Anyway let's don't go beyond that.[19]

In another passage from the White House transcripts, Nixon coached Haldeman and Dean on how to coach witnesses when he said, "But you can say I don't remember. You can say I don't recall. I can't give any answer to that that I can recall."[20] In an exchange with Haldeman on April 25, 1973, Nixon predicted that his pattern of deception would be successful in the end when he noted:

President: Bring it out and fight it out and it'll be a bloody god-damned thing . . . rough as a cob . . . we'll survive. . . . Despite all the polls and the rest, I think there's still a hell of lot of people out there, and from what I've seen they're—you know, they want to believe, that's the point, isn't it?[21]

Throughout the entire Watergate episode with Nixon's legacy of "inoperative statements," "stonewalling," "missing gaps," "fake polls," forged diplomatic cables, and "cover-ups," it was never quite clear just how far Nixon would go in the name of national security. John Ehrlichman had testified before the Senate Watergate hearings that the president had the "power to authorize an inherent break-in in matters concerning national security."[22] As the bizarre events of Watergate unfolded, Nixon's erratic and contradictory behavior only began to make sense if one assumed that (a) Nixon was involved in the cover-up and was therefore guilty, and (b) Nixon felt that the president was above the law and could order illegal acts in the name of national security. By August 1974 both of these assumptions seemed plausible.

Finally, in 1977 Nixon articulated his ethical and legal standards for presidential behavior in the Nixon-Frost interviews. Nixon told interviewer David Frost, "When the President does it that means that it is not illegal."[23] Moreover, Nixon told Frost:

If the President, for example approves something . . . approves an action because of national security, or in this case because of a threat to internal peace and order of significant magnitude, then the President's decision in that instance is one that enables those who carry it out, to carry it out without violating a law. Otherwise they're in an impossible position.[24]

In short, Nixon gave national security a bad name. By flagrantly throwing up what he called the "tent of national security" around his illegal actions, Nixon cheapened and degraded a legitimate competing value within a democratic polity—national security. From the myriad potential case studies of unilateral covert presidential deception within the Nixon administration, perhaps the program to overthrow the Salvador Allende regime in Chile is most instructive about Nixon's use of secret and deceptive presidential power.

The Programs to Undermine the Allende Regime in Chile

Between 1962 and 1974 three U.S. presidents engaged in various covert actions to prevent Salvador Allende from coming to power in Chile and to remove him from power once he was elected. The Kennedy and Johnson administrations directed the Central Intelligence Agency to op-

pose Chilean Marxists in the FRAP (Popular Action Front) and partic-
ularly Allende, their presidential candidate in the 1964 Chilean presidential elections. Money was channeled to the centrist party, the Christian
Democrats, and their presidential candidate, Eduardo Frei, and the CIA
underwrote more than half the total cost of the 1964 Frei campaign.[25]
The CIA also organized campaigns of propaganda against the Chilean
Marxists as well as published misinformation under the banner of the
Chilean Communist party.[26] Moreover, the CIA established major contacts
within the Chilean press, organized labor, peasant groups, and other
important blocs in order to direct those groups to support Frei and to
oppose Allende. Between 1962 and 1964 the CIA had been authorized
by two presidents to spend about $3,440,000 to insure that Frei would
win the 1964 presidential election.[27] On September 4, 1964, Frei won the
election over Allende by taking 55.7 percent of the vote. One CIA study
self-servingly concluded that "U.S. intervention enabled Eduardo Frei to
win a clear majority in the 1964 election, instead of merely a plurality."[28]

During 1964-68 the Johnson administration through the CIA continued
to oppose Allende by supporting various sectors of Chilean society to pre-
pare them for the upcoming 1970 presidential election. Thus, when Nixon
came to the presidency in 1969, he was faced with ongoing institutionalized
programs conducted by the CIA that would support almost anyone who
opposed Allende in Chile.

Publicly, Nixon announced a new era of relations with countries in
Latin America and dubbed it "Action for Progress." Nixon declared:

We must be able to forge a constructive relationship with nations [Latin
American nations] historically linked to us if we are to do so with nations
more removed. A new spirit and a new approach were needed to pursue
this objective in the Americas. It meant recalling our special relationship
but *changing our attitude to accomodate the forces of change.* And it
meant translating our new attitude into an action program for progress
that offers *cooperative* action rather than paternal promises and panaceas.[29]
(emphasis added)

In addition, Nixon announced that the goal of his administration's policy
toward Latin American countries would be "independent, self-reliant
states linked together in a vital and useful association," in which "the
United States should contribute, not dominate."[30] Nixon outlined five

principles which would guide his new "Action for Progress" approach to Latin America:

1. A firm commitment to the inter-American system, to the compacts which bind us in that system—as exemplified by the Organization of American States and by the principles so nobly set forth in its charter.
2. Respect for national identity and national dignity, in a partnership in which rights and responsibilities are shared by a community of independent states.
3. A firm commitment to continued United States assistance for hemispheric development.
4. A belief that the principle future pattern of this assistance must be U.S. support for Latin American initiatives, and that this can best be achieved on a multilateral basis within the inter-American system.
5. A dedication to improving the quality of life in this new world of ours—to making people the center of our concerns, and to helping meet their economic, social and human needs.[31]

Despite Nixon's public proclamations about his new attitude toward Latin America, Nixon entered into covert programs in Chile that violated the principles of U.S. recognition of independent, self-reliant states and noninterference. The CIA, with direct authorization from the 40 committee, funneled money into various Chilean political groups to attempt to stop Allende in the 1970 presidential election. The first discussion of such action within the 40 committee took place on April 17, 1969, when it was suggested that if the United States were going to try to influence the 1970 presidential election in Chile, it would have to move quickly. Allende was running again and his platform, which included "nationalization of the copper mines, accelerated agrarian reform, socialization of major sectors of the economy, wage increases, and improved relations with socialist and communist countries,"[32] greatly concerned Nixon and National Security Advisor Henry Kissinger.

Finally, in March 25, 1970, the 40 committee approved a joint proposal formulated by the CIA and the American Embassy in Chile that called for "spoiling operations" against Allende. The 40 committee approved $125,000 for the operation against Allende's new coalition party, Popular Unity.[33] Only the U.S. State Department opposed this initial intervention into Chilean politics for the 1970 presidential election, whereas the move was supported by Nixon, Kissinger, CIA Director Richard Helms, U.S. Ambassador Edward Korry, and the Department of Defense.[34]

In June 1970 the board of directors of International Telephone and Telegraph became concerned about a possible Allende victory in Chile and had one of their directors, John McCone (former CIA director and still a consultant with the agency), initiate talks with CIA Director Helms on ITT's desire to challenge Allende. The CIA refused ITT's first offer to distribute ITT funds within Chile to oppose Allende, but CIA advised ITT how it could channel its own funds to stop Allende.[35] On June 27, 1970, the 40 committee approved $300,000 for anti-Allende propaganda within Chile as the September election neared. Finally, on September 4, 1970, Allende won 36.3 percent of the vote for a plurality over his closest opponent, Jorge Alessandri, who had 35.3 percent, but the ultimate outcome was to be decided by a vote in the Chilean Congress in late October 1970.

Given this situation, Nixon responded in two modes. *Track I* became the name of Nixon's efforts through the 40 committee to apply political, social, and economic pressures on the Chilean Congress to vote against Allende. By September 14, the 40 committee had approved $250,000 for Ambassador Korry to influence the Chilean Congress, and one month later they approved $60,000 more for Korry's use. *Track II* was Nixon's more aggressive approach to deal with Allende that included plans for a military coup d'etat against Allende.[36] Track II planning by-passed the 40 committee, the State Department, and the U.S. ambassador to Chile. It concerned only Nixon, Kissinger, Helms, and the CIA. As the Church committee outlined it, Track II began when Nixon secretly informed Helms "that an Allende regime in Chile *would not be acceptable* to the United States and instructed the CIA to play a direct role in organizing a military coup d'etat in Chile to prevent Allende's accession to the Presidency"[37] (emphasis added).

In planning a military coup against Allende, the CIA ran into a formidable roadblock in the person of Chilean Commander of the Army Rene Schneider. Schneider believed in free elections and the Chilean tradition of noninterference by the military. In order to get Schneider removed from the situation, the CIA supplied machine guns and ammunition to younger officers in the Chilean Army who wanted to kidnap Schneider to initiate the coup.[38] On October 22, 1970, two days before the Chilean Congress was to vote for the presidency, General Schneider was killed during a kidnap attempt, but the Church committee concluded that the assassination was carried out by a different group of conspirators from the group being supplied by the CIA.[39]

Despite the efforts of Track I and Track II, Allende was selected by the Chilean Congress to be president over Alessandri by 153 to 35 votes on October 24, 1970. The political propaganda, the economic pressure, the social pressure, the CIA infiltration, the proposed bribes, the ITT intervention, and the aborted coup all failed. Nixon was faced with a new political reality that he had tried to prevent—a freely elected Marxist president in a Western democracy. Nixon's public posture, given this kind of political reality, was clear: he said in October 1969 that "we will deal with governments as they are."[40] Moreover, in early 1971 Nixon reiterated his position when he said, "We are prepared to have the kind of relationship with the Chilean government that it is prepared to have with us."[41]

Unfortunately, Nixon's covert position on Allende and Chile did not live up to his principle of noninterference. Nixon and Kissinger were faced with a choice after Allende had been elected to the presidency in Chile: (a) they could acknowledge Allende's victory and establish a policy of peaceful coexistence and noninterference, or (b) Nixon and Kissinger could refuse to recognize the new political reality in Chile and attempt to overthrow the Allende regime. The evidence indicates that Nixon, in consultation with Kissinger and Helms, opted for the latter choice. Between November 3, 1970 (Allende's inaugural day), and September 11, 1973, when Allende died in the military takeover, Nixon and Kissinger engaged in a wide array of covert and some overt actions that were designed to make it difficult for Allende to govern.

Nixon and Kissinger viewed Allende's free election as a Marxist "takeover." As Kissinger told the Subcommittee on Multinational Corporations of the Committee on Foreign Relations in the United States Senate in 1973:

So I don't think we should delude ourselves that an Allende takeover in Chile would not present massive problems for us, and for democratic forces and for pro-U.S. forces in Latin America, and indeed to the whole Western Hemisphere. . . . It is one of those situations which is not too happy for American interests.[42]

Thus, the 40 committee started modestly by sending $25,000 to the Christian Democrats in November 1970, but by January 1971 the committee approved $1,240,000 to fund an initial program to "destablize" Allende's regime. The money would go covertly to support opposition candidates, newspapers, radio stations, and all anti-Allende groups.[43]

In March 1971 the 40 committee approved $185,000 to support the Christian Democratic party, specifically. Later in May 1971 the committee approved $77,000 to support a Christian Democratic newspaper and $250,000 for the Christian Democratic party to pay off its short-term debts.[44] In the summer of 1971, the 40 committee approved CIA plans to spend $700,000 in support of the Santiago newspaper *El Mercurio,* and they authorized $150,000 for anti-Allende candidates in the Chilean by-election.[45] The 40 committee also made nine other authorizations and program approvals for covert action up until Allende's death on September 11, 1973:

November 5, 1971: $815,000 to support two opposition candidates and to induce a split in Allende's Popular Unity Coalition.
December 15, 1971: $160,000 to support two candidates in January 1972 by-elections.
April 11, 1972: $965,000 for more support to *El Mercurio.*
April 24, 1972: $50,000 for another effort to split Popular Unity Coalition.
June 16, 1972: $46,500 to support a candidate in a Chilean by-election.
September 21, 1972: $24,000 to support an anti-Allende businessmen's group.
October 26, 1972: $1,427,666 to support opposition political parties and private sector organizations in the March 1973 congressional elections.
February 12, 1973: $200,000 for more support to anti-Allende parties in the congressional elections.
August 20, 1973: $1,000,000 to support opposition political parties and private sector organizations. (This money was never spent.)[46]

The CIA under Nixon's authorization directed multi-faceted covert programs against Allende from 1970 to 1973 in order to disrupt the political climate within Chile. The CIA had made contacts and infiltrated about every sector of Chilean life, including the major newspapers, the military, the business community, the labor community, and the political community. The CIA covertly directed a propaganda campaign against Allende from within, and they helped organize the internal attack to disrupt the Chilean economy. This three-year covert war by the CIA against Allende appeared in concert with other U.S. diplomatic, military, and economic pressures. Although rhetorically Nixon recognized the integrity of the independent state of Chile and its free democratic process, privately he gave the orders to make "the economy scream."[47] The United States decreased bilateral aid to Chile from $35 million in 1969 to $1.5 million in 1971 and cut back on Export-Import Bank Credits from $29 million in 1969 to nothing in 1971.[48] Moreover, the United States withheld Inter-American Development Bank loans from Chile, which had amounted to $46 million in 1970, but only $2 million in 1972.[49] While trying to make "the economy scream," the United States increased its military sales to the Chilean army in order to help build a coup network.

The results of the Nixon-Kissinger covert and overt attempts to harass Allende from inside Chile are difficult to measure. One point is clear, however: because of American interference Chile was a much different state to govern from what it would have been if Nixon had believed in his public rhetoric about the sovereignty of Chile. The secret war against Allende ended dramatically on September 11, 1973, when the military junta led by General Augusto Pinochet overthrew Allende by force. Allende died in the military takeover and the new junta announced to the world that Allende had committed suicide. But their official version of the circumstances surrounding Allende's death remained highly suspect.

The junta abolished all political parties, called off free elections indefinitely, and suspended civil liberties such as free speech and free press. Many people died during the coup and the junta set up massive detention centers to relocate political prisoners. Within months of the coup, horror stories about the junta's political executions and torturing of political prisoners began to filter out of Chile, and Chile soon became known in the world press as a nation where "grievous violations of human rights" were occurring.[50]

Explanation of the Nixon Administration's Covert Response: Applying the Framework

At first glance it is not readily apparent why Nixon would enter into covert programs to oppose Salvador Allende. Ironically, during this time, the Nixon administration was moving toward "detente" with the Soviet Union and the People's Republic of China. These diplomatic moves make it more difficult to explain Nixon's singular anticommunist line against

Allende. The framework for understanding covert responses within the presidency, perhaps, can be helpful in this case.

Personality-Private Motives

Particularly when one moves into the second phase of the Nixon administration's response to Allende, that is after Allende won a plurality in the 1970 election, the personality and private motive explanation of actors becomes important. After Nixon had worked so long in trying to prevent Allende's election in Chile, he was determined not to let Allende run a successful government in Chile. Nixon viewed Allende as a Marxist who posed a personal challenge to Nixon's toughness. The decision to escalate the covert response came out of an environment of covert activity that was shaped by three strong personalities: Nixon, Kissinger, and Helms. Each man's world view and passion for secrecy drew the actors into a predictable covert response.

Nixon felt that if Chile voted in a Marxist president, then the rest of Latin America would turn "red." As Nixon told David Frost, his feelings about Allende in 1970 could be summarized in the following fashion:

Nixon: If Allende should win the election in Chile, and then you have Castro in Cuba, what you will have in effect in Latin America is a red sandwich, and eventually it will all be red. . . .

Frost: You've got little Cuba and little Chile and all those enormous countries in between, I mean, you're really saying that Brazil should feel itself surrounded by Cuba and Chile?

Nixon: All that I can say is that as far as Brazil is concerned, as far as Argentina is concerned, the other countries in that part of the hemisphere. . . . I can testify to the fact that many of their governments are potentially unstable. I can testify to the fact also that *they do have a problem of subversion.* I don't mean that it was an immediate threat, but I mean *that if you let one go, you're going to have some problems with others.*[51] (emphasis added)

Nixon, a man of many internal contradictions, showed symptoms compatible with classic definitions of "paranoia." As Bruce Mazlish, William Safire, and others have observed, Nixon feared that other people were out to "get him."[52] But nowhere have Nixon's paranoid tendencies been better described than in Nixon's own admission of his obsessive paranoia. In the Nixon-Frost interviews, Nixon confessed to his paranoid tendencies in the following exchange:

Frost: . . . Isn't there in that whole conversation . . .
Nixon: *A paranoic attitude?*
Frost: Yes.
Nixon: Yeah, I know. I understand that and it gets back to the statement that I made, rather an emotional statement the day I left office and I said, "Don't hate other people because hatred destroys yourself." Yeah I want to say here that I have a temper. . . .

> *That atmosphere has to be understood in the context of the times. . . . And call it paranoia, but paranoia for peace isn't that bad.*[53] (emphasis added)

Perhaps the Nixon administration's response to Allende in Chile was another case of Nixon's self-styled "paranoia for peace." Nixon described the Chilean operation in his memoirs, and as he remembered it, "They encountered our unmistakable steel."[54] He discussed his belief that he had to remain strong in the face of communist expansion and that he had done so in his response to Allende.

It would be too easy to explain all of Nixon's covert responses with his complex psychological make-up. It is important to note that Nixon appeared to be psychologically compatible and stylistically comfortable with covert responses as part of his routine behavior within the White House, but Nixon's tendency toward secret behavior does not explain why some decisions were publicized and other decisions, such as Track II against Allende, were wrapped in a shroud of secrecy and deception.

Pragmatic Calculations Component

Why didn't Nixon publicize his actions against Allende and attempt to get congressional support for overt actions against him? Nixon realized that such publicity of his moves against Allende probably would have raised some public outcry. Covert actions offered Nixon an opportunity to escape criticism for his policy. Moreover, Allende would have been alerted publicly to the fact that Nixon was out to "get him," thus making the success of the operation less likely. As Nixon noted in a similar situation, "An action's either going to be covert or not."[55]

Perhaps Nixon also recognized the potential conflict of interest that was developing between the president, the Republican party, ITT, and the CIA. ITT had put pressure on the Nixon administration, particularly the CIA, to take actions to protect "American interests" in Chile. Translated, this meant that ITT wanted the Nixon administration to protect ITT from any moves by Allende that would nationalize ITT's holdings in Chile. The Nixon administration wanted to remain in good standing with ITT because of the upcoming 1972 presidential election in expectation that ITT would contribute heavily to the president's reelection bid. Thus, ITT's demands for action against Allende carried unusual influence within the Nixon administration. There is no solid evidence that a quid pro quo was ever transacted between the Nixon administration and ITT, but the ease with which ITT entered into the decision-making process regarding Allende carries these implications.[56] Covert action allowed the pragmatic Nixon to cover up possible wrongdoing within his administration.

Institutional Approach

Personality and pragmatic explanations are usually important in understanding foreign policy decisions in situations that are "nonroutine" or highly ambiguous in situations in which the decision is free from organizational constraints, and in "unanticipated events in which initial reactions are likely to reflect cognitive 'sets.' "[57] Before Allende's election in 1970, the Chilean situation was none of the above. Thus, the institutional part of the framework to explain presidential covert action might be helpful in explaining Nixon's behavior up until 1971.

The institutional approach would argue that during 1969-70 Nixon was engaging in presidential behavior that had become institutionalized since 1958—namely, to stop Allende from winning the popular vote in Chile. As John Marks has noted, Eisenhower had adopted this position as early as 1958.[58] Later the Kennedy and Johnson administrations would adopt this form of accepted and expected presidential behavior—that is, when Allende runs for the presidency in Chile, a U.S. president should filter money to Allende's opposition parties and engage in electoral propaganda against Allende. This form of presidential behavior had become routinized by the time Nixon took over the presidency in January 1969. During the first few months of the Nixon presidency, a time when presidents learn by on-the-job training, one can *imagine* the following exchange between Nixon and Helms in 1969:

Nixon: What are we doing in Chile?
Helms: When Allende runs we support his opponents.
Nixon: Okay. Fine. Now what are we doing in Peru?

Although we have no record of any existing secret tape that would confirm such an exchange between Nixon and Helms, this kind of institutional explanation of Nixon's covert response in Chile seems plausible.

The Nixon administration's post-1970 behavior against Allende might be considered an extension of the institutionalized action of the past, except that Nixon changed the rules of the game. By entering into the highly secretive and deceptive Track II program, the Nixon administration was no longer just tampering with electoral politics in Chile. Nixon, Kissinger, and Helms were engaged in the practice of inciting a coup against Allende. This radically changed the stakes of the game.

Bureaucratic Politics

The bureaucratic view of the Nixon administration's response to Allende would focus on the process by which the decision emerged in the environment of bargaining between the president, the national security advisor, the director of CIA, the secretary of state, the 40 committee, the Department of Defense, and the Joint Chiefs. The roles and stands of each group in the formulation of the initial response have not been completely revealed. However, enough evidence exists to piece together the following bureaucratic explanation.

In tandem with Nixon, Kissinger helped define the world view and the options for the Nixon administration. Kissinger had an overwhelming impact on U.S. foreign policy from 1969 to 1976. He often acted as more than just a member of the foreign policy-making elite; Kissinger at times acted as the "U.S. foreign policy president."

Kissinger reveled in secrecy and high palace intrigue. While the United States was publicly claiming to be neutral in the Pakistan-India confrontation in 1971, Jack Anderson revealed that Kissinger was covertly supporting Pakistan. Kissinger became outraged at that "national security" leak. Earlier in 1969 Kissinger had become outraged at the *New York Times'* leak of the secret bombing of Cambodia, and Kissinger felt that Ellsberg's leak of the Pentagon Papers was detrimental to the national interest. Kissinger's paranoia over national security leaks was matched only by Nixon's.

As Marks has written, Kissinger thought that an Allende victory in Chile would adversely influence Argentina, Bolivia, and Peru.[59] Kissinger maintained that Chile would provide a "contagious example" to "infect" NATO allies in southern Europe, and he was especially worried about Allende's democratic path to power.[60] As Kissinger told the 40 committee in a secret meeting, "*I don't see why we need to stand by and watch a country go Communist due to the irresponsibility of its own people*" (emphasis added).[61] Kissinger's world view and his personality characteristics, which included a penchant for secrecy and unilateral action, closely resembled Nixon's psychological make-up. Given this situation, Allende would soon become another Nixon-Kissinger target in their "paranoia for peace" reactions.

In this bureaucratic interplay between secretive personalities in the upper echelon of the national security bureaucracy, Nixon, Kissinger, and Helms seemed to reinforce each other's attraction to secret actions. Allende presented a Marxist challenge to the stability of their perception of the world order. The bureaucratic solution that emerged, Track II, was designed to deal with Allende in the most efficient and quickest way that Nixon and Kissinger could conceive. Nixon would simply order the CIA to do everything possible to keep Allende from being sworn in after the election.

On September 15, 1970, Nixon met with Kissinger, Helms, and Attorney General John Mitchell in the oval office. Nixon ordered Helms to block Allende's assumption of the presidency in Chile. Nixon ordered that no one else was to know about this Track II effort to encourage a coup in Chile. The State Department, the Department of Defense, the 40 committee, the U.S. ambassador in Chile, Congress, the press, and the American people were all excluded from knowledge about Nixon's secretive and deceptive plan. As Helms testified to the Church committee, "If I ever carried a marshal's baton in my knapsack out of the Oval Office, it was that day."[62]

Perhaps the most interesting personality involved in the program to "get" Allende was CIA Director Helms, who served from 1966 to 1972. Helms was the quintessential secret bureaucrat who routinely engaged in secret and deceptive programs as part of his job. Yet Helms had a passion for secrecy which went beyond the tendencies exhibited by Nixon and Kissinger, and unlike Nixon and Kissinger, Helms never leaked anything to anyone at any time. As Thomas Powers has cogently observed, "Like Lyman Kirkpatrick, Helms thought that secrets should be secret from 'inception to eternity.' "[63] Helms has never provided any information to investigators about the Ellsberg break-in, the assassination plots, the Watergate break-in, CIA domestic intelligence, why he destroyed his personal files, or any other activity that he was in a position to know about during 1966 to 1972 when he served as CIA director. Helms always seemed to have a severe case of amnesia before the Senate investigators of the various committee hearings he testified at in the 1970s.

One of his lies under oath finally caught up with Helms. During questioning by Senator Stuart Symington in the Foreign Relations Committee hearings on Helm's confirmation as ambassador to Iran, the following exchange took place:

Symington: Did you try in the Central Intelligence Agency to overthrow the government of Chile?
Helms: No, sir.
Symington: Did you have any money passed to the opponents of Allende?
Helms: No, sir.[64]

These statements were a total dissembling of the truth and they eventually became the basis for a charge of perjury made by the Department of Justice against Helms in 1977. Later, the charge would be changed to a misdemeanor for failing to answer questions accurately before a Senate committee, when the Helms case was plea bargained by Attorney General Griffin Bell and the Justice Department. Helms pleaded "no contest" and was fined $2,000 and placed on a one-year probation.[65]

The Carter administration apparently felt that the Helms case was too "hot" to handle; to try to convict Helms of perjury would have required a long trial in which possible national secrets could have leaked out. No one knew what Helms would say on the stand, and the feeling of some people in the Justice Department was that the risk of national security damage was greater than the possible benefits of convicting an ex-CIA director for lying to the Senate. Helms clearly knew too much about everything.

Even after the Church committee had completed its investigation into covert action in Chile from 1963 to 1973, Helms was never really forthcoming with details of the operations. In 1974 at a press conference, President Gerald Ford became the first American president to admit that the United States had been involved in covert actions against Chile, and he added, *"I think this is in the best interests of the people of Chile and certainly in our best interests"* (emphasis added).[66] Later, during the Nixon-Frost interviews in May 1977, Helms's original boss in the Chilean operations, Nixon defended his actions against Allende. Yet Helms would never supply any details because he felt that this would betray the covertness of the "covert operation." Much like G. Gordon Liddy of Watergate break-in fame, who never once talked about the operation to anyone, Helms felt that his silence in the name of national security was an honorable and dignified action.

It did not matter at all to Helms that everyone else had botched the cover of an operation and that investigators knew some aspects of the covert operation; Helms would not supply any information about the specifics of the covert action. Liddy had said that "when the prince approaches his lieutenant, the proper response of the lieutenant to the prince is 'Fiat voluntas tua' (Yes, thy will be done),"[67] and Helms was likewise an able presidential servant. Secrets were sacred to Helms.

Why did Helms remain silent? Thomas Powers has presented three compelling reasons: to protect himself from self-incrimination, to protect the CIA from congressional oversight, and, most important, to protect the secrecy system. Powers described Helms's view of secrets in the following fashion:

The CIA's belief in secrets is almost metaphysical. Intelligence officers are cynical men in most ways, but they share one unquestioned tenet of faith which reminds me of that old paradox which is as close as most people ever get to epistemology: if a tree falls in the desert, is there any sound? The CIA would say no. The real is the known; if you can keep

secrets, you can determine reality. If no one knows we tried to kill
Castro, *then we did not do it.* If ITT's role in Chile is never revealed,
then commercial motives had nothing to do with the Allende affair. . . .
So it wasn't just himself and the CIA that Helms was protecting when
he kept secrets. It was the stability of political "arrangements," the notion of a Free World, the illusion of American honor. Only Helms would
not have admitted it was an illusion, perhaps not even to himself. *If no
one knows what we did, he would have thought, then we aren't that sort
of country.*[68]

Helms received some support for his defense of the secrecy system in
the name of national security, which required that he lie under oath to a
committee of the U.S. Senate. Presidential observer Hugh Sidey defended
Helms and columnist Joseph Kraft argued that the principle of equality
before the law does not apply to the head of the intelligence community
because "his [Helms'] responsibility not to divulge secrets to unauthorized
people mitigates the offense of not coming totally clean with a congressional committee asking vague questions in regions outside its formal area
of responsibility."[69] Senator Richard Lugar, on the Senate Intelligence
Committee in 1977, stated, "I'm really in doubt whether prosecution of
someone in the role of intelligence duties is appropriate at all."[70] Finally
Helms's defense attorney, Edward Bennett Williams, proclaimed that
Helms should wear his conviction like a "badge of honor."[71]

However, District Judge Barrington Parker was not convinced by any
of the arguments in favor of Helms's right to withhold information. Parker
ruled:

It is indeed unfortunate that there are those in public office who are so
divided in their loyalties. You gave your solemn oath to testify truthfully.
You, however, failed. You dishonored your oath and you stand before
this court in disgrace and shame. There are those in the intelligence community . . . who feel they have a license to operate outside the law, it
may be that you were encouraged by others to believe that withholding
of information was proper, but from this day forward, *let there be no
doubt, no one is above the law.*[72] (emphasis added)

Once again, the behavior of the Nixon administration in the covert
programs to undermine the Allende regime in Chile can partly be explained with the four parts of the framework. The end result of the ac-

tion was that a democratic regime was overthrown and replaced by a repressive military junta. Nixon responded to the charge that he had indirectly overthrown Allende by saying, "Allende was overthrown eventually not because of anything that was done from the outside, but because his system didn't work in Chile and Chile decided to throw it out."[73] Kissinger responded to the charge by saying, "The CIA had nothing to do with the coup, to the best of my knowledge, and I only put that qualification in case some mad man appears down there, who, without instructions, talked to somebody."[74] Yet the evidence presented by the Church committee suggests that Nixon and Kissinger played a much more important role in making it difficult for Allende to govern than they have been willing to talk about publicly. The United States did not plan and execute the overthrow of Allende; Nixon and Kissinger were not personally responsible for Allende's death. However, from 1970 to 1973, the secret and deceptive behavior of Nixon and Kissinger encouraged and aided such an outcome.

Summary

In the Nixon case study, all four components of the framework to explain secretive and deceptive action appear to be useful. With respect to Track I of the program to eliminate Allende, I think the personality explanation fits best, followed by the institutional approach. However, personality explanations most often do not fit well and this is the case with Track II of the program to "get" Allende. Here the pragmatic component best fits the Nixon case, with the bureaucratic politics explanation fitting second best. Thus, all four explanations come into play for Nixon, and his decisions to engage in secret and deceptive programs cannot just be written off as the "Nixon personality."

The Nixon case is made much more complex by the special relationship between Nixon and Kissinger. This relationship was one that started with Kissinger doing secret and deceptive work for the 1968 Nixon presidential campaign. Kissinger used his ties with the Johnson administration in October 1968 to routinely pass on secret information to the Nixon camp about the status of the Paris peace talks and Johnson's true positions. As Nixon noted in his memoirs, "One factor that had most convinced me of Kissinger's credibility was the length to which he went to protect his secrecy."[75]

Kissinger never really stopped doing secret and deceptive work for Nixon. As investigative reporter William Shawcross has shown in his brilliant work *Sideshow: Kissinger, Nixon and the Destruction of Cambodia,* Kissinger in consultation with Nixon waged a systematic policy of routine secrecy and deception with regard to Cambodian policy.[76] The secret bombing of Cambodia was a plan designed by Nixon and Kissinger apparently for pragmatic reasons. As Nixon has explained:

Maximum precautions were taken to keep the bombing secret, for several reasons. . . . We knew that because of Cambodia's neutral status, Sihanouk could not afford to endorse our actions officially. Therefore, as long as we bombed secretly, we knew that Sihanouk would be silent; if the bombing became known publicly, however, he would be forced to protest publicly . . . the North Vietnamese would find it difficult to protest since they were officially denying that they had any troops in Cambodia. *Another reason for secrecy was the problem of domestic antiwar protest. My administration was only two months old, and I wanted to provoke as little public outcry as possible at the outset.*[77] (emphasis added)

When the leaks in the secret Cambodian bombing developed, the paranoia of Nixon and Kissinger bloomed. They embarked on a new secret program, a program to wiretap potential leakers of "national security" information. However, the sources of the leaks were never discovered, and this had a new consequence for "open government." Nixon described a new, even more secret tendency that developed within his administration:

When our efforts to discover the source of the leaks failed, we began conducting our foreign policy planning in smaller groups. It is an ironic consequence of leaking that instead of producing more open government, *it invariably forces the government to operate in more confined and secret ways.*[78] (emphasis added)

This certainly was the case in the Nixon-Kissinger era of U.S. foreign policy.

Notes

1. See, for example, Ronald E. Pynn, ed., *Watergate and the American Political Process* (New York: Praeger, 1975); David Wise, *The American Police State* (New York: Random House, 1976); Theodore White, *Breach of Faith* (New York: Dell,

1976); Leon Jaworski, *The Right and the Power* (New York: Reader's Digest Press, 1976); Jimmy Breslin, *How the Good Guys Won: Notes from an Impeachment Summer* (New York: Ballantine, 1975); and Arthur Schlesinger, Jr., *The Imperial Presidency* (New York: Popular Library, 1974), for works citing Nixon's abuses of power.

2. See James Barber, *The Presidential Character,* 2nd ed. (Englewood Cliffs, N.J.: Prentice-Hall, 1977); Erwin Hargrove, "Presidential Personality," in his *The Power of the Modern Presidency* (New York: Alfred Knopf, 1974); and Fred I. Greenstein, "A President Is Forced to Resign: Watergate, White House Organization and Nixon's Personality," in *America in the Seventies: Problems, Policies and Politics,* ed. Allan P. Sindler (Boston: Little, Brown, 1975), pp. 526-39.

3. William F. Mullen, *Presidential Power and Politics* (New York: St. Martin's Press, 1976), p. 50.

4. See Carl Bernstein and Bob Woodward, *All the President's Men* (New York: Warner *Paperback Library,* 1975); Bob Woodward and Carl Bernstein, *The Final Days* (New York: Simon & Schuster, 1976); John Dean, *Blind Ambition* (New York: Simon & Schuster, 1976); Jaworski, *The Right and the Power;* White, *Breach of Faith;* and Aaron Wildavsky, "The System Is to Politics as Morality Is to Man: A Sermon on the Presidency," in *Perspectives on the Presidency,* ed. A. Wildavsky (Boston: Little, Brown, 1975), pp. 526-39.

5. For sources on "it can happen here," see Wise, *The American Police State,* and Morton Halperin, Jerry Berman, Robert Borosage, and Christine Marwick, *The Lawless State* (New York: Penguin Books, 1976). For reasons why "it can't happen here," *see* Jaworski, *The Right and the Power,* and Greenstein, "A President Is Forced to Resign."

6. For reforms to restrain the president, *see* Charles M. Hardin, *Presidential Power and Accountability: Toward a New Constitution* (Chicago: University of Chicago Press, 1974), pp. 182-97; William F. Mullen, *Presidential Power and Politics,* pp. 222-68; and Richard Goodwin, "Dismantling the Presidency: Advise, Consent and Restrain," *Rolling Stone,* March 14, 1974, pp. 13-15. For arguments on the Nixon presidency as a failure of a weak presidency, *see* Theodore Sorensen, *Watchmen in the Night: Presidential Accountability After Watergate* (Cambridge, Mass.: The MIT Press, 1975).

7. *See* Richard Johnson, *Managing the White House* (New York: Harper & Row, 1974); Dan Rather and Gary Gates, *The Palace Guard* (New York: Warner, 1975); Stephen Hess, *Organizing the Presidency* (Washington, D.C.: The Brookings Institution, 1976) and Richard P. Nathan, *The Plot that Failed: Nixon and the Administrative Presidency* (New York: John Wiley & Sons, 1975).

8. Victor Lasky, *It Didn't Start with Watergate* (New York: Dial Press, 1977).

9. For a response to the countless overoptimistic accounts about how the system worked during Watergate and how "it can't happen again," see Halperin et al., in *The Lawless State,* "Have the Crimes Stopped?" pp. 239-54.

10. Hardin, *Presidential Accountability,* p. 1.

11. Thomas I. Emerson, "The Danger of State Secrecy," pp. 58-68.

12. See Bombing of Cambodia Hearings, Senate Committee on Armed Services, 93rd Cong., 1st sess., 1973; Impeachment of Richard M. Nixon, Report, Committee

on the Judiciary, House of Representatives, 93rd Congress, 2nd Session, 1974, pp. 217-19; *and see* Morton Halperin and Daniel Hoffman, "The Secret Bombing of Cambodia," in their *Top Secret: National Security and the Right to Know* (Washington, D.C.: New Republic Books, 1977), pp. 14-21.

13. Text of Nixon Letter to Thieu, *New York Times*, May 1, 1975, p. 16.

14. Jaworski, *The Right and the Power*, pp. 32-36.

15. Ibid., "The Case Against the President," pp. 176-90.

16. White, *Breach of Faith*, p. 438.

17. Wise, *The American Police State*, pp. 274-321; and Halperin et al., *The Lawless State*, pp. 59-132.

18. White, *Breach of Faith*, pp. 412-15.

19. *The White House Transcripts* (New York: New York Times-Bantam, 1974), pp. 163-64.

20. Ibid., p. 171.

21. White, *Breach of Faith*, pp. 415-16.

22. John Ehrlichman, Testimony Before the Select Committee on Presidential Campaign Activities of the United States Senate: Watergate and Related Activities, 93rd Cong., 1st sess., 1973, Book 6, pp. 2599-601.

23. Richard Nixon-David Frost Interview, text in *Indianapolis Star*, May 20, 1977, p. 12.

24. Ibid., pp. 12-13.

25. "Covert Action in Chile 1963-1973," Staff Report of the Select Committee to Study Governmental Operations with Respect to Intelligence Activities, United States Senate, December 18, 1975, 94th Cong., 1st sess. (Senator Frank Church, Chairman), p. 15.

26. Ibid., p. 15.

27. Ibid., p. 57.

28. Ibid., p. 17.

29. Richard Nixon, "U.S. Foreign Policy for the 1970s: A New Strategy for Peace," A Report to the Congress by the President, February 18, 1970, p. 41.

30. Ibid., p. 44.

31. Ibid., p. 45.

32. "Covert Action in Chile 1963-1973," p. 20.

33. Ibid., p. 58.

34. Ibid., pp. 42-43.

35. Ibid., p. 12.

36. Ibid., pp. 25-26.

37. Ibid., p. 23.

38. Wise, *The American Police State*, p. 221.

39. "Alleged Assassination Plots Involving Foreign Leaders," Church Committee Interim Report (Washington, D.C., 1975), p. 226.

40. Cited in Charles Meyer testimony, Multinational Corporations and United States Foreign Policy, Hearing before Subcommittee on Multinational Corporations of the Committee on Foreign Relations, U.S. Senate, 93rd Cong. (Washington, D.C.: U.S. Government Printing Office, 1973), Part I, p. 402.

41. "Covert Action in Chile 1963-1973," p. 26.

42. Ibid., p. 27.

43. Ibid., p. 59.

44. Ibid.

45. Ibid.

46. Ibid., pp. 60-61.

47. Ibid., p. 33.

48. Ibid., p. 33 and *see* Table on p. 34.

49. Ibid., p. 37 and *see* Table on p. 37.

50. Ibid., p. 61.

51. Graham Hovey, "Nixon Defends Efforts to Topple Chile's Allende," from the Nixon-Frost Interview, New York Times News Service, Louisville, *The Courier-Journal,* May 26, 1977, p. A-10.

52. Bruce Mazlish, *In Search of Nixon* (New York: Basic Books, 1972), pp. 84-85; and William Safire, *Before the Fall* (New York: Belmont Towers, 1975), pp. 307-15.

53. Nixon-Frost Interviews, text in the *Indianapolis Star,* May 20, 1977, p. 13.

54. Richard Nixon, *RN: The Memoirs of Richard Nixon* (New York: Grosset & Dunlap, 1978), p. 490.

55. Nixon-Frost Interviews, text, p. 12.

56. Wise, *The American Police State,* p. 234, talks about ITT's entrance into domestic politics in the 1972 election.

57. Ole Holsti, "Foreign Policy Formation Viewed Cognitively," in *Structure of Decision,* ed. R. Axelrod (Princeton, N.J.: Princeton University Press, 1976), pp. 29-30.

58. Halperin et al., *The Lawless State,* p. 19.

59. John Marks, Ibid., p. 17.

60. Seymour Hersh, "Kissinger Called Chile Strategist," *New York Times,* September 11, 1974.

61. Seymour Hersh, "Censored Matter in Book about CIA," *New York Times,* September 11, 1974.

62. Richard Helms, quoted in William Colby, *Honorable Men: My Life in the CIA* (New York: Simon & Schuster, 1978), p. 303.

63. Thomas Powers, "The Rise and Fall of Richard Helms: Survival and Sudden Death in the CIA," *Rolling Stone,* December 16, 1976, p. 54.

64. Joseph Kraft, "In Defense of Helms," *Indianapolis Star,* November 9, 1977, column.

65. Lee Byrd, "Judge Fines ex-CIA Chief $2,000, Places Him on a Year's Probation," Louisville, *The Courier-Journal,* November 5, 1977, p. 1.

66. Gerald Ford News Conference of September 15, 1974, text in *New York Times,* September 16, 1974.

67. Harry Rosenthal, "Liddy Says He Would Repeat His Role in Break-in if a President Asked Him To," (AP) Louisville, *The Courier-Journal,* September 9, 1977, p. A-3.

68. Powers, "The Rise and Fall of Richard Helms," p. 54.

69. See Hugh Sidey, "Staying a Step Ahead of Them," *Time* November 14, 1977, p. 23; *and see* Kraft, "In Defense of Helms."

70. Richard Lugar, Louisville, *The Courier-Journal*, November 9, 1977, p. B-1.

71. Lee Byrd, "Judge Fines ex-CIA Chief," p. A-6.

72. Ibid., p. A-1.

73. George Hovey, "Nixon Defends Efforts to Topple Chile's Allende," p. A-10.

74. Seymour Hersh, "CIA Chief Tells," *New York Times*, September 8, 1974.

75. Richard Nixon, *RN*, p. 324.

76. William Shawcross, *Sideshow: Kissinger, Nixon and the Destruction of Cambodia* (New York: Simon & Schuster, 1979). This British investigative reporter wrote what is perhaps the definitive account of a secret and deceptive program by Nixon and Kissinger in the destruction of Cambodia. By using the Freedom of Information Act to its fullest extent, Shawcross was able to get important documents concerning the secret bombing of Cambodia out of the Pentagon.

77. Richard Nixon, *RN*, p. 382.

78. Richard Nixon, *RN*, p. 390.

6. GERALD FORD:
THE END OF THE
SECRET PRESIDENCY?

Gerald Ford came to the presidency under extraordinary circumstances and during times that placed unprecedented pressures on him to conduct an "open" presidency. An open presidency presumably is one that values truth, honesty, disclosure, and publicity in its relationship with Congress, the press, and, most important, the public. After Lyndon Johnson's "credibility gap" and Richard Nixon's Watergate excesses, Ford was called upon to supply the leadership that would restore a modicum of trust between the public and its president. It was readily apparent that Ford would not be another "Nixon," nor could he have been one. Nixon's conduct within the presidency pushed some of the institution's systemic problems to their ultimate extremes and crushed the Nixon administration. Clearly Ford could not carry on an "imperial presidency." There seemed to be a vast reservoir of support for the president from a public who wanted to believe in the possibility of presidential integrity once again. As Joe McGinniss noted, it was the "Selling of the President 1974. . . . This time we, the people are not only the consumers but the merchandisers as well . . . creating an idol whom history suggests, we will eventually feel compelled to destroy."[1]

As mentioned in Chapter 2, Ford was called upon to manage presidential responses to the intense year of congressional investigations into the intelligence community. The Church committee and the Pike committee demanded access to much of the information on intelligence activities that was lodged within the presidential secrecy system. The Ford administration's responses set the tempo of the investigations and limited the scope of the inquiries. Ironically during this period, when presidential uses of the intelligence community were becoming increasingly questioned, the Ford administration entered into a paramilitary, covert CIA intervention in Angola. Once again, as in previous administrations, the Ford administration did not inform Congress of the full extent and intent of its actions. We will look at the Angolan case briefly in an effort to ascertain whether the secret presidency has ended in the post-Watergate period.

Secrecy and the Ford Administration

There were some promising signs which indicated that Ford would establish an unpretentious and honest leadership. His presidential model was Harry S. Truman, who had been at that time, through some historical revisionism, portrayed as an open and honest president. Ford even toasted his own English muffins.[2] In the public arena Ford constantly professed candor and openness:

In a political sense, there is one problem that currently underlies all of the others. That problem is making government sufficiently responsive to the people. If we don't make government responsive to the people, we don't make it believable. And we must make government believable if we are to have a functioning democracy. (Jacksonville, Florida, December 16, 1971)

I believe and hope that I have been honest with myself and with others, that I have been faithful to my friends and fair to my opponents, and that I have tried my very best to make this great government work for the good of all Americans. (Senate confirmation, November 1, 1973)

Truth is the glue on the bond that holds government together, and not only government but civilization itself. (Senate confirmation, November 1, 1973)

I believe that truth is the glue that holds government together, not only our government but civilization itself. (At the presidential swearing-in ceremony, August 9, 1974)

In all my public and private acts as your President, I expect to follow my instincts of openness and candor with full confidence that honesty is always the best policy in the end. My fellow Americans, our long national nightmare is over. (August 9, 1974)[3]

Presumably Ford's goals at the beginning of his two-and-one-half-year administration were to restore confidence in the presidency and to increase the morale of the nation. His original Gallup approval rating of 71 percent in August testified that Ford was on the correct track to fulfill his goals.[4] Then came Ford's pardon of Nixon, which helped to lower Ford's popularity to 50 percent within one month of office. Besides its devastating impact on the concept of justice and the idea that no man is above the law, the pardon was important to understanding Ford's concept of an open presidency. In making this decision, unlike others, Ford apparently did not consult with many advisors. It represented an intense personal decision developed in a cloud of secrecy. Ford presumably changed his mind about the pardon because he had reminded congressional confirmation committees earlier that "the American people would not stand for a pardon," and that he did not intend to grant one.

In spite of the relentless charges from increasing numbers of conspirologists that Ford had pardoned Nixon as a quid pro quo, and despite the courageous questioning from Congresswoman Elizabeth Holtzman, no evidence has been produced to indicate that Ford acted illegally, unethically, and certainly not unconstitutionally. The important point to emphasize, however, is that within one month Ford acted as three presidents before him had; on a major decision he closed the decision-making process to dissenters, secretly developed his own response, and then took unilateral, nonreciprocal action without adequately assessing the costs of his action.[5]

The pardon was not the only instance when Ford abruptly changed his mind. He had repeatedly said that under no circumstances would he run for president in 1976. Of course, Ford quickly changed his mind once in office and ran the presidency with an eye toward the upcoming election, much like any other incumbent during his first term. These examples of Ford's change of mind (I will not pardon—I do pardon; I will not run— I am running) can probably be dismissed, since the logic of running for the presidency is much different from the logic required for actually being president. Yet they are important items in evaluating the "openness" and "candor" of Ford's presidency. These events in and of themselves, of course, do not represent conscious lying and deception on Ford's part, but as Richard Reeves notes, "The ironic thing about Ford's constant professions of candor and openness is that what he really means is that he tries to be as honest as a politician can."[6]

There were very few attacks on Ford's personal morality during the administration. Besides the usual charges that while serving as congressman from Michigan he was backed by special interests in financing his congressional campaigns, it was claimed that Ford led the blocking of the early Watergate probe in the House Banking Committee in 1972. These charges were sensationalized during the campaign in 1976, but in the denouement it became obvious that Ford was not backed by special interests any more than most other members of Congress were, and that his campaign "irregularities" were more like campaign regularities for the typical congressional race. Moreover, though Ford did try to halt the early Watergate investigation, he was the House minority leader and could not have been expected to take any other position at that time.[7] Ford's action could not in any way be described as part of the general Watergate cover-up, John Dean to the contrary.

Regardless of the innumerable "Jerry Ford" jokes, the incessant attacks on his intellectual abilities, and the claims of his clumsiness (or perhaps because of these), Ford left office with relatively high popularity among the American people. Except for Dwight Eisenhower, Ford appears to have ended his presidency in better physical condition and more liked than other president since World War II.[8] The office has not been kind to incumbents, and Ford survived relatively well. The new president, Jimmy Carter, thanked Ford for restoring trust in government. Public opinion polls indicated that the percent of Americans who had "highly favorable" opinions of the United States had increased from 1973 to 1976.[9] Holding Ford to his presumed original goal of restoring confidence in the nation, by most crude measures it appears that this had been accomplished. However, it is not clear to what degree Ford contributed to this development, other than that he did not attempt to subvert the constitution in Nixonian fashion. One might contend that no matter who served in the presidency after Nixon and Watergate, the restoration of national confidence was predictable.

More important, Ford established the new parameters of the "secret presidency" during the post-Watergate period and he provided the new presidential model (which President Jimmy Carter appears to have adopted), which attempts to give the *appearance* of an open presidency while maintaining most of the institutional arrangements of the secret presidency that had developed since World War II. In short, Ford provided a leadership style that promotes the incumbent's honesty, truthfulness, and openness in symbolic terms rather than substantive changes within the institutionalized secret presidency. Ford's incredible achievement, then, becomes having sold presidential openness to a nation that was ready to buy such a scarce commodity without making any substantive institutional changes that might insure a less secret presidency.

Ford and Carter included, presidents today are no more forthcoming or open than pre-Watergate presidents in matters of national security or matters that the president deems necessary to justify presidential secrecy. It is the appearance of openness that has changed. After the experiences of Vietnam and Watergate, there has been a recognition by presidents and presidential candidates that they must at least appear open. Ford and Carter mastered this principle early in the post-Watergate days.

Even in areas where Congress had thought it had made its intent well known, such as the War Powers Resolution of 1973 and the Hughes-Ryan Amendment to the Foreign Assistance Act of 1974, Ford managed to act unilaterally without consulting Congress. Two examples are illustrative: the *Mayaguez* affair and the CIA intervention in Angola. In the *Mayaguez* affair, most members of Congress felt that they had been *informed* rather than *consulted* on Ford's decision to use military force to secure the release of the commercial ship, the S. S. *Mayaguez,* which had been captured by Cambodian forces.

On May 15, 1975, Ford ordered a U.S. Marine attack on the island of Koh Tang to liberate the American crew, and forty-one Americans lost their lives in the operation.[10] In a study made by the General Accounting Office, the comptroller general of the United States concluded that "hasty action and faulty intelligence" were responsible for the deaths.[11] According to the report, the Marine assault and the U.S. bombing of the Cambodian mainland did not result in the release of the crew because the Cambodians had already begun to release them before the assault began. A survey of Congress showed that most members felt the *Mayaguez* situation was a crisis that *required* the president to consult with Congress under the War Powers Resolution of 1973 rather than inform Congress after the fact of a unilateral decision he had made.[12]

The secrecy surrounding the *Mayaguez* affair was very short-lived. Secrecy was necessary to maintain the surprise effect of the assault on the Cambodians, and it was not used as a domestic political tool by Ford to hide his foreign policy actions from Congress and the people. Indeed Ford had informed the subcommittees of the appropriate committees in

Congress under his interpretation of the War Powers Resolution. More important, after the operation was concluded, Ford publicized his version of events and the *Mayaguez* affair was changed into a public event instead of a covert operation. There was no effort to cover up by Ford, but rather there was a concerted effort by the administration to publicize the "John Wayne-bravado" aspects of the operation, which marked the last show of military force by the United States in the Indochina war.[13]

In 1975, while the Church committee and the Pike committee were engaged in the so-called Year of Intelligence investigations, the CIA under Ford's directive became involved in the civil war in Angola through covert action. Pursuant to the Hughes-Ryan Amendment, which requires the president to notify the Senate and House Armed Services, Appropriations, and Foreign Relations Committees when he directs a covert action plan in the name of national security, Ford notified six subcommittees of the covert actions in Angola. Unfortunately, the Ford administration did not tell Congress the complete story about the Angolan operation. It is to this case study that we now turn.

The Angolan Intervention

In 1975 the CIA spent over $31 million in military hardware, transportation costs, and cash payments in order to back covertly two of the three contending factions in the Angolan Civil War: the National Front for the Liberation of Angola (FNLA) and the National Union for the Total Independence of Angola (UNITA).[14] Both factions opposed the Soviet-backed Popular Movement for the Liberation of Angola (MPLA). Again, Congress was presented with after-the-fact information and was not consulted in the decision-making process. Ford and Secretary of State Kissinger alone made the decision to become involved in Africa through covert action during the very year that Congress was investigating past covert actions.[15] Although many members of the appropriate subcommittees voiced their objections to covert intervention in Angola during the executive session briefings, the members were reluctant to break the secrecy imposed by the Ford administration since Ford was acting within the letter (but not the intent) of the Hughes-Ryan Amendment.[16]

Once again an administration had cut off public debate and acted unilaterally. It was not until after the press began to report stories implying a possible covert role by the CIA in the Angolan Civil War that Congress moved to take public action on the matter. By January 1976 both the Senate and the House voted to end all appropriations and assistance to Angolan factions over the intense objections of Ford and Kissinger. Evidently the lessons of the 1960s with regard to covert intervention had not been learned yet by Ford and Kissinger.

The secrecy of the operation was clearly intended to cut off possible public reprobation and congressional opposition rather than to give strategic advantages to the operation inside Angola. As Harry Rositzke has observed, "The use of covert action, not to achieve a foreign purpose in secret, but to evade Congressional scrutiny, degrades the covert instrument into a domestic political tool."[17] This certainly was the case in Ford's secretive and deceptive response in Angola. Yet Ford was never able to understand this criticism of his Angolan intervention. Ford argued that he decided on a *covert* response in Angola for three reasons: (1) it would be more effective than an open response, (2) American allies had requested covert action, and (3) the Angolan recipients of support requested *covert* support rather than *overt* support.[18] Ford did not mention the fact that this was probably the only way his administration could have intervened, given the mood of Congress and the public.

One of the lessons of the Angolan intervention was that Congress must be wary of the post-Watergate "open presidency." The secrecy involved in the reporting of Angolan information by the Ford administration was legitimate and within presidential discretion as provided by the Hughes-Ryan Amendment. Unfortunately, the apparent deception that Kissinger and Colby engaged in to cover up the scope of CIA involvement in Angola was not legitimate.

Much as the Kennedy administration's Operation Mongoose, the Johnson administration's secret bombing of Laos, and the Nixon administration's Track II plots against Allende, the Ford administration engaged in a unilateral decision without consulting Congress. Moreover, Kissinger and Colby may have consciously misled the various subcommittees who took up the Angolan intervention. This is the view of former chief of the CIA Angolan Task Force, John Stockwell, and a secret Senate Intelligence Committee study.[19]

According to Stockwell, the CIA conveniently labeled paramilitary specialists and technicians sent to Angola as "intelligence gatherers." This enabled Kissinger and Colby to deny under questioning by various members of Congress that the United States was involved in a military venture in Angola. When Senator Dick Clark of the Senate Foreign Relations Committee became suspicious of CIA involvement in Angola, he was sent by the committee to Angola to gather data on the problem. As Stockwell noted, Clark maintained that the CIA was sending arms directly to Angola, that Americans were fighting in the conflict, and that the CIA was working covertly with South Africa, but he did not have the evidence to contradict the CIA cover story.[20] Furthermore, Colby was able to work a gambit on the Senate Foreign Relations Committee by sharing Angolan information with it after receiving the oath of members not to reveal publicly any Angolan information. Thus Stockwell perceptively argued that "this [gambit] was the flaw of the Hughes-Ryan Amendment, aside from the fact that it did not specify that CIA briefings of congressional committees must be complete or accurate."[21]

Since Senator Clark had to accept publicly the CIA lie that the agency was not involved in Angola, Clark and Senators John Tunney and Alan Cranston proposed an amendment to the budget for the Defense Appropriations Bill which stated that no defense funds could be used in Angola in 1976 except for intelligence gathering purposes. The Senate approved the amendment 54 to 22 and the House concurred 323 to 99 to force Ford to take action on the amendment. In February 1976 Ford signed the amendment into law and the CIA paramilitary covert operation in Angola was effectively ended.[22]

In July 1978 after a year of secret study by the Senate Intelligence Committee, reporter Seymour Hersh gained access to the committee's report on potential lying by Kissinger and Colby over the Angolan intervention. Some senators and staff members believed that CIA documents on Angola "not only contradict the testimony of Kissinger and Colby but also indicate that they knew at the time that their testimony was incorrect."[23] Kissinger told the Senate Foreign Relations Committee in January 1976 that the CIA was not involved in recruiting mercenaries to fight in Angola. However, one former CIA official maintained that the 40 committee, led by Kissinger, approved $1.3 million to recruit Portuguese mercenaries for combat in Angola.[24] The Senate Intelligence Committee did not know how to resolve this contradiction.

Thus the Ford administration, particularly Kissinger and Colby, seemed content to relay open and honest information to the appropriate members of Congress when it related to *past* deeds of the CIA, but on matters of current covert operations during the Ford administration, Kissinger and

Colby were less than candid. By giving incomplete and inaccurate testimony on Angola, the Ford administration was able to prolong its attempts at covert intervention. More important, the Ford administration was able to convey the symbol of the open presidency about past deeds at the same time it maintained the secret presidency in its own current covert operations.

Explanation of Ford's Defense of the Secrecy System: Applying the Framework

It becomes apparent that personality explanations do not help in explaining Ford's exceptionally strong defense of the presidential secrecy system. By all accounts Ford cannot be labeled as "paranoid," "manipulative," "authoritarian," "cabalistic," or "active-negative," but rather as a normal, well-adjusted presidential personality type.[25] If any president had cause to develop symptoms of paranoia (a feeling that one's enemies lurk everywhere) while in office, Ford could have been that president given the fact that two assassination attempts on Ford occurred within the span of one month. However, Ford handled that situation with extraordinary courage as he tried to keep the myth alive that the president could still walk among the people anywhere in the United States. Indeed, James David Barber was once moved to pronounce Ford as an "active-positive," a classification for the normal, well-adjusted, "great" presidential personalities.[26]

Ford's personality could be an important variable if one could demonstrate that Ford was so passive that he had virtually no assertiveness in the face of the charismatic Kissinger when formulating foreign policy. Although this might be analytically tempting, most accounts maintain that Ford had the final say in foreign policy decisions. Even though Kissinger had a tendency to try to dominate decisions, Ford seems to have been in control in the foreign policy arena.

The pragmatic calculations explanation for Ford's secrecy may not be helpful in some specific instances of Ford's defense of presidential secrecy, but it is helpful in explaining part of Ford's overall approach to the problem. Ford once said that he would gladly share secrets with all 212 million Americans if such information would go no further, but in his view this could not logically be done. He recognized the calculus of pragmatic calculations that considers the need to promote national security, the strategic advantages gained from secrecy, ongoing foreign policy commitments, the domestic political environment, and the need to conceal incompetence, inefficiency, wrongdoing, personal embarrassment, or administrative error. But these cost-benefit calculations do not totally explain Ford's entire presidential style within the "open" secret presidency.

The bureaucratic politics explanation for Ford's maintenance of the presidential secrecy system has special attraction. Within the organization structure of the secrecy system, Ford was reduced to a bargainer among competing equals. He did, however, have the power to structure his advice system.[27] This bureaucratic explanation of secrecy and deception stresses the organizational interests of the CIA, the State Department, military intelligence, the Department of Defense, NSA, and the FBI, among others, to maintain the presidential secrecy system. In this bargaining system, for example, Colby pressured Ford to maintain a strong covert capability and to keep current CIA secrets. Kissinger also becomes a central figure in the defense of the presidential secrecy system. His strong personality comes into play because Ford relied primarily on Kissinger to structure his diplomatic, intelligence, foreign policy, and national security options. Kissinger's "passion for secrecy" thus becomes an important influence in Ford's defense of the secrecy system, according to the bureaucratic explanation.[28] Organizational output within the national security bureaucracy would often reflect Kissinger's personal influence.

When political scientists become political advisors, there is often a need to cut the gap between expertise and decision making by means of the briefing. Kissinger wrote about the problems of the dynamics in the encounter between decision maker and expert during his days as a scholar. As Kissinger described the process, and no doubt later practiced it himself:

Now briefings reward theatrical qualities. They put a premium on the ability to package information and *to present a fore-ordained result.* Every briefer worth his salt says, "Interrupt me at any point with a question." Usually the victim of the briefing is very proud if he can formulate a question. The briefer has heard the question a hundred times before and it is like throwing a fast ball across the middle of the plate to Mickey Mantle. *He gives a glib response which is overwhelming.* All this creates a state of mind where the policy maker may have the uneasy feeling of knowing he is being taken, even though he doesn't quite know how. This magnifies the sense of insecurity.[29] (emphasis added)

There is no evidence to suggest that Kissinger did not try to play this "Mickey Mantle" game with Ford. Indeed, Kissinger's power may have exceeded his ability to structure options as secretary of state in the Ford administration to the point where Kissinger made some decisions as Ford acquiesced. Ford's autobiography is particularly revealing on this point. Leonid Brezhnev once asked Ford in Vladivostock, "Why did you have to bring Henry Kissinger with you?" Ford replied, "Well, it's just very hard to go anywhere without him."[30]

It was Kissinger who became the policy advocate rather than an option-presenter in the Mayaguez incident, the Angolan intervention, the destruction of Cambodia, the Pike committee confrontation, and other decisions that Ford would be called upon to make. There is no evidence to suggest that Ford ever disagreed with Kissinger or rejected any of Kissinger's single options. John Hersey, in his minute by minute account of a week in the life of President Ford, was informed by Ron Nessen that he would be unable to observe any Ford-Kissinger meetings on foreign policy. Hersey was told, "Nobody, but nobody—except Brent Scowcroft and occasionally Secretary of Defense James Schlesinger—goes in with Henry to discuss foreign policy with the President."[31] For Kissinger, by being the only foreign policy voice that the president listened to, it was easy to play the "Mickey Mantle" game with the president. It was especially easy since he most often talked to the president in secret and alone about foreign policy.

Finally, the institutional explanation for explaining Ford's defense of presidential secrecy and deception appears to supply an adequate explanation of the Ford case. Ford apparently believed that he was protecting the institution of the presidency from intrusion by the disclosure-conscious Congress. In the post-Watergate morality with its emphasis on openness in government, Ford was concerned that an impulsive Congress might push too far for disclosures that would weaken the president's future capacity for covert action or destroy his ability to protect secrets. Ford once claimed that "the ethical tone [of my administration] will be what I make it,"[32] but he might have added that the openness of his administration would also be what he would make it. Regardless of Ford's protestations of openness, he was essentially engaged in preserving an institution that derives much power from its secrecy. Ford promised the public that all intelligence abuses had ended by 1973 and he personally vouched for the fact that the CIA was not engaged in any illegal, immoral, or unconstitutional activities. Thus, this promise was supposed to end the controversy about secrecy and deception in the White House.

To insure that the CIA would be brought under control, Ford made numerous minor organizational changes within the intelligence community, including the establishment of an Intelligence Oversight Board.[33] However, these changes did not fundamentally protect the country from CIA wrongdoing since they were basically *internal* safeguards. The secrecy system, as usual, was still controlled for the most part by the president. The nation had to rely on the president's word and moral character that all intelligence community abuses had ceased. Given the attractive Ford personality and his veritable "boy scout" image, the idea that the intelligence crisis was over became an easy notion to sell.

In short, Ford ran an "open" secret presidency. His success in adopting this contradictory style can be seen in the fact that President Carter also apparently adopted the Ford style of the symbolically open presidency combined with defending the institutionalized secret presidency.[34] Carter even thanked Ford for leaving the intelligence community in "good shape" with regard to intelligence safeguards. In true Ford fashion, Carter even promised that the CIA would never engage in any illegal, immoral, or unconstitutional acts while he was the president. After all of the revelations about abuses within the presidential secrecy system, the final line in the struggle between disclosure and secrecy seemed to be still nothing more than the presidential plea of "Trust me."

Notes

1. Joe McGinniss, quoted in Theodore Sorensen, *Watchmen in the Night* (Cambridge, Mass.: The MIT Press, 1975), p. 4.

2. The English muffins were toasted by Ford specifically for the White House photo opportunity for newspeople. Marilyn Berger, NBC White House reporter, noted that Ford did not toast his own muffins by the end of his presidency on January 20, 1977, but rather ate what the White House cooks prepared for breakfast. In a similar fashion, at the beginning of his presidency Ford allowed the press to cover his comings and goings by helicopter on the White House grounds, but by late June 1976 Ford moved the press photographers away from the landing area

so no more of the "Ford Bumps Head" pictures could be shot. See AP Wire Story, *Gary Post-Tribune,* June 20, 1976, p. 1.

3. David LeRoy provides the Ford quotes in his *Gerald Ford: Untold Story* (Arlington, Va.: R. W. Beatty, 1974), pp. 105-7; *and see* John Hersey, *The President* (New York: Alfred Knopf, 1975), p. vii.

4. *Gallup Poll, Indianapolis Star,* January 16, 1977, sect. 2, p. 16.

5. Jerald terHorst, *Gerald Ford and the Future of the Presidency* (New York: The Third Press, Joseph Okpaku Books, 1974), pp. 225-40, for the secret aspects of the pardon decision making. Bob Woodward and Carl Bernstein give accounts of Alexander Haig's role in pushing for the pardon in their *The Final Days* (New York: Simon & Schuster, 1976), pp. 325-26. Leon Jaworski's account of the pardon dissents from the view that Ford's decision was secretive and unexpected in Jaworski, *The Right and the Power* (Houston: Gulf Publishing and Reader's Digest Press, 1976), pp. 239-51.

6. Richard Reeves, *A Ford, Not a Lincoln* (New York: Harcourt, Brace, Jovanovich, 1975), p. 97.

7. See LA Times Story, "Ford Led Blocking of Early Watergate Probe, Letter Shows," *Indianapolis Star,* October 20, 1976, p. 14; *and see* John Dean, *Blind Ambition* (New York: Simon & Schuster, 1976), pp. 139-42.

8. Truman and Johnson did not leave the presidency at the heights of their popularity since both suffered from increasingly unpopular wars. Although Kennedy may have been more popular than Ford after Kennedy's assassination, Ford at least left office alive. Finally, Nixon left the White House by fleeing in a helicopter because his support had sunk to an all-time low. When Ford left office, he had at least a 48 percent approval rating, as witnessed by his November 1976 election showing.

9. *Gallup Poll, Indianapolis Star.*

10. Actually 18 Marines died during the assault and 23 members of the Air Force died in a helicopter crash during a related mission two days earlier. See the Report of the Comptroller General of the United States, *Seizure of the Mayaguez, Part IV,* submitted to the Subcommittee on International Political and Military Affairs, House Committee on International Relations, October 4, 1976.

11. "Ford Disputes Criticism on Handling of Mayaguez," Associated Press, Louisville, *The Courier-Journal,* October 6, 1976, p. A-6.

12. Report of the Comptroller General, *Mayaguez Part IV,* p. 153. Some problems with the survey include the fact that not all members of Congress responded, but, more important, Democratic members tended to think that the president informed them rather than consulted with them, whereas Republican members tended to believe that the president had consulted with them rather than merely informed them.

13. The only charges of "cover-up" surrounding the Mayaguez centered on the reluctance of the White House to allow the House Subcommittee to see the Comptroller General's Third Report, "A Study of Crisis Management," in an unclassified form. As Dante Fascell, chairman of the Subcommittee on International Political and Military Affairs noted, (the report) "was originally submitted to the subcom-

mittee in classified form at the insistence of the President's Advisor for National
Security [Brent Scowcroft]. His decision was made despite the fact that the Department of State and Defense, which provided the information on which the report
is based, had no objection to its release in an unclassified form. Negotiations between
the subcommittee and the special advisor eventually led to an agreement that substantial portions of the report could be declassified and released." See *Mayaguez,
Part IV,* p. vi.

14. See the Pike Committee Report, *Village Voice,* February 16, 1976, p. 85.
For other helpful sources on the secret war in Angola, see Harry Rositzke, *The
CIA's Secret Operations* (New York: Reader's Digest Press, 1977), pp. 181-83;
CIA's Secret War in Angola (Intelligence Report, Vol. 1, No. 1, Center for National
Security Studies, 1975); Hearings before the Senate Select Committee on Intelli-
gence Activity, 94th Cong., 1st sess., November 20, 1975; Morton Halperin and
Daniel Hoffman, *Top Secret: National Security and the Right to Know* (Washington,
D.C.: New Republic Books, 1977), pp. 21-24; and Hearings before the Senate Com-
mittee on Foreign Relations, Nomination of Nathaniel Davis, 94th Cong., 1st sess.,
February 19, 1975.

15. Pike Report, *Village Voice,* February 16, 1976, p. 85.

16. Halperin and Hoffman, *Top Secret,* p. 23.

17. Rositzke, *The CIA's Secret Operations,* p. 182.

18. "Gerald R. Ford: Presidential Decisions," NBC Interview by John Chancellor,
April 26, 1978.

19. See John Stockwell, *In Search of Enemies: A CIA Story* (New York: W. W.
Norton, 1978), and Seymour Hersh, "Shadow Cast on Colby, Kissinger: Study
Questions Angola Testimony," New York Times News Service, Louisville, *The
Courier-Journal,* July 16, 1978, p. A-13.

20. Stockwell, *In Search of Enemies,* pp. 179 and 229-30.

21. Ibid., pp. 229-30.

22. Ibid., p. 231.

23. Hersh, "Shadow Cast on Colby, Kissinger" p. A-13.

24. Ibid., p. A-13.

25. See Doris Kearns Goodwin, "Ford and Carter: The Character of the Candidates," *Redbook,* November 1976, pp. c-1 to c-8; John Hersey, *The President*
(New York: Alfred Knopf, 1975); Bud Vestal, *Jerry Ford, Up Close: An Investigative Biography* (New York: Coward, McCann, and Geoghegan, 1974); terHorst,
Gerald Ford and the Future of the Presidency; and Dean Fischer, "The Ford-
Carter Character Test: Team Player Makes Good," *Time,* October 4, 1976, pp. 22-
27.

26. David Broder, "Carter Would Like to Be an 'Active Positive' " *The Washington Post,* July 16, 1976, p. A-12; and James David Barber, "Picking a President,"
Psychology Today, July 1976.

27. Ford has generally received high marks for his organization of the White
House. Stephen Hess has noted that Ford was one of the few modern presidents
that moved "expeditiously" when he felt he needed to make organizational changes,
in Hess, *Organizing the Presidency* (Washington, D.C.: The Brookings Institution,

1976), p. 187. *See also* I. M. Destler, "National Security Advice to U.S. Presidents: Some Lessons from Thirty Years," *World Politics,* January 1977, pp. 143-76.

28. Kissinger's "passion for secrecy" has been documented in David Wise, "How Kissinger Bugged His Friends," *New Times,* October 29, 1976, pp. 25-28; and Wise, *The American Police State* (New York: Random House, 1976). *See also* William Shawcross, *Sideshow: Kissinger, Nixon and the Destruction of Cambodia* (New York: Simon & Schuster, 1979).

29. Henry Kissinger, in Kissinger and Brodie, *Bureaucracy, Politics and Strategy,* Security Studies Project, U. of California at L.A., 1968, p. 5.

30. Gerald R. Ford, *A Time to Heal: The Autobiography of Gerald R. Ford* (New York: Harper & Row/Reader's Digest, 1979).

31. John Hersey, *The President,* p. 120.

32. Quoted in Sorensen, *Watchmen in the Night,* p. 30. Evidently Ford did not feel that CIA payments to foreign leaders were inappropriate because Ford, as "open" president, did not even tell incoming President Carter that the CIA was paying money to King Hussein of Jordon. See Bob Woodward, "CIA Reportedly Paid Millions to Hussein," LA Times-Washington Post News Service, Louisville, *The Courier-Journal,* February 18, 1977, p. 1.

33. The Intelligence Oversight Board was retained by Carter but it does not represent an effective outside check against illegal activities by the intelligence community.

34. While conducting a symbolically open presidency with fireside chats, presidential phone-ins, and Kennedyesque news conference performances, Carter and his Director of Central Intelligence Stansfield Turner have called for fewer members of Congress to handle classified information and some penalties for government officials who disclose classified information. See "Punishment for Leaking Secrets Studied," LA Times-Washington Post News Service, Louisville, *The Courier-Journal,* March 10, 1977, p. A-4. Carter also was very upset at the release of the CIA-Hussein payments story by the *Washington Post* and Turner indicated that the CIA was investigating the Hussein leak with disciplinary action in mind.

7. JUSTIFIABILITY OF SECRET AND DECEPTIVE ACTIONS

As Max Weber has noted, "There is no absolutely 'objective' scientific analysis of culture."[1] Values can pervade one's research during every step of the investigation. The problems that political scientists select for research within the broad spectrum of "political reality" are only slices of empirical reality. The researcher's own biases, value system, and ethnocentric concerns act as perceptual lenses in filtering one's experience and perception of political reality. The researcher's selective perception and selective retention can act as barriers to intersubjective testability and independent verification of political reality.

On the general descriptive and explanatory level of political occurrences (case studies), the preceding considerations present immense problems for the objective study of secretive and deceptive presidential behavior. The question of values in social science research presents implicit problems for one's phenomenological account of these four case studies. As one attempts to explain secretive and deceptive behavior after first describing such behavior, one is engaging in an activity that can be conducted within the confines of "empirical" political science. The methodological techniques and the sophisticated tools for analyzing political reality go far in the struggle to eliminate the researcher's values systematically in the process of description and explanation. Yet the process can never be fully protected and insulated.

However, this book is concerned with more than just describing and explaining the secret presidency. This chapter seeks to make reasoned judgments as to whether a particular secretive and deceptive action by a president was justified. The elusive concept of the term "justified," when used as a normative yardstick for judging presidential behavior, calls for the researcher to explicitly state his or her value positions on secrecy and deception. In this manner, the researcher enumerates for the reader the values that guide the analysis. By alerting others to the values that guide him in a normative discussion of secrecy and deception by presidents, the researcher puts the reader in a better position to evaluate his claims.[2]

Stern objections to this kind of normative articulation of values have been raised. For example, some might argue that "values are not something to be discarded, nor even something to be made explicit in order to be separated from empirical matter, but are ever-present and permeate empirical analysis through and through."[3] Others such as Ernest Nagel argue that the alleged role of value judgments in (1) the selection of problems, (2) the determination of the contents of conclusions, (3) the identification of fact, and (4) the assessment of evidence, does not indicate the intrinsic "impossibility of securing objective conclusions in the social sciences."[4] Nagel contends that social science ought to be *wertfrei*, free from valuations. However, that conclusion in itself is a normative value-statement about the way scientific research should be conducted. For many scientists the essence of the scientific enterprise is the struggle toward unbiased judgments. As May Brodbeck has noted, "An objective report is one in which the reporter's feelings, wishes, or values do not consciously or unconsciously distort his description of the situation,"[5] and science strives for objectivity.

There is substantial disagreement over the tactics and strategies to use in resolving the subjective-objective problem within social science. I maintain that in the pursuit of objectivity, the first step is to acknowledge one's subjectivity. Specification of operative values diminishes the power value judgments take on when they are disguised as statements of facts. Gustav Bergman thus has concluded, "The motive power of a value judgment is often greatly increased when it appears within the rationale of those who hold it not under its proper logical flag as a value judgment but in the disguise of a statement of fact."[6]

Normative standards serve to assert "a preference for some value or values of a normative variable over others, or to assign priorities among the normative variables in a cluster."[7] In this vein, then, some organizing value framework regarding secrecy and deception in presidential behavior can be set forward. The values are generated from two traditions: public law analysis and ethical philosophy. Norman C. Thomas has recently urged political scientists to assign the public law approach a higher priority than in the past and not to leave it "almost entirely to lawyers."[8] The public law approach centers on "The analysis of presidential powers in terms of custom and usage and acts of constitutional interpretation by presidents, Congress and the federal judiciary."[9]

Likewise, Sissela Bok has recently called for a public discussion on lying and deception within U.S. foreign policy. As she explains, "In the conduct of foreign policy, a national discussion of the purposes and limits of deception could set standards for allowable deception in times of emergency. Examples of past deception held necessary for national defense could be debated and procedures set up for coping with similar choices in the future."[10] This chapter will attempt to respond to the goals articulated by Thomas and Bok.

Value Framework

1. A president can be said to have taken unjustified actions in taking secret or deceptive actions that are unconstitutional, illegal, or unethical. Such actions may ultimately be necessary but they are not justified.

Of course, presidential scholars can never establish the "unconstitutionality" of any specific covert activity; only the courts, and specifically the Supreme Court, can be the final arbiters of the constitutionality of presidential action. However, scholars can present constitutional arguments centering on particular presidential action given the Supreme Court's previous record. The only guidelines that scholars have to interpret what presidential behavior might be illegal can be found in the U.S. Criminal Code and various Supreme Court interpretations. In any event, great disagreements exist over exactly what constitutes constitutional and legal presidential action.

"Unethical" presidential actions are even more difficult to articulate. The morality of secret and deceptive presidential action can only be defined by observers in relation to a set of acceptable presidential actions that are best described as fitting within the "American political culture." Observers of presidential behavior, such as Congress, various elites, the press, foreign nations, and the public, have come to expect certain parameters for presidential behavior that incumbents must act within or risk facing public reprobation. As Clinton Rossiter has explained:

The presidency, like every other instrument of power we have created for our use, operates within a grand and durable pattern of private liberty and public morality, which means that it operates successfully only when the President honors the pattern by selecting ends and means that are "characteristically American."[11]

Although there are many problems when considering behavior that is "characteristically American" (no agreement has been reached as to what precisely constitutes American behavior as opposed to un-American behavior), the idea that a president must behave in certain accepted ways and follow a set of presidential norms seems obvious. Those norms by most accounts demand that the president not engage in systematic lying or deception, or commit a "breach of faith."[12] Presidents should not value power above all other values, abuse power, or "justify immoral acts in terms of one's authority and position."[13] Moreover, presidents should not engage in behavior while in office that is motivated "by a desire for personal material gain."[14]

2. Means and ends must be compatible. Presidential goals and ends do not justify the use of certain means, just as the use of acceptable means in a legitimate process does not automatically justify the ends. National security must compete with other goals and values. Even major questions of national security cannot by themselves be reason enough to engage in unconstitutional, illegal, or unethical behavior. Francis Rourke has observed:

Since democratic communities exist to serve other values besides national security, the extent to which the practice of withholding information furthers security interests must always be measured against the possibility that it may at the same time *exact so high a price in terms of other values which are equally central to the well-being of a democratic community that it simply cannot be justified.*[15] (emphasis added)

The modern president has enough legitimate means at his disposal in the 1980s that he can act swiftly to "save the nation" with constitutional, legal, and perhaps ethical means.

3. The notion that "other nations do it" does not by itself justify a president's resorting to secretive and deceptive actions. Other nations do a lot of things. Other nations use torture, engage in political murders, violate human rights, hold political prisoners, eliminate dissent, practice genocide, and establish concentration camps. The use of such practices by other nations cannot alone serve as justification for presidential actions. Secret and deceptive acts must be evaluated on their own merits and they cannot be categorically justified by the argument that the Soviets or the Cubans engage in deceptive practices so therefore the United States must engage in this kind of activity to protect national security. The idea behind this argument is that international politics is a "dirty game" and participants must be willing to play by these rules. However, the United States commands a powerful strategic position in this game of international politics, and it is not clear to what degree, if any, the United States's strategic advantages would diminish if it decided unilaterally to play the game without resorting to deceptive actions.

4. If an open and public alternative to the covert policy exists, then the policy maker should select the open and public alternative.

Presidential secrecy is neither all good nor all evil. There is a legitimate need to keep some presidential behavior secret, as Chapter 8 will demonstrate. Yet this level of legitimate presidential secrecy must be drawn narrowly so that abuses of the secrecy system will not occur. This value argues that openness is preferable to secrecy.

5. If a truthful statement or option to a false statement is available, then the president should select a truthful statement.

As in Value 4, deception is neither all good nor all evil. A certain amount of presidential deception may be justified to maintain national security or other competing values within the democratic polity. However, the guidelines for the legitimate use of presidential deception must be drawn very narrowly. This last value simply argues that a truthful statement is preferable to deception.

These five values will serve as a guide to the analysis of secrecy and deception within the presidency. To summarize, a president should not engage in secret or deceptive action:

1. that is unconstitutional, illegal, or unethical;
2. when means and ends are not compatible;

3. just because "other nations do it";
4. when an open action would suffice;
5. or when an honest action would achieve the same goal.

Other normative-value statements might be implicit from these five positions, and they will evolve in the analysis of the four case studies that follow. One benefit of making reasoned judgments about the justification of past presidential actions is that public discussion of past failures can decrease the probability of future failures.

Charles L. Stevenson noted about ethical learning of officers that "A judgment of his past failure will make him ashamed of himself and induce him to choose differently in any roughly similar case that may arise."[16] In the same spirit, judgments about justifications of covert actions will be advanced to further the process of presidential value learning.

Justifiability of Kennedy's Covert Response Against Castro

Was the Covert Action against Castro Unconstitutional?

The National Security Act of 1947, which established the Central Intelligence Agency under the direction of the National Security Council, is often cited by proponents of covert action as the statutory basis for covert operation, specifically the passage that directs the CIA to perform those "other functions and duties related to intelligence affecting the national security as the National Security Council may from time to time direct."[17] However, critics of covert action respond that this passage does not specifically refer to covert action, nor does the legislative intent and legislative history of the National Security Act indicate that Congress knew it was approving a covert action arm of U.S. foreign policy.[18]

Perhaps the best statement of the argument for the constitutionality of presidential covert action was prepared in 1962 in a secret memorandum by the CIA for then General Counsel to CIA Lawrence Houston. (See Appendix for the contents of the secret memo.) The analysis argues that the president, through various Supreme Court rulings and through his commander-in-chief powers, has the constitutional right to engage in covert actions to protect American property, lives, and national security. However, the constitutional case for covert action is not at all as clear as the CIA memo would lead one to believe. Even former President Harry Truman said in 1963, "I never had any thought when I set up CIA that it would be injected into peacetime cloak and dagger operations."[19] However interesting this pursuit of understanding the 1947 National Security Act and its relationship to establishing the statutory basis for covert action might be, it ignores the fact that the CIA operates not so much from statutory authority as through secret national security directives. These still secret directives, which presumably ordered covert operations during the Truman and the Eisenhower administrations, were the basis for CIA legitimacy and the basis on which Kennedy came to perceive covert action as not only constitutional but necessary in a hostile world.

Throughout the 1950s Congress gave its implicit approval of covert intervention and covert operations by acquiescing to the executive on these matters. The Supreme Court has never ruled per se on the specific question of whether covert action is unconstitutional. The Court has preferred to grant the president broad powers during times of crisis in the president's role as commander-in-chief and top national security manager. Even during times of intense oversight by Congress, the legislative branch has accepted the constitutionality of some covert actions when Congress was consulted. In 1974 an amendment to the Foreign Assistance Act prohibited covert operations in foreign countries "other than those intended solely for obtaining intelligence," with one exception. Those covert operations which the president approves of in writing and reports to the appropriate congressional committees are not prohibited.[20] Thus Congress gave approval in principle to the idea of covert action. Another example of congressional reluctance to condemn uniformly the use of covert action is in the House Judiciary Committee's action toward Nixon in the impeachment resolutions of 1974. Among the laundry list of charges that were considered, the committee refused to accept the "secret" bombing of Cambodia or U.S. involvement in the overthrow of Allende in Chile as legitimate reasons for impeachment.[21]

Regardless of congressional acquiescence, Supreme Court obfuscations, and presidential precedents for covert action, critics of covert action do not agree that presidential covert action is therefore constitutional. They point out that unilateral presidential covert action can expand the already too broad presidential war-making powers. The Constitution is clear on this point: Congress shall have the legislative power to declare war and the president shall be commander-in-chief. Most covert actions against foreign nations by unilateral covert presidential orders are unconstitutional, according to critics, because they represent for all intents and purposes, a presidential declaration of war.

Supporters of covert action would argue that the covert action does not involve a presidential declaration of war, but rather it falls within the legitimate interests of the executive under his grant of constitutional power as commander-in-chief. Moreover, they argue that the precedent established by twentieth-century presidents in regard to making unilateral decisions over war and peace in the name of national security has been justified.[22] In a cold war environment with a common set of assumptions about communism, covert action is not only viewed as constitutional but necessary in the national interest.[23]

In the face of these two arguments, covert action remains constitutionally vague and murky. Specifically with respect to the Kennedy administration's covert actions against Castro, one can summarize the discussion by noting that Kennedy's actions were no more unconstitutional than other covert actions were thought to be at that time. Strong arguments can be made to support the president's prerogative to make national security decisions as commander-in-chief. With respect to other covert action precedents set by previous presidents, Kennedy not only was following in their footsteps, but he was engaging in covert action more frequently and broadening the scope of covert activity. In short, his actions were constitutionally questionable, but ultimately defensible under a broad interpretation of the president's commander-in-chief powers according to current understanding of the national security interests involved.

Was the Program to Eliminate Castro Legal?

Obviously under the U.S. Criminal Code it is against the law to murder another individual, to conspire to murder another individual, or to have been a willing accomplice to murder done by agents acting under you.[24] Clearly the Criminal Code laws on murder and murder conspiracy do not apply when the president of the United States is involved in carrying out his national security role as commander-in-chief. However unfortunate, there were and are no laws that make it illegal for the president to authorize the murder of a foreign head of state. Some may claim that the president has no legal authority to engage in this kind of activity, though the matter has never been tested in the Courts. Even Ford's Executive Order 11905, which states that "No employee of the United States Government shall engage in, or conspire to engage in, political assassination" (1976), does not provide protection against future presidents engaging in this kind of activity. The order does not make the penalties clear, and, more important, it is not clear how the order will be enforced on U.S. presidents. In sum, on the domestic level, it is still not an illegal act for the president to plot to eliminate a foreign head of state in the pursuit of a foreign policy objective.

On the international level, the act of plotting to assassinate another head of state is unquestionably illegal under international law. Of course, international law has never been one of the great operational constraints on U.S. foreign policy. Under the Charter of the United Nations, members are specifically forbidden to engage in political assassination because it violates each country's rights to territorial integrity and political independence.[25] In the international arena, political assassination is viewed as another form of covert intervention that flagrantly violates common understandings of international law. Richard Falk has listed six categories of instances in which CIA covert action violates international law. Political assassination falls within his second category of instances, which "involves the international law violations that arise from the spectrum of covert activities carried on in a foreign society without the knowledge and consent of the territorial government and inconsistent with its political independence as a sovereign state."[26] In sum, on the international level, political assassination as a tool for foreign policy is clearly illegal.

Critics of this view charge that it is naive and unrealistic to label covert action as illegal on the international level. Moreover, they charge, such a view is largely irrelevant given the ineffectiveness of the international law system and its inability to carry out justice by dealing out penalties and sanctions to offending nations. Besides, the argument goes, other nations engage in this kind of "illegal" nation-state behavior and the United States must engage in it to protect its national interests.

Although the criticisms of those who apply international law to covert action are at times compelling, one must recognize the virtues of being a law-abiding citizen in the international community. If a nation enters into an agreement (such as the United Nation's Charter) that demands respect for certain principles of international law, then that nation should abide by those principles of legitimate law. If a nation systematically violates international law because other nations systematically violate international law, the system inevitably becomes weaker. Consistent adherence to the principles to which the nation has committed itself by joining various international organizations is a leadership quality that foreign policy makers should pursue.

Was the Program to Eliminate Castro Unethical?

By most religious standards, including the Judeo-Christian ethic, it is immoral to murder another human being. When one head of state plots the death of another, the character of the act remains essentially immoral. However, there are degrees of complicity about this basically immoral act, and there are extenuating circumstances that make some offenses less immoral than others. The rightness or wrongness of a political assassination attempt can be thought of as existing on a continuum ranging from slightly immoral to absolutely immoral. The following discussion will consider some of the extenuating circumstances.

When the alleged assassination plots surfaced in 1975 and Kennedy's apparent involvement became more evident, Congress, the press, and the public stated their reactions in terms of moral outrage. The idea that a president of the United States may have been involved in an assassination plot against a foreign leader was morally repugnant to most Americans who used the benefit of perfect 1970s' hindsight. Yet no written evidence could be produced to prove that Kennedy had ordered the assassination of Castro. Moreover, Castro was never assassinated, though it was not for the lack of effort. Therefore, how can Kennedy be charged with committing an immoral act in this case?

Richard Nixon's defenders seized upon the opportunity to point out that even Nixon had never considered political assassination as a tool of U.S. foreign policy. Victor Lasky concluded:

Whatever else can be said of Nixon, there was one thing he did not do in his five and a half years in office. As far as the record shows, he did not discuss the pros and cons of murdering foreign leaders who had aroused his ire. This is precisely what Kennedy did in a conversation with George Smathers. . . .[27]

The implication is clear—Nixon never ordered anyone to be killed while he was in the White House. But this assertion has problems of definition and relativity. In some sense, all presidents who are engaged in the conduct of foreign war may be said to have "murdered foreigners." It would be a difficult task indeed, to get a majority of peasants who had survived the "secret bombing" of Cambodia to agree with the proposition that "Nixon never ordered anyone to be killed while he was in office." In the same vein, Nixon is not beyond possible complicity in the overthrow and eventual death of Salvador Allende in Chile.

Most Americans do not think of presidents as murderers when they conduct wars and carry out their commander-in-chief powers. When the lives of masses of people are inexorably tied to the day-to-day decisions of presidents, ethical principles such as "Thou shall not kill" are quickly dismissed as being naive or irrelevant. It is ironic that mass homicide can be more easily tolerated by the American public than the idea that an American president could plot to take the life of a foreign head of state. The latter act is usually equated with the act of a common criminal, and it is discomforting to view one's president as a common criminal in view of the "symbolic function" that the president fulfills for the political system.[28] If a president conspires to assassinate foreign leaders, he is viewed as a deceptive, manipulative conspirator by many. His actions usually indicate the impotence of his overt foreign policy toward the nation against which he conspires. Political assassination as a national foreign policy tool, according to this view, is the policy of morally and politically weak presidents.

Some would suggest that the resolution of the moral problem depends upon who is being assassinated and who is doing the assassinating. Rositzke argues that the plotting of Hitler's murder by German Jews or German generals, and the assassination of the Dominican dictator Trujillo are "at least open moral questions even by professed American standards of morality."[29] Although Germans were obviously not the *only* people to suffer under Hitler, for Rositzke, the defense of "tyrannicide" only approaches possible morality when it involves "the murder of a dictator by *his own people.*"[30] Thus assassination plots against foreign leaders cannot be absolved by the "tyrannicide" arguments.

Still others would suggest that it is impossible to resolve the moral question of presidential assassination plots against foreign leaders because, they argue, the behavior is characteristically *amoral.* As Richard Barnet has noted, "Conspirators, according to popular understanding of the term, are men who plot to commit acts they know to be wrong."[31] Subordinates in the CIA involved in the planning of the plots to eliminate Castro apparently did not think the acts were morally wrong. CIA plotters acting in Kennedy's name operated in an amoral world dominated by national security interests, according to this view.

However, Kennedy could differentiate moral from immoral foreign policy actions. In 1961 Kennedy told reporter Tad Szulc that he was morally opposed to the use of political assassination.[32] More important, Kennedy's rhetoric in his foreign policy statements and speeches indicates that he could distinguish between the high ideals of morality in American foreign policy and the unacceptable use of an immoral American foreign policy action. The key question then becomes whether Kennedy was involved in the *immoral* plots to assassinate Castro. This is a central question on which reasonable people can easily disagree after being presented with the available evidence.[33]

In conclusion, by all accounts, assassination plots against foreign heads of state are unethical. The Kennedy administration should have adopted an open and honest response to the Castro problem rather than select a closed and deceptive one. Although the Church committee dismissed the assassination plots as aberrations in the conduct of U.S. foreign policy, these plots can more accurately be described as the culmination of interventionist logic and covert action ideology. To condemn Kennedy personally for the use of possible assassination plots in the conduct of his foreign policy on the grounds that such plots in particular are unethical seems to be a rather parochial view. To argue that assassination plots are any more or less moral than the whole history of previous American political, economic, and military intervention around the globe is absurd. The assassination plots must be placed in the context not of the "Cold War," or "the climate of the times," but rather in the historical context of the systematic behavior of the United States as an overt and covert interventionist nation. In this view, assassination is conceptualized as just one more tool for political, economic, and military intervention and connotes nothing extraordinary. The rightness or wrongness of the plots as an abuse of power can only be judged after one makes a value judgment about the whole history of unilateral covert American political, economic, and military intervention in general. That particular judgment is beyond the scope of this chapter, but suffice it to say, the Kennedy administration was not behaving in uniquely "un-American" ways.[34]

Justifiability of the Johnson Administration's Covert Action in Laos

Was Johnson's Covert Action in Laos Unconstitutional?

By allowing the CIA to direct the actions of organized native tribes-men in Laos, Johnson was essentially involved in a large-scale paramilitary operation that was kept secret from Congress and the public. Covert para-military operations conducted by the executive branch for an extended period of time cannot be classified as legitimate covert action in the name of national security. They are examples of unilateral presidential war mak-ing. When the paramilitary operation is conducted in a neutral country, in secret, and in response to a situation that does not seem to directly affect the security of the United States, that particular operation's con-stitutionality becomes highly doubtful. Unlike the potential national security threat that Castro posed for Kennedy, the situation in Laos posed no significant and immediate threat to national security. Johnson, who condoned the bureaucratic structure that allowed the CIA to conduct the Laotian ground war, was involved in unconstitutional action, as I evaluate the situation (though the constitutionality of paramilitary operations has never been decided by the courts).

A strong but ultimately unconvincing constitutional argument can be made in support of Johnson's secret CIA ground war in Laos. One might argue that Johnson merely was acting pursuant to the Tonkin Gulf Resolu-tion (1964) in which Congress approved and supported the determination of the president "to take all necessary measures to repel any armed attack against the forces of the United States and to prevent further aggression . . . including the use of armed force, to assist any member or protocol state of the Southeast Asia Collective Defense Treaty requesting assistance in defense of its freedom."[35] It could also be argued that the president was merely exercising his valid constitutional duties as commander-in-chief. According to this line of thought, Johnson would be viewed as a president who, like presidents before him in analogous situations, was involved in protecting the lives of American soldiers.

In defense of Johnson's actions one might string together a set of Supreme Court rulings such as *United States* v. *Curtiss-Wright Export Corporation* (1936), *United States* v. *Pink* (1942), and *Missouri* v. *Holland* (1920)[36] to argue that Johnson's actions were constitutional.

U.S. v. *Curtiss-Wright* (1936) dealt with the constitutionality of Franklin Roosevelt's unilateral embargo of arm shipments to Bolivian revolutionaries using the discretionary power that had been granted to him by a joint resolution passed by Congress in 1934. Justice Sutherland in the majority opinion maintained that the president was the sole organ in the federal government in matters of foreign policy and that these powers were "very plenary and exclusive."[37] He wrote that this power was "a power which does not require as a basis for its exercise an act of Congress, but which, of course like every other governmental power, must be exercised in subordination to the applicable provisions of the Constitution."[38] In *U.S.* v. *Pink* (1942) the Court upheld the validity of executive agreements and argued that in some cases they could be inforced as valid internal and domestic law.[39] Finally, *Missouri* v. *Holland* (1920) could be cited because Justice Holmes in the majority opinion argued that the treaty power was broader than the enumerated powers of Congress.[40]

Taken together, the weight of these three cases in regard to the constitutionality of Johnson's actions in Laos from 1964 to 1968 would suggest that Johnson spoke for the American people in matters of foreign relations in a "plenary and exclusive" manner, that Johnson's secret agreement with Souvanna Phouma was a valid exercise of presidential power and was binding on the nation, and that the treaty signed by the United States in the Southeast Asia Treaty Organization (SEATO) that in Johnson's view obligated the United States to defend the security interests in Southeast Asia was broader than the enumerated powers of Congress. Like Franklin Roosevelt, Johnson argued that he was using discretionary powers in Southeast Asia that Congress had granted him through congressional resolution. Johnson also argued that he was living up to U.S. treaty obligations and executive agreements.

Although the constitutional argument in support of the Johnson administration's ground war in Laos is compelling at times, it is ultimately ill-founded. The *Curtiss-Wright* decision does give judicial support to the idea of broad presidential powers in foreign relations, but it clearly does not give the president the power to engage in secret wars or unconstitutional behavior. Justice Sutherland said the president's foreign affairs power "must be exercised in subordination to the applicable provisions of the Constitution,"[41] and in the case of the secret war in Laos, the applicable provision in the Constitution is that Congress shall have the power to declare war. Covert paramilitary operations that Congress has not explicitly approved amount to presidential declarations of war, which are by definition unconstitutional. Likewise, even though the *Pink* decision upheld the validity of executive agreements, the Court *did not* argue that presidents could engage in unconstitutional behavior and have such behavior legitimized by secret executive agreements. If this were the case, a president such as Nixon, for example, could have made a secret executive agreement with a foreign head of state to repeal the First Amendment, and this would be legitimate. Fortunately the Court has refused to pass on the final determination of constitutional questions to the president.[42]

Similarly, the decision in *Missouri* v. *Holland,* while posing theoretical questions about the possible power a president might have in pursuing treaty obligations, does not provide constitutional justification for a president to unilaterally engage in a covert ground-war operation because the president believes he is operating within the intent of a treaty that was ratified by the Senate. As Kelly and Harbison observed about the implications of *Missouri* v. *Holland:*

The treaty in question did not touch upon the fundamentals of the social order . . . did not impair or damage the interests of any powerful vested right . . . [did not] involve the sanctity of private property, nor even work any very important practical change in the extent of federal power. The theoretical implications of the opinion were in fact not subsequently translated into reality. The national government has not since brought about any significant change in its authority through the treaty-making power.[43]

Besides, with respect to the SEATO treaty, Laos was never a signatory nation, and Laos was removed from the "protocol area" by the Geneva Accords of 1962.[44]

Finally, any claim by the president that the secret ground war in Laos was necessary to protect American troops in South Vietnam is irrelevant. Even though this might have been a concern in the president's decision-making process, it was never articulated. When Johnson decided to keep the operation secret to protect Laotian neutrality, he lost all claim to legitimate paramilitary action because Congress was not informed.

The secret air war in Laos presents the same kinds of constitutional problems that the Johnson administration's paramilitary operation in Laos presented. However, one minor difference exists in that some members of Congress were selectively informed about some aspects of the bombing, but the entire Congress, as noted before, was never informed about the scope of the bombing in Laos. Although it is generally accepted that after Congress has declared war or authorized discretion in using warlike responses to security emergencies, the president maintains control of the tactics and strategies to be used in the conflict; it is not a general principle that the president can control tactics and strategies when no authorization or state of war exists. Indeed, the legislative history of the Tonkin Gulf Resolution would suggest that Congress did not mean for it to be a continuous justification for presidential war making in Indochina.[45] The measure reacted to a specific situation and it did not provide for, nor did it appear to envision, the escalation of the war to the extent that over 500,000 troops would be stationed in South Vietnam. Later the president would present Congress with a circular and perpetual "fait accompli"— that is, he would argue that U.S. troops in Southeast Asia were not "making war" but were involved in protecting the security of U.S. troops and citizens who were already there.[46]

The conclusion of this discussion is that Johnson's secret paramilitary ground operations conducted by the CIA in Laos and the Johnson administration's secret bombing of Laos from 1964 to 1968 were both unconstitutional. Though one might argue that the president as commander-in-chief has a responsibility to respond in emergency situations in a definitive manner when the consultation process would do substantial damage to the success of the response, this argument hardly fits the Laotian situation. The president had ample time to consult with Congress within the five-year period if he had wanted to. Johnson's response was hardly a response to an emergency situation in that his conduct of the secret Laotian war was systematic and sustained over the years.

Even though Johnson entered into the secret war in Laos at Souvanna Phouma's request, this rationale cannot justify secret presidential war making. Not only did the agreement protect Laotian neutrality deceptively, it also made Johnson's presidential action unaccountable. As Henry Kissinger testified before the Church committee:

I do not believe in retrospect that it was a good national policy to have the CIA conduct the war in Laos. I think we should have found some other way of doing it. And to use the CIA simply because *it was less ac-*

countable for very visible major operations is poor national policy. And the covert activities should be confined to those matters that clearly fall into a gray area between overt military action and diplomatic activities, and not to be used simply for the *convenience of the executive branch and its accountability.*[47] (emphasis added)

In allowing the president to engage in secret discussions with foreign leaders and to classify the results of their specific executive agreements, the United States must be ready to handle the systemic consequences of such practice. The consequences are:

1. maximization of commitment in secret discussions with foreign governments; then minimization of the risk of commitment in statements made to the American public.
2. maximization in public of the importance of our friendly relationship with a foreign government; then minimization, and often classification of that government's obstructiveness, failures, and noncooperation.[48]

Was the Secret War in Laos Illegal in the Domestic and/or International Arena?

Other than the fact that the Johnson administration's paramilitary venture in Laos and its secret bombing of Laos were, as I argued, unconstitutional acts, the actions do not specifically violate any statutes within the U.S. Criminal Code. For example, there are no laws against unilateral secret bombings by presidents. However, in the international arena, the validity of the presidential actions seem more questionable. It is not clear whether Johnson violated international law by agreeing to Souvanna's request for U.S. intervention. After all, the United States was not making war *against* Laos but against the North Vietnamese troops *within* Laos. To be sure, Johnson was involved with the internal struggles within Laos by supporting Souvanna over the Pathet Lao, but the main interest of the U.S. policy toward Laos was in Laos as a battlefield on which to fight North Vietnam.

Johnson did not want to claim the international right to violate the neutrality of Laos, nor did he want to publicize the fact that Souvanna had requested military support in violation of his publicly stated neutrality.

Since North Vietnam never publicly acknowledged that its troops were using Laos and Cambodia as sanctuaries during the Indochina war (they never acknowledged that their troops had ever crossed into South Vietnam for that matter), Johnson could not publicly claim U.S. involvement in neutral Laos or the United States would be viewed as the first violators of Laotian neutrality. Even though some international law interpretation would have backed Johnson's actions if he had publicly claimed the right to intercede in Laos, since Laotian neutrality had been violated by North Vietnam, Johnson selected a policy of nonacknowledgment of the U.S. commitment in Laos. As John Moore has remarked:

> It is well established in the customary international law of the rights and duties of belligerents toward neutral states that a belligerent power may take action to end serious violations of neutral territory by an opposing belligerent when the neutral power is unable to prevent belligerent use of its territory and when the action is necessary and proportional to lawful defensive objectives.[49]

If a neutral country is unable or unwilling to maintain its neutral status, and the violation of such neutral status by one offending nation seriously jeopardizes the security of another nation, then the injured nation has the international right to attempt to defend itself within the borders of the neutral country. But Johnson made no such public claim, nor did U.S. security appear to be threatened.

One scholar has concluded that in ambiguous situations such as the violation of a neutral country, when both sides do not admit publicly to their violations, diplomats and statesmen "must sometimes lie in order to tell the truth."[50] According to James Payne, four principles guide the dynamics of the interaction between belligerents:

1. When an opponent is violating or preparing to violate the status quo in a manner not yet publicly known and one is not ready to respond, one does not acknowledge the facts of this action.
2. A refusal to acknowledge one's own violation of the status quo (assuming ambiguity in the public knowledge of the facts exists) weakens the severity of the violation.
3. If the other side also denies knowledge of an unannounced viola-

tion, the action practically ceases to be a violation and the status
quo in question tends to be "unviolated."

4. Assuming ambiguity in the public knowledge of the action has been
   preserved, the violation of the status quo will "occur" only when
   the fact of the violation becomes public knowledge.[51]

Payne's status quo framework applied to the secret war in Laos concludes
that Johnson was telling a "lie" in order to tell the truth about our real
intentions in Laos. Payne's subtle and complex argument follows these
lines, as I interpret his reasoning for the Laotian case study:

a. Most nations (U.S., Laos, People's Republic of China, Soviet Union,
   etc.) knew that North Vietnam was violating the neutrality of
   southern Laos in order to conduct the war against South Vietnam.
b. North Vietnam did not want to *claim* any inherent right to violate
   the neutrality of Laos, but wanted to take temporary action
   covertly.
c. Laos did not want to acknowledge publicly that its neutrality had
   been violated because that would have been a call for overt warlike
   action on its part to repel violators of its neutrality.
d. Laos asked the United States to protect its neutrality, which was
   being violated covertly.
e. Johnson agreed to take covert steps to protect Laotian neutrality,
   but he did not announce his actions publicly because that would
   have been a signal that the United States claimed the right to
   violate the status quo, which had not been broken publicly.

Thus, fitting Payne's framework to the Johnson administration's deceptive behavior, one can see that all sides were willing participants in the
charade that Laotian neutrality was not being violated. The nations involved manipulated their mutual perceptions of the situation so that no
violation appeared to be taking place, when in fact clear violations of
neutrality were occurring every day.

As a justification of Johnson's secret behavior in Laos, Payne's notion
that Johnson had to "lie in order to tell the truth" (that is, the real U.S.
intention) is patently absurd. Even though three nation-states such as
North Vietnam, the United States, and Laos agree that no violation of
neutrality has occurred, one would be hard pressed to convince the native

Laotian tribespeople, who were being decimated by the bombing and the armed incursions, that Laos was still a neutral country. If a nation such as the United States enters into such international agreements as the United Nations Charter and the SEATO Treaty that honor the concept of neutrality, then it is obligated not to violate neutrality covertly. The president, by conducting diplomacy in a manner that allowed "lying in order to tell the truth," and armed confrontation to keep a country neutral, showed disrespect for international law. In short, Johnson's secret war in Laos was arguably illegal from the viewpoint of international law.

Was the So-called Secret War in Laos Unethical?

The morality of the Johnson administration's actions must be seen in the context of a president responding to a legitimate plea for help from Souvanna Phouma. However, Johnson did not enter into the secret agreement out of purely altruistic motives. By violating Laotian neutrality, Johnson could carry out his main policy goal of harassing North Vietnam troops within Laos. The moral problem of that response centers not on the ultimate goal, but on the methods selected to implement such a policy. A covert ground war organized by the CIA and condoned by the president poses certain ethical problems. Rather than systematically involving ethnic tribes to fight for the United States over a five-year period, Johnson should have been willing to commit the United States to an overt military action, if he deemed the national security stakes to be so important. In addition, Johnson's five-year policy of covertly bombing targets in northern, central, and southern Laos destroyed large numbers of Laotian peasants and leveled numerous villages. The bombing also created many more homeless refugees in the Indochina conflict.

It is not clear to me how this systematic destruction of Laos aided in keeping that country neutral and out of the Indochina conflict, nor is it clear to me how the massive bombing of an essentially peasant nation on the other side of the globe directly affected the immediate national security interests of the United States. The bombing and the "scorched-earth" policy in Laos during the Johnson years seem unjustified when weighed against other competing American interests. But Johnson would never suffer any great public reprobation over his specific Laotian policy precisely because it was kept hidden so effectively from Congress and the public.

Justifiability of the Nixon Administration's Response to the Allende Regime in Chile

The Nixon administration's efforts to engage in covert activities to keep Allende from being elected by funneling money to opposition parties was probably constitutional. Besides the many precedents for this practice (for example, the CIA filtered money into selected European political parties during the 1940s to keep them vigorous in the face of the Marxist challenge), Nixon had taken the required steps to notify the appropriate committees in Congress. The Church committee found that prior to 1973 there had been some twenty meetings in which CIA briefed the House and Senate Armed Services and Appropriations Committees and their intelligence subcommittees about possible covert electoral action in Chile.[52]

Yet the CIA never mentioned the secret "Track II" approach that encouraged the attempted military coup against Allende in 1970, which resulted in the death of General Schneider. Therefore, one might make the case that "Track II" had no congressional oversight at all. However, it is still not clear whether this kind of unilateral covert action (encouraging a coup in a foreign country) is unconstitutional. Presidents acting in the name of national security and fulfilling their roles as foreign policy managers and commanders-in-chief historically have been given broad latitude for their actions. Nixon, acting in this capacity, probably could make a strong case for the constitutionality of his actions in trying to topple Allende in Chile.

The legality of the entire affair to overthrow Allende in Chile is another matter. Domestically, the legality of the operation is complicated by the entrance of ITT into the decision-making process. The Logan Act clearly forbids private citizens to engage in or conduct U.S. foreign policy, but ITT played a crucial role in destabilizing Allende's regime. At one point in the process, ITT offered the CIA over $1 million to prevent Allende's election, but the CIA refused to pass the money on into Chile. Still, the CIA did instruct ITT on how to filter ITT's own money directly into Chile. The CIA-ITT relationship was further complicated by the fact that former CIA Director John McCone was a member of the ITT board of directors. Nixon was pushed to take action by ITT in order to protect ITT holdings in Chile. Nixon moved to protect these interests even before Allende had expropriated any U.S. multinational corporation's property, partly because Nixon wanted to protect his working relationship with ITT for the upcoming U.S. presidential election in 1972. In summary, the ITT involvement was probably illegal in the domestic sense and it represented an extreme conflict of interest in the covert operation against Allende.

On the international level, Nixon's efforts to weaken the Allende regime by covert means were clearly illegal. Nixon violated the UN Charter, the OAS agreements, and his own rhetoric recognizing the right of Chile to self-determination. Covert intervention violated the spirit and letter of international law, but Nixon suffered no great international sanctions or reprobation for his efforts that resulted in a democratic society being transformed into an authoritarian military regime.

Finally, Nixon's efforts to topple Allende were unethical when judged by the standards of American rhetoric and justice. Nixon encouraged the overthrow of a freely elected regime by force in the "Track II" coup attempt. Nixon's efforts to destabilize Chile also helped make it impossible for Allende to govern. This helped set the stage for the military coup against Allende in 1973. Allende lost his life in the takeover, and the junta directed a series of repressive measures that brought it international reprobation for its massive violations of human rights.

Of course, Nixon did not directly overthrow or kill Allende himself, but he did encourage the military takeover indirectly. The Nixon administration also helped set the atmosphere that made a military takeover possible. In his fear of the self-proclaimed Marxist, Allende, Nixon lost sight of the fact that Allende had won a free election (despite U.S. efforts to help the opposition) by using a free press, freedom of dissent, and the electoral process. Ironically, in the end it was not Allende but rather the military junta that called off all elections, banished political parties, closed down the free press, muzzled dissent, arrested political enemies, and executed central opponents to the new regime.

Justifiability of Ford's Covert Responses During the Year of Intelligence

Not one of the Ford administration's covert responses in the case study during the "Year of Intelligence, 1975-1976," including the obstruction of the Pike committee as discussed in Chapter 2, the secrecy surrounding the early handling of the Mayaguez affair, and the covert intervention in

Angola as discussed in Chapter 6, can be accurately labeled unconstitutional or illegal. In arriving at these responses mostly because of institutional pressures to maintain the secret presidency, Ford did not appear to abuse his powers or break any laws. Although Ford was clearly within the letter of the law on all three responses, unfortunately, he was not behaving consistently with the intent of the congressional measures that required consultation with Congress.

None of Ford's responses should be termed unethical. They were, in Ford's view, actions by the president to defend the presidency against encroachments by Congress. Ford believed he was acting consistently with his responsibility to maintain presidential secrets in the national interest, his duty to defend property and lives of Americans abroad, and his discretionary power to respond to a request for help by various Angolan factions.

Most important, Ford's actions in regard to secrecy and deception indicate that even at a time of intense efforts at congressional oversight, the president still maintains control over the secrecy system. During the Pike committee investigations, the Ford administration engaged in a wide variety of tactics to hinder a full investigation of covert actions. The Ford administration finally convinced a majority of the House that the president should be allowed to sanitize the Pike committee's report to protect national secrets, as judged by the president. During the Mayaguez affair, the Ford administration informed Congress of its actions rather than consulting with Congress. Finally, the Ford administration did not give Congress an accurate picture of the scope of its covert intervention in Angola when it tried to comply with the Hughes-Ryan Amendment. All of these actions are justifiable from the perspective of the president in the confrontation for information between the executive and Congress. Perhaps Ford's responses may be about as "open" and "honest" as we can reasonably expect in the American political system of separated powers.

Notes

1. Max Weber, " 'Objectivity' in Social Science," in *Readings in the Philosophy of the Social Sciences,* ed. May Brodbeck (New York: Macmillan, 1968), p. 85.
2. Gunnar Myrdal, *Value in Social Theory* (London: Routledge and Kegan Paul, 1958), p. 261.
3. Paul Streeten, ibid., p. xiii.
4. Ernest Nagel, "The Value-Oriented Bias of Social Inquiry," in Brodbeck,

ed., *Readings*, p. 113. *See also* Don Bowen, "Objectivity as a Normative Standard," *The Journal of Politics*, 39, no. 1, (February 1977): 201-10, for a counterpoint, and F. Oppenheim, " 'Facts' and 'Values' in Politics: Are They Separable?" *Political Theory* (February 1973).

5. Brodbeck, "Values in Social Science," in Brodbeck, ed. *Readings*, p. 79.

6. Gustav Bergman, "Ideology," in Brodbeck, ed., *Readings*, p. 129. *See also* George Carey, "Beyond Parochialism in Political Science," in *The Post-Behavioral Era: Perspectives on Political Science,* ed. George Graham and George Carey (New York: David McKay, 1972), pp. 37-53, where Carey argues that "behavioral analysts were quick to adopt value-free positions in analysis professionally, but that their values affected clearly their own research, and more critically, the discipline as a whole," p. 9.

7. Eugene Meehan, *Value Judgment and Social Science* (Homewood, Ill.: Dorsey Press, 1969), p. 111.

8. Norman C. Thomas, "Studying the Presidency: Where Do We Go from Here?" *Presidential Studies Quarterly,* 7, no. 4 (Fall 1977): 173.

9. Ibid., p. 172.

10. Sissela Bok, *Lying: Moral Choice in Public and Private Life* (New York: Pantheon Books, 1978), pp. 98-99.

11. Clinton Rossiter, *The American Presidency,* rev. ed. (New York: Mentor Books, 1962), p. 43.

12. Theodore White, *Breach of Faith* (New York: Dell, 1976). For White, Nixon's mistake was obvious, as he noted: "The true crime of Richard Nixon was simple: he destroyed the myth that binds America together, and for this he was driven from power. . . . That faith holds that all men are equal before the law and protected by it; and that no matter how the faith may be betrayed elsewhere, at one particular point—the Presidency—justice will be done beyond prejudice, beyond rancor, beyond the possibility of a fix. It was that faith that Richard Nixon broke, betraying those who voted for him even more than those who voted against him." ` See p. 409.

13. Harold Lasswell and Arnold Rogow, *Power Corruption, and Rectitude* (Englewood Cliffs, N.J.: Prentice-Hall, 1963), p. 59.

14. Ibid., p. 59; *and see* C. Van Woodward, ed., *Responses of the Presidents to Charges of Misconduct* (New York: Dell, 1974), in his article, "The Conscience of the White House," introduction.

15. Francis Rourke, *Secrecy and Publicity* (Baltimore, Md.: Johns Hopkins University Press, 1961), p. 225.

16. Charles L. Stevenson, *Facts and Values: Studies in Ethical Analysis* (New Haven and London: Yale University Press, 1963), p. 144.

17. See William Colby, "The View from Langley," in *The CIA File,* ed. Robert Borosage and John Marks (New York: Grossman Publishers, 1976), pp. 183-84. For the counterpoint, see Church Committee Final Report, Book I, p. 131.

18. Robert Borosage, "The King's Men and the Constitutional Order," in Borosage and Marks, eds., *The CIA File,* pp. 130-31; and see Church Committee Final Report, Book I, p. 132.

19. Quoted in Harry Rositzke, *The CIA's Secret Operations* (New York: Reader's Digest Press, 1977), p. 151. Rositzke notes that Truman's statement was inconsistent with his authorization of covert activity in Italy, Greece, Turkey, and the Philippines. Merle Miller in his *Plain Speaking: An Oral Biography of Harry S Truman* (New York: Berkeley Medallion, 1974), recorded Truman's view of the CIA on pp. 419-21. Truman said, "Now as nearly as I can make out, those fellows in the CIA don't just report on wars and the like, they go out and make their own, and there's nobody to keep track of what they're up to. They spend billions of dollars on stirring up trouble so they'll have something to report on. . . . It's become a government all of its own and all secret. They don't have to account to anybody."

20. The Hughes-Ryan Amendment, Public Law 92-559, December 30, 1974, and see Church Committee Final Report, Book I, pp. 134-35.

21. See White, *Breach of Faith*, p. 407, and Appendix A, "The Articles of Impeachment," pp. 437-41.

22. The problem of who shall declare war and who shall make war has been a problem that has confronted Congress and the executive since the establishment of the Constitution. The literature on the confrontation is voluminous. See, for example, "Documents Relating to the War Power of Congress, The President's Authority as Commander-in-Chief and the War in Indochina," Committee on Foreign Relations, United States Senate, July 1970; Edward S. Corwin, *The President: Office and Powers* (New York: New York University Press, 1957), pp. 227-62; Arthur Schlesinger, Jr., *The Imperial Presidency* (New York: Popular Library, 1974), pp. 47-204; Ronald Moe, ed., *Congress and the President* (Pacific Palisades, Calif.: Goodyear, 1971), Chaps. 15, 16, and 17; Louis Fisher, "War Powers: A Need for Legislative Reassertion," in *The Presidency Reappraised*, ed. Rexford Tugwell and Thomas Cronin (New York: Praeger Publishers, 1974), pp. 56-73; William Mullen, *Presidential Power and Politics* (New York: St. Martin's Press, 1976), pp. 98-109; and Louis Fisher, *The Constitution Between Friends* (New York: St. Martin's Press, 1978), pp. 214-46.

23. The common set of assumptions that has characterized the conduct of U.S. foreign policy since World War II can be seen in Graham Allison, "Cool It: The Foreign Policy of Young America," *Foreign Policy*, no. 1 (Winter 1970-71): 144-60; John Donovan, *The Cold Warriors* (Lexington, Mass.: D. C. Heath, 1974); Richard Barnet, *Roots of War* (Baltimore, Md.: Penguin, 1973), pp. 95-136; Ernest May, "The Nature of Foreign Policy: The Calculated versus the Axiomatic," *Daedalus*, 91 (Fall 1962): 666-67; *and see* Morton Halperin, Priscilla Clapp, and Arnold Kanter, *Bureaucratic Politics and Foreign Policy* (Washington, D.C.: The Brookings Institution, 1974), pp. 11-12.

24. Margaret Gentry, "Levi to Study Section on Assassination Plots," Louisville, *The Courier-Journal*, June 11, 1975, p. 2. AP.

25. Quincy Wright, "Non-Military Intervention," in *The Relevance of International Law*, ed. Karl Deutsch and Stanley Hoffman (New York: Schenkman Publishing, 1968), p. 12.

26. Richard A. Falk, "CIA Covert Operations and International Law," in Borosage and Marks, eds., *The CIA File*, pp. 142-58.

27. Victor Lasky, *It Didn't Start with Watergate* (New York: Dial Press, 1977), p. 8.

28. See Alfred de Grazia, "The Myth of the President," in *The Presidency,* ed. Aaron Wildavsky (Boston: Little, Brown, 1969), pp. 49-73; Bruce Miroff, *Pragmatic Illusions* (New York: David McKay, 1976), p. 6; Louis Brownlow, "What We Expect the President to Do," in Wildavsky, ed., *The Presidency,* p. 35; George Reedy, *The Twilight of the Presidency* (New York: New American Library, 1971), p. 28; Thomas Cronin, "The Textbook Presidency and Political Science," paper delivered to the Annual Meeting of the American Political Science Association. September 1970; Thomas Cronin, *The State of the Presidency* (Boston: Little, Brown, 1975), pp. 25-51; William Mullen, *Presidential Power and Politics* (New York: St. Martin's Press, 1976), Chap. 3, pp. 110-55; *and see* John Orman, "The Macho Presidential Style," *Indiana Social Studies Quarterly,* 29, no. 3 (Winter 1976-1977): 51-60.

29. Rositzke, *The CIA's Secret Operations,* pp. 199-200.

30. Ibid., p. 200.

31. Barnet, *Roots of War,* p. 126.

32. Tad Szulc, "Cuba on Our Mind," in *The Assassinations,* ed. Peter Dale Scott, Paul Hoch, and Russell Stetler (New York: Vintage Books, 1976), pp. 382-83.

33. See "Alleged Assassination Plots," Church Committee Interim Report; and Rositzke, *The CIA's Secret Operations,* pp. 201-3. Kennedy's indirect complicity in the assassination plots against Trujillo by the Dominicans and against Diem in South Vietnam appears to be more plausible than any direct complicity against Castro. Trujillo was assassinated with arms supplied by the CIA after the Kennedy administration expressed interest in removing Trujillo from office, and Diem was assassinated in 1963 after Kennedy determined that Diem should be replaced. In neither case can Kennedy be directly tied to the death of the foreign head of state. Kennedy did not order the death of Trujillo, but the CIA supplied the Dominican coup with the tools to murder Trujillo. Kennedy did not order the death of Diem, but his actions led to the anti-Diem coup that eventually took Diem's life. American officials knew about the assassination plotting in both instances but took no steps to inform either Trujillo or Diem of plots against their lives. In both situations American foreign policy was deemed to be in a better position without Trujillo and Diem as heads of state.

34. Michael Parenti, ed., *Trends and Tragedies in American Foreign Policy* (Boston: Little, Brown, 1971), pp. 119-228.

35. The Tonkin Gulf Resolution, 78 Stat. 384, approved August 10, 1964.

36. See *United States* v. *Curtiss-Wright Export Corporation* (1936) 299 U.S. 304; *United States* v. *Pink,* (1942) 315 U.S. 203; and *Missouri* v. *Holland* (1920), 252 U.S. 416.

37. Quoted in Alfred H. Kelly and Winfred A. Harbison, *The American Constitution: Its Origins and Development,* 4th ed. (New York: W. W. Norton, 1970), p. 824.

38. Ibid., p. 824.

39. Ibid., p. 825.

40. Ibid., pp. 686-87.

41. Ibid., p. 824.

42. *Marbury* v. *Madison* (1803) established the constitutional principle that the Supreme Court would have judicial review of the legislative acts.

43. Kelly and Harbison, *The American Constitution*, p. 688.

44. See "Indochina: The Constitutional Crisis," prepared by students of the Yale Law School, in Documents Relating to the War Powers of Congress, the President's Authority as Commander-in-Chief and the War in Indochina, Committee on Foreign Relations, U.S. Senate, July 1970, pp. 81 and 48f.

45. See "The War in Southeast Asia: A Legal Position Paper," prepared by Root-Tilden Scholarship Program of students from New York University School of Law, 1970, in Documents, Committee on Foreign Relations, ibid., pp. 105-6.

46. "Indochina: The Constitutional Crisis," Documents, Committee on Foreign Relations, pp. 79 and 41f. *See also* "Congress, the President, and the Power to Commit Forces to Combat," *Harvard Law Review*, 81, no. 8 (June 1968): 1771-805, printed in Documents, ibid., p. 64.

47. In Foreign and Military Intelligence, Book 1, Church Committee Final Report, p. 157, *and see* Kissinger Testimony, November 21, 1975, p. 54.

48. See "Security Agreements and Commitments Abroad," report to the Committee on Foreign Relations (Senator Stuart Symington, Chairman) U.S. Senate, December 21, 1970, p. 17. One example of a president maximizing commitment in public discussions was when President Nixon talked with President Theiu of South Vietnam in regard to a possible U.S. show of force if North Vietnam would overrun South Vietnam after the peace agreement of January 1973. In this case it was Theiu who was ultimately deceived, rather than Congress or the American people.

49. John N. Moore, "Legal Dimensions of the Decision to Intercede in Cambodia," in Documents, Senate Foreign Relations Committee, p. 129. *See also* John Stevenson, "On Issues of International Law Involved in United States Military Actions in Cambodia," Documents, p. 94.

50. James L. Payne, *The American Threat: The Fear of War as an Instrument of American Foreign Policy* (Chicago: Markham, 1970), p. 83.

51. Ibid., pp. 84-86.

52. Chile Report, Church committee, p. 49.

8. SECRECY, DECEPTION, AND PRESIDENTIAL POWER IN A SYSTEM OF DEMOCRATIC ACCOUNTABILITY

After surveying various uses of secrecy and deception by the Kennedy, Johnson, Nixon, and Ford administrations, including an attempted assassination, secret wars, organized coups, paramilitary maneuvers, withholding information, and lying, it becomes necessary to advance some guidelines about how such presidential behavior can be held accountable. Perhaps one central lesson of all the case studies in Quadrant I (secretive and deceptive) is the fact that four presidents were virtually *unaccountable* in the area of their covert foreign policy. Although the case studies represented a skewed selection from the universe of cases involving presidential management of foreign policy, by specifically focusing on aspects of secrecy and deception, it is possible to advance some generalizations about presidential behavior in this area.

First, the resort to secrecy and deception by presidents in the 1960s and 1970s cannot be explained fully by any one of the components of the framework. The single components of each framework are most useful in understanding the phenomenon when they are used in combination. Recent presidents have faced pragmatic, bureaucratic, and institutional pressures to engage in secretive and deceptive acts. Some presidents have resorted to this kind of behavior because they have been more psychologically comfortable handling problems in a secret and deceptive action because of their own private motives. Explanation of deception by presidents is a complex task, but the four components of the framework taken together highlight reasons for this kind of behavior within the modern presidency.

Some components of the framework to explain presidential secrecy and deception worked better than others when applied to the various case studies. For example, the best fitting approach to explain the secrecy and deception of Operation Mongoose and the assassination plots against Castro was the pragmatic component, followed closely by the bureaucratic politics component. The secret ground war in Laos is best understood by using the bureaucratic politics component and the pragmatic approach to secrecy and deception. The secret bombing in Laos can best be understood by focusing on the pragmatic approach and the personality perspective. Track I of the program to eliminate Allende can best be explained with the personality approach and the institutional component of the framework; Track II of the program can be understood by using the pragmatic focus and the bureaucratic politics component. Finally, the obstruction of the Church and the Pike committees can best be explained by using the institutional component in tandem with the bureaucratic politics explanation for secrecy and deception, and the Angolan covert intervention can best be understood by using the bureaucratic politics component first and then the institutional perspective (see Table 4).

For those who keep score, by giving 2 points for the best fitting component in the framework and 1 point for the second best, the following tally emerges:

    1. Pragmatic-calculations component   9 points
    2. Bureaucratic politics component   8 points
    3. Institutional component   4 points
    4. Personality component   3 points

This tally suggests that in the various case studies of secret and deceptive presidential action that were used here, the pragmatic-calculations and the bureaucratic politics components seemed to work best.

Second, although the case studies selected were from Quadrant I behavior of the framework to explain secretive and deceptive presidential behavior, they focused entirely on foreign policy and national security decision making. In the 1960s and 1970s secrecy and deception in the White House also began to find its way into domestic policy making with increasing regularity. The consequences of secrecy and deception in domestic politics have still not been realized, but enough data in the form of case studies have been revealed about domestic covert behavior to make it possible to apply the framework to domestic policy cases.

TABLE 4: Explaining Covert Presidential Behavior

Case	President	Date	Best Fit
A. *Programs to Eliminate Castro*			
1. Operation Mongoose	John Kennedy	1961-63	1. pragmatic 2. bureaucratic
2. Assassination plots		1961-63	1. pragmatic 2. bureaucratic
B. *Secret War in Laos*			
1. CIA ground war	Lyndon Johnson	1963-68	1. bureaucratic 2. pragmatic
2. Secret bombing		1964-68	1. pragmatic 2. personality
C. *Programs to Eliminate Allende*			
1. Track I	Richard Nixon	1969-73	1. personality 2. institutional
2. Track II		1969-70	1. pragmatic 2. bureaucratic
D. *Programs to Control Secrecy System*			
1. Obstruction of Church and Pike committees	Gerald Ford	1974-76	1. institutional 2. bureaucratic
2. Angolan covert intervention		1975	1. bureaucratic 2. institutional

In his memoirs, Richard Nixon indicates that he had once wanted to be an FBI man but his application to the agency as a young man was misplaced. Had it not been for this small bureaucratic foul-up, Nixon suggests that he would have gone on to be a "G-man" instead of the president.[1] Nixon neglected to mention that he had it both ways, since some argue that Nixon did become an FBI man while in the White House, judging from Nixon's programs to quell dissent and to stop "national security" leaks. Of course, Kennedy even engaged in the domestic surveillance of Dr. Martin Luther King, Jr., and Johnson engaged in programs of counterintelligence and domestic surveillance such as the FBI's COINTELPRO action. A study of these various unilateral covert actions in the domestic arena would be beyond the scope of this book; in fact it would, indeed, be another book. However, using the framework to explain Quadrant I behavior, as illustrated in Table 5, could be instructive in these cases.

TABLE 5: Domestic Spillover: Explaining and Evaluating Domestic Covert Presidential Behavior

Case	Explanation	Evaluation: Violates Public Democratic Norms		
		Unconstitutional	*Illegal*	*Immoral or Unethical*
John Kennedy and the domestic surveillance of Martin Luther King, Jr. (1963)	1. pragmatic 2. bureaucratic	Questionable	Questionable	Yes
Lyndon Johnson and the Federal Bureau of Investigation's COINTEL-PRO action (1964-68)	1. bureaucratic 2. personality	Questionable	Yes	Yes
Richard Nixon and the plumbers program to stop national security leaks (1969-73)	1. personality 2. institutional	Yes	Yes	Yes

Third, it is all too easy to adopt a posture of moral indignation and self-righteousness about past presidential uses of deception in foreign policy. (See Table 6.)

Journalists, muckrakers, historians, and political scientists have the benefit of considerable hindsight in their analysis of crisis decision making, but presidents must make decisions under pressure of deadlines and without the benefit of moral tutors on the consequences of each decision. Thus, while it is easy to be appalled at assassination plots, secret bombings, the overthrow of democratic governments, lying, and withholding information, it should also be easy to understand why presidents and national security leaders in the past *did not* become appalled at these specific acts when they considered the available options to meet a perceived national security threat.

Kennedy, Johnson, Nixon, and Ford were not evil men who conspired to deceive Congress and the public. These presidents were human beings who, like most other human beings, had great capacities for both good and evil. In their minds, if they admitted any deception at all, they probably saw it as well-intentioned and for the public's own good. The problem with this noble kind of lie is that it can lead to one of the most serious kinds of deception in presidential behavior: self-deception. If the president deludes himself into believing that a deceptive course of action is "right," then he may not experience his misstatements of fact as deception.

Accountability: Secrecy and Reforms

Secrecy still poses a central problem in keeping the post-Watergate presidency accountable for its actions. If one group does not know what the other is doing, it is impossible for the former to keep the latter accountable. As was previously demonstrated, the post-Watergate president still basically controls the presidential secrecy system even though Congress has made some efforts to regain access to information. It is still a fact of political life that the president controls national secrets and Congress does not. The fact that the House of Representatives voted almost two to one not to release the Pike Committee Report on covert operations and secrecy until after the executive had sanitized it, which meant that the report would never be released officially, illustrates Congress' amazing deference to the president. In effect, the House was agreeing with the principle that the president should control national security secrets, free from unilateral determinations by Congress of what should or should not be classified.

It is not entirely clear to me why Congress should not have equal access to state secrets. Moreover, who should have the power to define what a state secret is? Who is to be held accountable, by whom, for what reason, and in what way? The chief executives in the case studies presented here challenged any system of accountability by controlling information. In a democracy, information is a tremendous power resource. If one can monopolize certain information, one's power is increased. To be held accountable, one must be responsible for and liable to be called upon to account for one's actions. If an individual controls the facts about covert operations on the domestic and foreign front, then that person negates any system of accountability.

The first step toward some new system of accountability for presidential secrecy is for Congress to legislate the categories of information that the president can legitimately withhold from Congress, the press, and the public. This would require the elimination of the current classification system, which has operated through executive order, to be replaced by a congressional definition of legitimate presidential secrets.

What should Congress allow the executive to keep secret? The executive *might* be allowed to keep the following categories of information secret from Congress, the press, and the public:

1. *Specific details about the development of ongoing diplomatic negotiations.* Secrecy protects negotiators by giving them flexibility, and disclosure of the bargaining posture could ruin the negotiations. For example, the secrecy that surrounded Kissinger's efforts to negotiate a breakthrough in United States-China relations should be protected. Indeed, there was evidence that if the early trial efforts toward détente had been publicized, the People's Republic of China would have balked in the talks. The emphasis in this category of information is on the "ongoing" details of negotiations in foreign affairs. The "outcomes" of secret negotiations must not be acceptable categories of information for the executive to routinely withhold from Congress, the press, and the public.

2. *Covert intelligence-gathering means.* The president should not be asked to reveal the methods, sources, and technology of intelligence gathering that are currently in use. Public disclosure of this information

TABLE 6: Evaluating Covert Presidential Behavior

Case	Violates Public Democratic Norms for Presidential Behavior			
		Illegal		Unethical or
	Unconstitutional	Domestic	International	Immoral
A. *Kennedy and the Programs to Eliminate Fidel Castro*				
1. Bay of Pigs 1961	No, but Questionable	No	Yes	—
2. Operation Mongoose 1961-63	No	No	Yes	—
3. Assassination plots 1961-63	No	No	Yes	Yes
B. *Lyndon Johnson and the secret war in Laos*				
1. CIA ground war 1963-68	Yes	No	Questionable	—
2. Secret bombing 1964-68	Yes	No	Questionable	Yes
C. *Richard Nixon and the Programs to Eliminate Salvador Allende 1969-73*				
1. Track I	No	Yes	Yes	Questionable
2. Track II	No	Yes	Yes	Yes
D. *Gerald Ford and the Programs to Maintain Control of the Presidential Secrecy System*				
1. Obstruction of Church and Pike committees 1974-76	No	No	No	No
2. Angolan covert Intervention 1975	No	No	No	No

could seriously harm intelligence gathering. The identity of current intelligence-gathering operatives should not be revealed publicly by the executive. However, there may be certain situations in which this information could be shared with the appropriate committees of Congress in secret session if it was directly related to a policy question.

3. *Defense contingency plans, military plans, troop movements, strategy, weapons research and development.* The president should be allowed to use secrecy to protect this kind of information, especially during times of declared war. This specific kind of detailed and technological national security information also needs to be protected by the executive from disclosure to Congress, the press, and the public during time of peace, however, during peacetime, the burden of proof that information legitimately falls within this very narrow national security category should fall on the president.

4. *The nature of presidential advice.* The president should not have to reveal the specific details of the exchanges within his advisory structure. The confidentiality of advisors' stated opinion should be protected to guard the presidential decision-making process. One exception to this rule would be when the need for evidence in a criminal trial outweighs the particular claim by the executive that his communications within his office should be privileged.

5. *Details about the ongoing negotiations of other nations, their covert intelligence gathering means, their defense and weapons plans, and the nature of their executive advice.* The president should not be required to reveal information about other nations in these categories if he chooses not to. Disclosure of this kind of information could compromise, embarrass, or hurt the national security of allies.

These five categories of information might be presumed by Congress to hold the legitimate status of "executive secrets." They represent, it seems to me, legitimate national secrets that should be kept from disclosure. Disclosure of the information could present grave problems for national security, and this information does not seem to be immediately relevant to the congressional need for information to make legislation. If, however, there is a congressional need for information in these five categories to make specific laws, then the Court should decide whether the president's specific claim of "executive privilege" overrides Congress' "need to know." If not, Congress, and only Congress could have access to this information in the form of secret sessions.

Of course, modern presidents might object to this narrow definition of legitimate categories for "executive secrets." The very fact that Congress would legislate such narrow categories might be viewed by some as a violation of the principle of separation of powers. Congress would be telling the president what he could and could not keep from them. Yet legislating the bounds of executive secrecy seems more democratic than allowing the president to determine by executive fiat what he can keep secret.

By limiting legitimate executive secrecy to these five categories of information, one can see that the president would be obligated to share with Congress much more information than currently is the practice. Outcomes of secret negotiations would have to be disclosed to Congress and secret executive agreements would not be allowed. Intelligence gathered by the CIA and other intelligence-gathering groups would be made available to specific committees and members of Congress upon request, since only intelligence-gathering means could be withheld by the executive. This sharing of CIA national security intelligence could be done in secret only if Congress so desired. Once a weapon has been researched and developed, all detail about the deployment of such a weapon must be made known to Congress. Although the nature of presidential advice is protected, the president could not legitimately engage in unilateral and secret action, once the decision had been reached, without informing Congress about the nature of his action.

Morton Halperin and Daniel Hoffman have developed a system of "Automatic Release" or "information necessary to congressional exercise of its constitutional power to declare war, to raise armies, to regulate the armed forces, to ratify treaties, and to approve official appointments."[2] *Their* system would require that the president automatically release the following kinds of information to Congress and the public:

1. Americans engaged in combat or in imminent prospect of combat;
2. American forces abroad;
3. nuclear weapons abroad;
4. financing of foreign combat operations or foreign military forces;
5. commitments to do any of the above; commitments of negotiations contemplating such commitments;

6. intelligence organizations: existence, budgets, and functions;
7. weapons systems: concepts and costs;
8. actions in violations of law.

This automatic release system developed by Halperin and Hoffman speaks to the issue of secrecy surrounding the so-called secret wars initiated by presidents, and their system is set up to further Congress' ability to take part in its constitutionally prescribed duties by providing it with information. As I view their system, none of the automatic releases would harm national security, but they would guard against covert presidential war making.

Any sound system of accountability would be well-advised to incorporate Halperin and Hoffman's "automatic release" system. But such a system of automatic disclosures by the president would be very difficult to enforce once it was legislated. How could Congress get the president or his advisors to publicly disclose actions he has undertaken that may be in violation of the law? Can we require presidents to incriminate themselves?

Some might argue that my five narrow categories of "executive secrets" combined with Halperin and Hoffman's "automatic release" system might harm national security. Indeed, they might. The guidelines defining what are legitimate presidential secrets might have been drawn too narrowly. The automatic releases might be asking the president to disclose too much. However, the recent history of abuses of the presidential secrecy system by Kennedy, Johnson, Nixon, and Ford indicate that the present system is just not working properly. This proposed new system would respond to some of the defects of the old system without endangering national security to any greater degree than covert presidential war making endangers national security. In short, too much presidential secrecy can pose as much of a threat to national security as too much openness. We have already experienced a record of too much secrecy and discovered the costs; this system asks that we risk "more openness" to test its potential as well.

The new system might also be criticized for not going far enough—the limits to presidential secrecy as specified by Congress are too broad and the automatic release specifications are too narrow.[3] Nevertheless, it is important to start to reform the classification system, and these suggestions are, in my estimation, a move in the right direction.

This new classification system with its five categories of legitimate executive secrets and its eight categories of automatic releases would leave a great deal of presidential information unaccounted for. The courts would act as the final arbiters for all uncategorized information as well as all disputes about proper categorization of information. But, given the Supreme Court's past reluctance to settle such disputes, this new system may not be any more manageable than the old one, though it seems clearly worth the effort and risks that have been given to past failures.

Accountability: Deception and Reforms

If designing guidelines for acceptable categories of secret information is difficult, the effort to specify when presidents may deceive Congress, the press, and the public is perhaps even more complex and controversial. If, as argued in Chapter 7, the president should not engage in a deceptive act (*a*) that is either unconstitutional, illegal, or unethical, (*b*) when means and ends are not compatible, (*c*) just because "other nations do it," (*d*) when an open action would suffice, or (*e*) when an honest action would achieve the same goal, then when can a U.S. president legitimately lie to Congress and the public? Are presidential lies for any reason ever justified?

It is a difficult task to hold presidents accountable for lying in public. As John Lovell has noted:

For individuals to tell deliberate falsehoods or to deceive others for the purpose of their own selfish advantage would be regarded as unethical, but for a statesman of one nation to lie to the statesman of another or otherwise intentionally deceive him, in order to advance the selfish interests of the nation is, under many circumstances, *judged to be not only proper but dutiful.*[4] (emphasis added)

Another scholar, James Payne, has even argued that statesmen must sometimes lie in order to communicate the truth of their actions.[5] For Rexford Tugwell, the problem is not stated in terms of why one president lies and another does not, but rather why do all presidents lie and only some face public reprobation? Tugwell concluded that, "as a rule, Presidents do not hesitate to deceive when it seems necessary to get their way or to defend themselves!"[6] Tugwell also observed:

There are so many illustrations of official deception, *and of the concurrence of those who might have objected,* that Johnson's departures from veracity concerning Southeast Asia appear in perspective as no different in kind, and very little worse in effect, than familiar ones in the past. . . . Apparently, it is only when hostility to a policy becomes general that the media begin to find and disseminate evidence that the public is being deceived.[7] (emphasis added)

One member of the Kennedy administration even asserted a presidential "right to lie" in order to save the nation.[8] Finally, Thomas Halper asks the probing question, "How can one deny the President the right to try to manipulate public opinion in support of the national interest as he sees it, while at the same time demand that he provide leadership?"[9]

The act of deception is perceived differently be deceivers and those who are deceived, as Sissela Bok has noted.[10] Liars often offer excuses for their statements which can be listed as the following types:

(A) Excuses that claim that the supposed lie is not really a lie, but a joke, perhaps, or an evasion, an exaggeration. Besides since it is impossible to objectively distinguish between truth and falsehood, the supposed lie cannot be proved to be one.

(B) Excuses that claim that the liar is not really responsible for his actions. He did not mean to deceive or mislead, or that he was forced or coerced into deceiving.

(C) Excuses that offer moral reasons why under certain circumstances their particular lie ought to be allowed.[11]

When people are deceived they are often hurt by the apparent disregard for the bond of trust that they thought had been established, or they can react by feeling sorry for themselves as a dupe. However, lies have consequences for both liars and the deceived that go beyond psychological dimensions. The action probably has costs and benefits for the self-interest of both the liar and the deceived.

An interesting problem in foreign policy arises when the liar and the deceived are one and the same. This situation can come about in two ways: through self-deception and when liars lie to liars. Irving Janis has done exploratory work essentially in the area of self-deception in his work on "groupthink."[12] In certain foreign policy decisions Janis argued that the president and his inner circle of advisors were "victims of group-

think" (or self-deception as I have labeled it). For example, Janis maintained that the Bay of Pigs decision and the decision to escalate the war
in Vietnam both showed classic symptoms of groupthink that include an
illusion of invulnerability, collective efforts to rationalize, an unquestioned
belief in the group's inherent morality, and stereotyped views of enemy
leaders as evil, among others.[13] With respect to liars lying to liars, a system
of escalation of lies develops. A liar adopts deceptive practices primarily
because he perceives that someone else has lied to him and therefore he
is justified in lying to other liars or to his enemies. The escalation of
covert activities by the Soviet Union and the United States during the
1950s and 1960s Cold War is a good example of this kind of phenomenon.

As a general rule in this new proposed system of accountability for
presidential deception, perhaps I should posit the notion that presidents,
in most circumstances, should never consciously lie to Congress, the press,
and the public. William Colby, former director of Central Intelligence
Agency, has noted why this must be the case. He said, "[After Watergate and Vietnam] I believe that an American official cannot any longer
lie to the American public and would be repudiated if he did."[14] Colby
maintains that officials can protect secrets without lying to the press by
answering sensitive questions with such responses as "I can't answer that
particular question," "I can't comment on that," or "As of now, I have
no comment that I can make." These kinds of responses protect national
security secrets without lying and misleading journalists, Congress, or the
public, according to Colby.

One problem with Colby's approach is that it puts the responsibility
on the press for asking the "right" questions, and even then an answer
may not be forthcoming. At one recent gathering of former presidential
press secretaries including Pierre Salinger, George Reedy, Ron Ziegler,
and Ron Nessen, all four press secretaries maintained that they had never
knowingly lied to the press.[15] Kennedy's press secretary Salinger said that
he had never lied about CIA assassination plots against Castro or Kennedy's
alleged affair with Judith Campbell (Exner), a friend of Mafia leader Sam
Giancana, precisely because the press never asked him about them.
Johnson's press secretary Reedy said he never personally lied for the
president about our involvement in Southeast Asia, but that he was passing
on the best information possible. Ziegler, Nixon's press secretary during
Watergate, said he never lied but was a victim himself of the Watergate
cover-up because the president misled him. Finally, Nessen, one of Ford's

press secretaries, argued that he had never lied in any fashion for Ford. Thus, if any lies were told from 1961 to 1976 by presidents through press secretaries, the press secretaries maintained that they did not know they were being used. Besides, the press did not ask the "right" questions.

Another problem of Colby's strategy is that at times a "No Comment," or an "I can't answer that," is an answer that gives away information, depending upon how the question is phrased. If the president makes the determination that he must keep his course of action secret from Congress and others, should he lie in this case to protect the secret? The following guidelines might be used:

1. A president may lie to Congress, the media, and the public in order to save the nation from a nuclear war. If the president must deceive the public in an effort to avoid a nuclear holocaust, then perhaps a lie is justified. But the burden of proof must be on the president, once the situation has passed, to show that it was his only option.

2. A president may lie to Congress, the media, and the public if a truthful statement or an evasive answer will not protect the legitimate "executive secrets" that were enumerated earlier, and if a lie is the only option that will protect:

a. the specific details of ongoing diplomatic negotiations;
b. covert intelligence-gathering means;
c. defense contingency plans, military plans, troop movements, strategy, weapons research and development;
d. the nature of presidential advice; or,
e. details about other nations' ongoing negotiations, covert intelligence-gathering means, defense and weapons plans, and the nature of executive advice.

After the confrontation has passed and the clamor for disclosure has settled, and after the cover story has been blown, it is the responsibility of the president to explain to the public why, in this particular case, deception was necessary.

3. Each case of presidential deception must be analyzed individually to examine the president's version of events as opposed to alternative versions. There can be no generalized unchallenged blanket presidential grants to lie.

4. In certain situations a president may lie in order not to cause undue alarm in Congress, press, or the public in the case of a constitutionally

declared war. For example, a president may lie, if it is his only option, about the conduct of the war and how the war is going to keep the public from panic. This exception applies only when the president acts as commander-in-chief during a constitutionally declared war. In times of peace, a lie about the state of the economy or about the nonexistence of unidentified flying objects, for example, cannot be justified on the grounds that the president is trying to avoid alarm.

In short, the president may not lie justifiably to the public if he takes action (a) that is unconstitutional, illegal, or unethical, (b) when means and ends are not compatible, (c) just because "other nations do it," (d) when an open act would suffice, or (e) when an honest action would achieve the same goal. He may lie justifiably (a) to save the nation from nuclear war, (b) to protect legitimate "executive secrets" if it is his only option, and (c) during a constitutionally declared state of war.

Again, these narrow categories of acceptable presidential deception face the same criticisms as the acceptability of "executive secrets." Some purists argue that the president should never lie under any circumstances and that the categories are extremely broad, giving the president a grant to engage in deception. No public official should ever assume that there will be any time that he or she can legitimately lie to Congress, the media, or the public, according to the purist line of thought. By allowing some deception, widespread distrust in a democratic nation is encouraged, some might contend. Yet others find the categories for allowable presidential deception to be extremely narrow. They believe the president would be weakened in his role as commander-in-chief and as foreign policy maker if these are the only times in which a president can justifiably lie.

Both views have an element of truth. The categories of justified presidential deception would have to be watched closely so that the president would not abuse this power. Likewise, there may be other instances in which the president would be justified in deceiving but which have escaped enumeration not because they were unworthy of inclusion but because they were simply overlooked. As Halper has observed, "What is one man's politics of leadership may be another's politics of deception."[16] However, the categories of deceptive behavior, as I have drawn them, would represent drastic changes in the level of allowable presidential deception.

The most obvious change would be the elimination of a unilateral covert operation initiated by the president since the president would not be allowed to lie in the form of a cover story. For all practical purposes this would eliminate the covert operation capability, except for the collection of intelligence. With respect to military action, the president would be able to engage in operations that meet the test of publicity to Congress, the media, and the public. Covert military operation would only be justified in case of a constitutionally declared war, or if Congress gave its consent.[17]

Conclusion: Accountability, Presidential Power, and Reforms

Since Vietnam, Watergate, and the CIA-FBI revelations, the topic of presidential accountability is once again a popular subject for scholars, president-watchers, and members of Congress. Charles Hardin has proposed to make the president more accountable to the electorate by changing the way in which we nominate and elect the president and members of Congress.[18] He advocates a parliamentary solution to the problem of presidential accountability, whereas Philip Kurland advocates much stronger congressional oversight.[19] Arthur Schlesinger, Jr., contends that we have to "de-imperialize" the presidency, and George Reedy maintains that we have to stop isolating the president.[20] Erwin Hargrove finds one solution in the possibility that the nation might elect better people as presidents, ones that have a "democratic character."[21] Norman C. Thomas finds hope in congressional reassertion of its will as central in holding the president accountable, and he places faith in the media as instruments to hold presidents accountable.[22] Thomas E. Cronin wants a regeneration of the political parties and a rebirth of citizen-politics to keep the chief executive ultimately in line.[23] Finally, the Ervin committee, the Rudino committee, the Church committee, and the Pike committee all made recommendations about the role of secret presidential power and how such power could be held accountable to Congress.[24]

Despite all of these calls for reforms in the accountability of the presidency, very little has changed with respect to the power of the institution. As noted earlier, Congress has emerged from its lack of oversight in the 1950s and 1960s to assert a new congressional will concerning foreign policy in the 1970s. For example, the War Powers Act of 1973 and the Hughes-Ryan Amendment of 1974 represent efforts by Congress to prevent so-called secret wars and unconstitutional wars. By law, the president must at least inform Congress of his troop deployment or his covert actions. The establishment of a permanent House and Senate Intelligence Committee also represents an effort by Congress to control secret and deceptive presidential actions. Yet these piecemeal efforts, in my estimation, do not go far enough.

Already post-Watergate presidents have argued that Congress has "tied" the president's hands in foreign affairs. Ford and Carter have both spoken publicly about some of the "unfortunate" consequences of congressional control of foreign policy making. The backlash against weakening presidential power in national security began before any comprehensive institutional remedies could be adopted by Congress. Even some critics of the theory of the strong presidency did not argue for changes that would weaken the institution.[25]

My proposals for reform in holding presidential power more accountable to Congress and the public center on the two most difficult challenges to the system of accountability: secrecy and deception. Presidential power is much more than the "power to persuade"; it is also the power to issue unilateral, nonreciprocal secret commands for action: therefore, any system of accountability must address itself to the problems of secrecy and deception. The current crisis in accountability is not a crisis of the lack of agents of accountability, but rather a crisis of the lack of information about secret and deceptive presidential actions. The problem of restraining the president, then, can be viewed as a problem of information control.

The agents of accountability in this political system do not lack the power to control the president; they lack sufficient information about presidential actions. Congress, the courts, the bureaucracy, the parties, the media, the electorate, and the public all appear to be able to control abuses of presidential power if they have adequate information about presidential actions. Congress can carry out adequate oversight only if it has the will and the legal authority to obtain the relevant policy information from the president. The courts can ultimately decide the constitutional aspects of troublesome areas of presidential power only if they have a will to challenge the presidential secrecy system. The bureaucracy can act as an agent of accountability by refusing to carry out commands that represent abuses of power only if they know what the president is doing. Political parties can only act as effective opposition to the president if they know about his covert actions. The media can only check presidential power if they are able to get information and willing to print or broadcast it. The electorate can only hold the president accountable every four years, and to do this effectively, they must have knowledge about the president's secret policies. Finally, if the weight of public opinion is to have any meaning at all in a system of accountability, it must be an informed public opinion represented by various informed groups within the public.

To regain control of the presidency, then, the political system must regain control of information about presidential activities. To do this I have suggested that Congress legislate categories of information that the president can legitimately keep secret. Moreover, Congress should articulate certain categories of deception that it considers justified. Of course, this legislation and articulation would run into monumental debate within Congress, but that is precisely what is needed at this point. Only by beginning a great national debate over presidential secrecy and deception can a resolution of the problems come about. The important national debate that began for a time after Vietnam and Watergate should not be allowed to wither away at least until the problem of presidential control of information has been resolved.

Some argue that the problem of accountability in a democratic polity may never be resolved. Besides, they argue, Congress cannot legislate the parameters of executive behavior. The president could merely veto such legislation and mount an intense national campaign to convince Congress to sustain his veto. The experience of the House vote on the Pike Committee Report shows the strength of such a presidential strategy. The possibility of a runaway, unconstrained presidency is one of the prices that a democratic polity built on the principle of separation of powers must pay. Halper wrote:

Instead of formal limitations, we must fall back on the *hope* that decision makers have been so inculcated with democratic values that they will not violate the *trust* which crises inevitably impose upon them. It is a matter of *faith,* and on this, as in most things, the people must take their chances.[26] (emphasis added)

Even Norman C. Thomas has essentially concurred with this view when he argues:

Awareness of the danger that abuse of presidential power can pose to freedom, the viability of the processes of electoral accountability, and the additional checks and balances . . . created by a resurgent Congress provide us with as much insurance as we can reasonably expect to obtain without changing the basic structure of government under the Constitution. . . . *In the final analysis there are risks that a free society must run and contingencies that cannot be anticipated regardless of how it chooses to approach the problem of securing executive accountability.*[27] (emphasis added)

However, I remain unconvinced that we have done all we can do, and I am uncomfortable leaving presidential accountability in the final sense to faith in the president's character and trustworthiness. Congressional efforts to legislate acceptable limits of presidential secrecy and to articulate allowable cases of presidential deception, if narrowly drawn, would be a major step to gain control of information that is a necessary condition of democratic accountability.

Notes

1. Richard Nixon, *RN* (New York: Grosset & Dunlap, 1978), p. 22.
2. Morton Halperin and Daniel Hoffman, *Top Secret* (Washington, D.C.: New Republic Books, 1977), pp. 58-65.
3. *Civil Liberties,* published by the American Civil Liberties Union, No. 314 (November 1976): pp. 4-6. The ACLU asked that "No information should be classified unless its disclosure would cause immediate irreparable damage to our national defense, i.e., technical details of weaponry, wartime military operations, and defensive military contingency plans in response to attack" (p. 6). Moreover, the ACLU publication called for an "End [of all] clandestine intelligence gathering except in times of war and in the investigation of crimes" (p. 5).
4. John Lovell, *Foreign Policy in Perspective: Strategy, Adaptation, Decision Making* (New York: Holt, Rinehart, Winston, 1970), p. 295.
5. James L. Payne, *The American Threat* (Chicago: Markham, 1970), pp. 83-86.
6. Rexford Tugwell, "On Bringing Presidents to Heel," in *The Presidency Reappraised,* ed. Tugwell and Thomas Cronin (New York: Praeger, 1974), p. 284.
7. Ibid., pp. 285-86.
8. Arthur Sylvester, Assistant Secretary for Public Affairs DOD, quoted in Theodore Sorensen, *Kennedy* (New York: Bantam, 1966), p. 359.
9. Thomas Halper, *Foreign Policy Crises: Appearance and Reality in Decision Making* (Columbus, Ohio: Charles E. Merrill, 1971), pp. 225-26.
10. Sissela Bok, *Lying: Moral Choice in Public and Private Life* (New York: Pantheon, 1978). *See also* Anthony Brandt, "Lies, Lies, Lies," in *Atlantic Monthly,* November 1977, pp. 58-63.
11. Bok, *Lying,* pp. 74-75.

12. Irving Janis, *Victims of Groupthink* (Boston: Houghton Mifflin, 1972).

13. Ibid., pp. 197-98.

14. William Colby, "How Can the Government Keep a Secret?" *TV Guide*, February 12, 1977, p. 3. *See also* Colby, "Why I Was Fired from the CIA," *Esquire*, May 1978, pp. 59-68; and Colby, *Honorable Men: My Life in the CIA* (New York: Simon & Schuster, 1978).

15. "Some of the President's Men," Documentary from Gonzaga University, Broadcast on PBS, May 16, 1978.

16. Halper, *Foreign Policy Crises*, p. 225.

17. See ACLU *Civil Liberties;* Richard A. Falk, "CIA Covert Operations and International Law," in *The CIA File*, ed. Robert Borosage and John Marks (New York: Grossman Publishers, 1976), p. 158; Ray S. Cline in his *Secrets, Spies and Scholars* (Washington, D.C.: Acropolis Books, 1976), wants to separate intelligence from covert activities of CIA. Colby in *Honorable Men*, wants to make covert capabilities more accountable to Congress; and Harry Rositzke, *The CIA's Secret Operations* (New York: Reader's Digest Press, 1977), wants to transfer covert capabilities to the Department of Defense.

18. Charles M. Hardin, *Presidential Power and Accountability: Toward a New Constitution* (Chicago: University of Chicago, 1974), pp. 184-85.

19. Philip Kurland and William Kenan, "Toward a Responsible American Presidency," in Roscoe Pound-American Trial Lawyers Foundation *The Power of the Presidency* (Cambridge, Mass.: June 1975), pp. 76-81.

20. Arthur Schlesinger, Jr., *The Imperial Presidency* (New York: Popular Library, 1973), and George Reedy, *The Twilight of the Presidency* (New York: New American Library, 1970).

21. Erwin C. Hargrove, "What Manner of Man?" in *Choosing the President*, ed. James David Barber (Englewood Cliffs, N.J.: Prentice-Hall, 1974), pp. 28-33.

22. Norman C. Thomas, "Recent Developments and Accountability: United States or Presidential Accountability Since Watergate," paper delivered at the 1978 Annual Meeting of the Midwest Political Science Association, April 21, 1978, Chicago.

23. Thomas Cronin, *The State of the Presidency* (Boston: Little, Brown, 1975), pp. 316-23.

24. See Ervin Committee (Watergate) Report; Rodino (House Judiciary Committee) Impeachment Report; Church (Senate Select Committee on Intelligence) Report; and Pike (House Select Committee) Report cited in bibliography.

25. See Schlesinger, *The Imperial Presidency*, and Ted Sorensen, *Watchmen in the Night* (Cambridge, Mass.: The MIT Press, 1975).

26. Halper, *Foreign Policy Crises*, p. 228.

27. Thomas, "Recent Developments and Accountability," pp. 32-33.

APPENDIX

SECRET MEMORANDUM, PREPARED FOR THEN GENERAL COUNSEL
LAWRENCE HOUSTON, CIA, JANUARY 1962, AUTHOR UNKNOWN

Memorandum Re: Constitutional and Legal Basis for So-Called *Covert
Activities of the Central Intelligence Agency*

This memorandum will discuss the constitutional and legal authority
for the Central Intelligence Agency to engage in covert activities. It is
understood that certain cold-war activities of a covert nature have been
engaged in by CIA almost from its inception, pursuant to an express
directive of the National Security Council, and that the Congress has repeatedly appropriated funds for the support of such activities.

I. Constitutional Powers of the President

"As a nation with all the attributes of sovereignty, the United States
is vested with all the powers of government necessary to maintain an
effective control of international relations." *Burnet v. Brooks,* 288 U.S.
378, 396. These powers do not "depend upon the affirmative grants of
the Constitution," but are "necessary concomitants of nationality."
United States v. Curtiss-Wright Corp., 299 U.S. 304, 318. "In the preservation of the safety and integrity of the United States and the protection
of its responsibilities and obligations as a sovereignty" the constitutional
powers of the President are broad 30 O.A.G. 291, 292. "The very delicate,
plenary and exclusive power of the President as the sole organ of the

federal government in the field of international relations . . . does not require as a basis for its exercise an act of Congress," although, like all governmental powers, it must be exercised in subordination to any applicable provisions of the Constitution. *United States v. Curtiss-Wright Corp., supra,* at p. 320. His duty to take care that the laws be faithfully executed extends not merely to express acts of Congress, but to the enforcement of "the rights, duties, and obligations growing out of the institution itself, our international relations, and all of the protection implied by the nature of the government under the Constitution." *In re Neagle,* 135 U.S. 1, 64. (1890).

Examples of the exercise of these broad powers are numerous and varied. Their scope may be illustrated by the following: The President may take such action as may, in his judgment, be appropriate, including the use of force, to protect American citizens and property abroad. *Durand v. Hollins* Fed. Cas. No. 4186 (C.C.S.D.N.Y. (1860)); *In Re Neagle, supra,* 135 U.S. at 64; *Hamilton v. M'Claughry,* 136 Fed. 445, 449-50 (D. Kansas, 1905); II Hackworth, Digest of International Law, 327-334; VI *Id.,* 464-5. Notwithstanding the exclusive power of Congress to declare war, the President may repel armed attack and "meet force with force." *Prize Cases,* 2 Black 635, 638 (1862). He may impose restrictions on the operation of domestic radio stations which he deems necessary to prevent unneutral acts which may endanger our relations with foreign countries. 30 O.A.G. 291.

Congress' grants of power to executive agencies in areas relating to the conduct of foreign relations and preservation of the national security from external threats are generally couched in terms which neither limit the powers of the President nor restrict his discretion in the choice of the agency through which he will exercise these powers. Thus, in establishing a Department of State in 1799, Congress directed that the Secretary should perform duties relating to "such . . . matters respecting foreign affairs as the President of the United States shall assign to the Department," and should "conduct the business of the department in such manner as the President shall direct." 1 Stat. 28; R.S. 202, 5 U.S.C. 156. More recently, in establishing the National Security Council, Congress gave it the function of advising the President "with respect to the integration of domestic, foreign, and military policies relating to the national security." 50 U.S.C. 402 (a).

From the beginning of our history as a nation, it has been recognized and accepted that the conduct of foreign affairs on occasion requires the use of covert activities, which might be of a quasi-military nature. See, *e.g.,* the acts of July 1, 1790, 1 Stat. 128, and Mar. 1, 1810, sec. 3, 2 Stat. 609. In a message to the House of Representatives declining to furnish an account of payments made for contingent expenses of foreign intercourse, President Polk reviewed that practice and stated:

"The experience of every nation on earth has demonstrated that emergencies may arise in which it becomes absolutely necessary for the public safety or the public good to make expenditures the very object of which would be defeated by publicity."

President Polk continued:

"Some governments have very large amounts at their disposal, and have made vastly greater expenditures than the small amounts which have from time to time been accounted for on President's certificates. In no nation is the application of such sums ever made public. In time of war or impending danger the situation of the country may make it necessary to employ individuals for the purpose of obtaining information or rendering other important services who could never be prevailed upon to act if they entertained the least apprehension that their names or their agency would in any contingency be divulged. So it may often become necessary to incur an expenditure for an object highly useful to the country; for example, the conclusion of a treaty with a barbarian power whose customs require on such occasions the use of presents. But this object might be altogether defeated by the intrigues of other powers if our purposes were to be made known by the exhibition of the original papers and vouchers to the accounting officers of the Treasury. It would be easy to specify other cases which may occur in the history of a great nation, in its intercourse with other nations, wherein it might become absolutely necessary to incur expenditures for objects which could never be accomplished if it were suspected in advance that the items of expenditure and the agencies employed would be made public." 4 Richardson, Messages and Papers of Presidents, 431, 435 (April 20, 1846).

Compare also Stuart, *American Diplomatic and Consular Practice* (1952) p. 195, (commenting on prevailing diplomatic practice of all countries), "actual cases of interference in the internal affairs of states to which the envoys are accredited are very numerous."

An early example of such a secret operation is afforded in the Lewis and Clark expedition of 1803. That expedition was authorized prior to the Louisiana Purchase by a statute providing:

"That the sum of two thousand five hundred dollars be, and the same is hereby appropriated for the purpose of extending the external commerce of the United States (2 Stat. 206)."

Congress used this cryptic language at the request of President Jefferson because, in the words of a present-day judge, the "expedition, military in character, would enter into lands owned by a foreign nation with which the United States was at peace and . . . the utmost secrecy had to be observed." *First Trust Co. of St. Paul v. Minnesota Historical Soc.,* 146 F. Supp. 652, (D.C. Minn. (1956)), aff'd *sub. nom. United States v. First Trust Co. of St. Paul,* 251 F. 2d 686 (C.A. 8). In his message to the Congress, President Jefferson stated:

"The appropriation of $2,500 'for the purpose of extending the external commerce of the United States,' while understood and considered by the Executive as giving the legislative sanction, would cover the undertaking from notice and prevent the obstructions which interested individuals might otherwise previously prepare in its way." (1 Richardson, *Messages and Papers of the Presidents,* 352 at 354.)

Under modern conditions of "cold war," the President can properly regard the conduct of covert activities as necessary to the effective and successful conduct of foreign relations and the protection of the national security. When the United States is attacked from without or within, the President may "meet force with force," *Prize Cases, supra.* In waging a world wide contest to strengthen the free nations and contain the Communist nations, and thereby to preserve the existence of the United States, the President should be deemed to have comparable authority to meet covert activities with covert activities if he deems such action necessary and consistent with our national objectives. As Charles Evans Hughes said in another context, "Self-preservation is the first law of national life and the Constitution itself provides the necessary powers in order to defend and preserve the United States." War Powers Under the Constitution, 42 A.B.A. Rep. 232 (1917). Just as "the power to wage war is the power to wage war successfully," *id.* 238, so the power of the President to conduct foreign relations should be deemed to be the power to conduct foreign relations successfully, by any means necessary to combat the measures taken by the Communist bloc, including both open and covert measures.

The exclusive power of Congress to declare war has been held not to prevent use by the President of force short of war to protect American citizens and property abroad. *A fortiori* it does not prevent his use of force short of war for other purposes which he deems necessary to our national survival. In either case the magnitude and possible grave international consequences of a particular action may be such as to render the approval or ratification of, the Congress if circumstances permit such action. But the necessity for obtaining such approval does not depend on whether the action is overt or covert.

II. Statutory Authority

There is no specific statutory authorization to any agency to conduct covert cold war activities. Nor is there any statutory prohibition, except to the extent, if any, that the prohibitions of the Neutrality Acts, 18 U.S.C. Chapter 45, against performance of certain acts by persons within the United States might be deemed applicable to such activities in particular circumstances. Hence the President is not restricted by act of Congress in authorizing such acts, or in assigning responsibility for them to such agency as he may designate.

Congress has authorized the Central Intelligence Agency, "for the purpose of coordinating the intelligence activities of the several government departments and agencies in the interest of the national security," to perform, *inter alia,*

"such other functions and duties related to intelligence affecting the national security as the National Security Council may from time to time direct." 50 U.S.C. 403 (d).

As previously noted, the National Security Council, which includes in its membership the President, the Vice President, the Secretary of State and the Secretary of Defense, has overall responsibility for advice to the President respecting all matters "relating to the national security."

We understand that in 1947, Secretary of Defense Forrestal asked the Director of Central Intelligence if CIA would be able to conduct covert cold-war activities, CIA advised at the time that it would conduct such activities if the National Security Council developed a policy that the United States would engage in such covert activities and assigned their conduct to CIA, and if the Congress appropriated funds to carry them out. In the latter part of 1947 the National Security Council developed a directive (NSC 10/2) setting forth a program of cold war activities and assigned that program to the Office of Policy Coordination under the Director of Central Intelligence, with policy guidance from the Department of State. The Congress was asked for and did appropriate funds to support this program, although, of course, only a small number of Congressmen in the Appropriations Committees knew the amount and purpose of the appropriation. The Office of Policy Coordination was subsequently combined with the clandestine intelligence activities in the Office of the Deputy (Plans) of CIA and the cold-war charter was assigned to CIA in coordination with the Department of State and Defense by NSC Directive 54/12.

A significant part of the strictly intelligence and counter-intelligence functions of CIA are clandestine in nature. It could perhaps be argued that many if not all of the covert activities assigned to CIA by the directives referred to above are at least "related" to intelligence affecting the national security within the scope of 50 U.S.C. 403 (d) (5) in the sense that their performance may need to be intimately dovetailed with clandestine intelligence operations, may involve use of the same or similar contacts, operatives and methods, and may yield important intelligence results. Alternatively, it would appear that the Executive branch, under the direction of the President, has been exercising without express statutory authorization a function which is within the constitutional powers of the President, and that the CIA was the agent selected by the President to carry out these functions. (The historic relationship between the two types of activity is indicated by the fact that the Office of Strategic Services, CIA's predecessor during World War II, engaged both in intelligence work, and in assistance to and coordination of local resistance activities. See Alsop and Braden, Sub Rosa, The O.S.S. and American Espionage (1946) p. 7.)

Congress has continued over the years since 1947 to appropriate funds for the conduct of such covert activities. We understand that the existence of such covert activities has been reported on a number of occasions to the leadership of both houses, and to members of the subcommittees of the Armed Services and Appropriations Committees of both houses. (See letter dated May 2, 1957, from Mr. Allen W. Dulles, Director, CIA to Senator Hennings, *Freedom of Information and Secrecy in Government,* Hearing before the Subcommittee on Constitutional Rights of the Senate Committee of the Judiciary, 85th Cong., 2d Session, p. 376 at 377:

"The Director of the Central Intelligence Agency appears regularly before established subcommittees of the Armed Services and Appropriation Committees of the Senate and of the House, and makes available to these subcommittees complete information on Agency activities, personnel and expenditures. No information has ever been denied to their subcommittees."

It can be said that Congress as a whole knows that money is appropriated to CIA and knows generally that a portion of it goes for clandestine activities, although knowledge of specific activities is restricted to the group specified above and occasional other members of Congress briefed for specific purposes. In effect, therefore, CIA has for many years had general funds approval from the Congress to carry on covert cold-war activities, which the Executive Branch has the authority and responsibility to direct.

It is well-established that appropriations for administrative action which Congress has been informed amount to a ratification of or acquiescence in such action. *Brooks v. Dewar,* 313 U.S. 354, 361; *Fleming v. Mohawk Co.,* 331 U.S. 111, 116; see also *Ivanhoe Irrig. Dist. v. McCracken,* 357 U.S. 275, 293-294; *Power Reactor Co., v. Electricians,* 367 U.S. 396, 409. Since the circumstances effectively prevent the Congress from making an express and detailed appropriation for the activities of the CIA, the general knowledge of the Congress, and specific knowledge of responsible committee members, outlined above, are sufficient to render this principle applicable. (Compare the cases of veiled, or contingent fund, appropriations referred to in Part I. And note the importance on the close contact between an agency and "its" committees. *E.g., Panama Canal Co. v. Grace Line Inc.,* 356 U.S. 309, 319.)

Source of Memo: Obtained by Tyrus Fain, ed., *The Intelligence Community* (New York: R. R. Bowker Co., 1977), pp. 708-20 under the Freedom of Information Act from the CIA in 1977.

SELECTED BIBLIOGRAPHY

Any bibliography on the presidency, secrecy, and political deception of necessity becomes a selected bibliography. This list does not purport to be comprehensive, but these are the selections that were most helpful to me as I worked on this project.

I. Secrecy, Deception, and Covert Activities

Adler, Renata. "Thinking the Unthinkable About the Nixon Scandal," *The Atlantic Monthly*. December 1976, pp. 76-95.

Agee, Phil. *Inside the Company: CIA Diary*. New York: Bantam Books, 1976.

Allison, Graham, and Szanton, Peter. *Remaking Foreign Policy: The Organizational Connection*. New York: Basic Books, 1976.

Anderson, Jack. *The Anderson Papers*. New York: Ballantine, 1974.

Baker, Carol M., and Fox, Matthew. *Classified Files: The Yellowing Pages, A Report on Scholar's Access to Government Documents*. New York: Twentieth Century Fund, 1972.

Berger, Raoul. *Executive Privilege: A Constitutional Myth*. Cambridge, Mass.: Harvard University Press, 1974.

Blackstock, Nelson. *COINTELPRO*. New York: Vintage, 1976.

Bok, Sissela. *Lying: Moral Choice in Public and Private Life*. New York: Pantheon Books, 1978.

Borosage, Robert, and Marks, John, eds. *The CIA File*. New York: Grossman Publishers, 1976.

Buncher, Judith, et al., ed. *The CIA and the Security Debate*. New York: Facts on File, 1976.

Cline, Ray S. *Secrets, Spies and Scholars*. Washington, D.C.: Acropolis Books, 1976.

Colby, William. *Honorable Men: My Life in the CIA*. New York: Simon & Schuster, 1978.

Copeland, Miles. *Without Cloak or Dagger*. New York: Simon & Schuster, 1974.

Cox, Arthur. *The Myths of National Security: The Perils of Secret Government*. Boston: Beacon Press, 1975.

Documents Relating to the War Power of Congress, the President's Authority as Commander in Chief, and the War in Indochina, Committee on Foreign Relations, United States Senate, July 1970.

Dorsen, Norman, and Gillers, Stephen, eds. *None of Your Business: Government Secrecy in America*. New York: Penguin, 1975.

Dubois, Larry, and Gonzales, Laurence. "The Puppet: Uncovering the Secret World of Nixon, Hughes and the CIA," *Playboy*. September 1976, pp. 74+.

Dulles, Allen. *The Craft of Intelligence*. New York: Harper & Row, 1963.

Ellsberg, Daniel. *Papers on the War*. New York: Pocket Books, 1972.

——. "The Rolling Stone Interview," *Rolling Stone*. November 8, 1973, pp. 34-56, and Part II, December 6, 1973, pp. 33-44.

Falk, Richard A. "President Ford, CIA Operations, and the Status of International Law," *American Journal of International Law*. April 1975, pp. 354-58.

Fink, Robert. "The Unsolved Break-ins 1970-1974," *Rolling Stone*. October 10, 1974, pp. 54-59.

Government Secrecy. Hearings Before the Subcommittee on Intergovernmental Relations of the Committee on Government Operations of the United States Senate, 93rd Congress, 2nd session.

Halper, Thomas. *Foreign Policy Crises*. Columbus, Ohio: Charles E. Merrill, 1970.

Halperin, Morton. "National Security and Civil Liberties," *Foreign Policy*. Winter 21, 1975-76.

——; Berman, Jerry; Borosage, Robert; and Marwick, Christine. *The Lawless State: The Crimes of the U.S. Intelligence Agencies*. New York: Penguin, 1976.

——, and Hoffman, Daniel. *Top Secret*. Washington, D.C.: New Republic Books, 1977.

Hearings and Final Reports of the Select Committee on Presidential Campaign Activities, United States Senate, 93rd Congress, 2nd session (Ervin-Watergate Hearings).

Hearings and Final Reports of the Select Committee to Study Government Operations with Respect to Intelligence Activities, United States

Senate, 94th Congress, Volumes 1-7, and Final Report Books 1-5 (Church committee).

Hersh, Seymour. "The Reporter Who Broke My Lai Massacre, the Secret Bombings of Cambodia and the CIA Domestic Spying Stories Interviewed," *Rolling Stone.* April 10, 1975, pp. 48-52 and 73-82.

———. "The Toughest Reporter in America Interviewed," *Rolling Stone.* April 24, 1975, pp. 45-48 and 62-72.

Kent, Sherman. *Strategic Intelligence for American World Policy.* Princeton, N.J.: Princeton University Press, 1966.

Kim, Young, ed. *The Central Intelligence Agency: Problem of Secrecy in a Democracy.* Lexington, Mass.: D. C. Heath, 1968.

Kirkpatrick, Lyman. *The Real CIA.* New York: Macmillan, 1968.

———. *The U.S. Intelligence Community.* New York: Hill and Wang, 1973.

Kohn, Howard. "The Hughes-Nixon-Lansky Connection: The Secret Alliances of the CIA from World War II to Watergate," *Rolling Stone.* May 20, 1976, pp. 40-50 and 72-92.

Lake, Anthony, and Gelb, Leslie. "Tale of Two Compromises: Pike and Kissinger," *Foreign Policy.* Spring 1976, pp. 224-37.

Lasky, Victor. *It Didn't Start with Watergate.* New York: Dial Press, 1977.

"Liars and Lying," *Salmagundi,* Spring 1975.

Machiavelli. *The Prince and Selected Discourses.* New York: Bantam, 1971.

Marchetti, Victor, and Marks, John. *The CIA and the Cult of Intelligence.* New York: Dell, 1975.

Marks, John. "The Case Against Kissinger," *Rolling Stone.* August 1, 1974, pp. 10-14.

Mayaguez Reports and Hearings Before the Committee on International Relations and Its Subcommittee on International Political and Military Affairs, House of Representatives, 94th Congress, 1st session, May, June, July, and September 1975.

Mayaguez Reports of the Comptroller General of the United States, October 4, 1976.

Mazlish, Bruce. *Kissinger: The European Mind in American Policy.* New York: Basic Books, 1976.

Mondale, Walter et al. "Reorganizing the CIA," *Foreign Policy.* Summer 1976, pp. 53+.

"National Security Issue," *Society.* March/April 1975.

Navasky, Victor. *Kennedy Justice.* New York: Atheneum, 1971.

Neir, Aryeh. *Dossier: The Secret Files They Keep on You.* New York: Stein and Day, 1975.

Nelson Rockefeller Report to the President by the Commission on CIA
   Activities. New York: Manor Books, 1975.
Nixon, Richard. *Submission of Recorded Presidential Conversations.*
   April 30, 1974.
Norton, R. "Risk Parameters Across Types of Secrets," *Journal of Counsel-
   ing Psychology.* September 1974, pp. 450-54.
Oglesby, Carl. *The Yankee and the Cowboy War: Conspiracies from Dallas
   to Watergate.* Mission, Ks.: Sheed Andrews and McMeel, 1976.
Pentagon Papers. New York: New York Times-Bantam Books, 1971.
Powers, Thomas. "The Rise and Fall of Richard Helms," *Rolling Stone.*
   December 16, 1976, pp. 47-55.
Ransom, Harry Howe. *Central Intelligence and National Security.* Cam-
   bridge, Mass.: Harvard University Press, 1958.
——. *The Intelligence Establishment.* Cambridge, Mass.: Harvard University
   Press, 1970.
——. "Strategic Intelligence and Foreign Policy," *World Politics.* October
   1974, pp. 131-46.
Rositzke, Harry. *The CIA's Secret Operations.* New York: Reader's Digest
   Press, 1977.
Rourke, Francis. "Administrative Secrecy: A Comparative Perspective,"
   Public Administrative Review. January 1975, pp. 1-42.
——. *Secrecy and Publicity.* Baltimore, Md.: Johns Hopkins University
   Press, 1961.
Schorr, Daniel. *Clearing the Air.* New York, 1977.
——. "My 17 Months on the CIA Watch: A Backstage Journal," *Rolling
   Stone.* April 8, 1976, pp. 32-38 and 79-98.
Schrag, Peter. *A Test of Loyalty.* New York: Touchstone, 1974.
"Security Agreements and Commitments Abroad." Report to the Com-
   mittee on Foreign Relations, United States Senate, December 21,
   1970.
Sheridan, Terence. "Tom Charles Huston: Don't Call Him Sonuvabitch,"
   Rolling Stone. October 25, 1973, pp. 51-56.
Shils, Edward. *The Torment of Secrecy: The Background and Conse-
   quences of American Security Policies.* New York: The Free Press,
   1956.
Sigal, Leon. "Official Secrecy and Informational Communications in
   Congressional-Bureaucratic Relations," *Political Science Quarterly.*
   Spring 1975, pp. 71-92.
Snepp, Frank. *Decent Interval.* New York: Random House, 1977.
Stockwell, John. *In Search of Enemies: A CIA Story.* New York: W. W.
   Norton, 1978.

Szanton, Peter, and Allison, Graham. "Intelligence: Seizing the Opportunity," *Foreign Policy*. Spring 1976, pp. 183-223.

Szulc, Tad. *Compulsive Spy: The Strange Career of E. Howard Hunt*. New York: Viking Press, 1974.

Ungar, Sanford. *The FBI*. Boston: Little, Brown, 1975.

——. *The Papers and the Papers*. New York: Dutton, 1972.

Village Voice. "Pike Committee Report on Intelligence," House Select Committee on Intelligence, 94th Congress, 1st Session, February 16, 1976 and February 23, 1976.

Weisband, Edward, and Franck, Thomas, eds. *Secrecy and Foreign Policy*. New York: Oxford University Press, 1974.

Weissman, Steve, ed. *Big Brother and the Holding Company*. Palo Alto, Calif.: Rampart Books, 1974.

White House Transcripts. New York: New York Times-Bantam Books, 1974.

Wiggins, James. *Freedom or Secrecy*, rev. ed. New York: Oxford University Press, 1964.

Wise, David. *The American Police State*. New York: Random House, 1976.

——. *The Espionage Establishment*. New York: Random House, 1967.

——. "How Kissinger Bugged His Friends," *New Times*. October 26, 1976, pp. 25-28.

——. *The Politics of Lying: Government Deception, Secrecy and Power*. New York: Vintage, 1973.

——. *The U-2 Affair*. New York: Random House, 1962.

——, and Ross, Thomas. *The Invisible Government*. New York: Random House, 1964.

II. The Presidency and Related Topics

Amlund, Curtis. *New Perspectives on the Presidency*. New York: Philosophical Library, 1969.

Bailey, Thomas. *Presidential Greatness*. New York: Appleton-Century-Crofts, 1966.

Ball, George. *Diplomacy for a Crowded World*. Boston: Little, Brown, 1976.

Barber, James. *The Presidential Character*. Englewood Cliffs, N.J.: Prentice-Hall, 1972 and 1977.

Berger, Raoul. *Impeachment: The Constitutional Problem*. Cambridge, Mass.: Harvard University Press, 1973.

Breslin, Jimmy. *How the Good Guys Won: Notes from an Impeachment Summer*. New York: Ballantine, 1975.

Burns, James. *The Deadlock of Democracy*. Englewood Cliffs, N.J.: Prentice-Hall, 1963.

——. *Presidential Government*. Boston: Houghton Mifflin, 1966 and 1973.

Califano, Joseph. *A Presidential Nation*. New York: W. W. Norton, 1975.

Commager, Henry. *The Defeat of America*. New York: Simon & Schuster, 1974.

Cornwell, Elmer. *Presidential Leadership of Public Opinion*. Bloomington: Indiana University Press, 1962.

Corwin, Edward S. *The President: Office and Powers*. New York: NYU Press, 1957.

Cotter, C. P., and Smith, J. M. *Powers of the President During National Crisis*. New York: Da Capo Press reprint of Public Affairs Press, 1972.

Cronin, Thomas. *The State of the Presidency*. Boston: Little, Brown, 1975.

Dean, John. *Blind Ambition*. New York: Simon & Schuster, 1976.

Fenno, Richard. *The President's Cabinet*. New York: Vintage, 1959.

Finer, Herman. *The Presidency: Crisis and Regeneration*. Chicago: University of Chicago, 1960.

Fisher, Louis. *President and Congress*. New York: The Free Press, 1972.

——. *Presidential Spending Power*. Princeton, N.J.: Princeton University Press, 1975.

Freud, Sigmund, and Bullitt, William. *Thomas Woodrow Wilson: Twenty-Eighth President of the United States. A Psychological Study*. New York: Avon, 1967.

Graber, Doris. *Public Opinion, the President and Foreign Policy*. New York: Holt, Rinehart and Winston, 1968.

Hamilton, Alexander; Madison, James; and Jay, John. *The Federalist Papers*. New York: Mentor Books, 1968.

Hardin, Charles M. *Presidential Power and Accountability: Toward a New Constitution*. Chicago: University of Chicago Press, 1974.

Hargrove, Erwin C. *Presidential Leadership*. New York: Macmillan, 1966.

——. *The Power of the Modern Presidency*. New York: Alfred Knopf, 1974.

Hilsman, Roger. *The Politics of Policy Making in Defense and Foreign Affairs*. New York: Harper & Row, 1971.

Hofstadter, Richard. *The American Political Tradition*. New York: Vintage, 1948.

Hughes, Emmet John. *The Living Presidency.* New York: Coward, McCann and Geoghegan, 1973.

James, Dorothy. *The Contemporary President.* New York: Pegasus, 1969.

Javits, Jacob. *Who Makes War.* New York: Morrow, 1973.

Jaworski, Leon. *The Right and the Power.* Houston, Tx.: Gulf Publishing, 1976.

Johnson, Richard. *Managing the White House.* New York: Harper & Row, 1973.

Kane, Joseph. *Facts about the Presidents.* New York: Ace, 1976.

Kessel, John. *The Domestic Presidency.* N. Scituate, Mass.: Duxbury Press, 1975.

McConnell, Grant. *The Modern Presidency.* New York: St. Martin's Press, 1967.

McGinniss, Joe. *The Selling of the President, 1968.* New York: Trident Press, 1969.

Mazlish, Bruce. *In Search of Nixon. A Psychohistorical Inquiry.* New York: Basic Books, 1972.

Mueller, John. *War, Presidents and Public Opinion.* New York: John Wiley & Sons, 1973.

Mullen, William. *Presidential Power and Politics.* New York: St. Martin's Press, 1976.

Nadar, Ralph; Petkas, Peter; and Blackwell, Kate. *Whistle Blowing.* New York: Grossman Publishers, 1972.

Nathan, Richard. *The Plot That Failed: Nixon and the Administrative Presidency.* New York: John Wiley & Sons, 1975.

Neustadt, Richard. *Presidential Power.* New York: John Wiley & Sons, 1960 and 1976.

Nixon, Richard. *Six Crises.* Garden City, N.Y.: Doubleday, 1962.

Novak, Michael. *Choosing Our King.* New York: Macmillan, 1974.

Polsby, Nelson. *Congress and the Presidency.* Englewood Cliffs, N.J.: Prentice-Hall, 1971.

Polsby, Nelson, and Wildavsky, Aaron. *Presidential Elections,* 3rd ed. New York: Scribners, 1971.

Rather, Dan, and Gates, Gary. *The Palace Guard.* New York: Warner, 1975.

Reedy, George. *The Presidency in Flux.* New York: Columbia University Press, 1973.

——. *The Twilight of the Presidency.* New York: World, 1970.

Rossiter, Clinton. *The American Presidency,* rev. ed. New York: Harcourt, Brace and Jovanovich, 1960.

Schlesinger, Arthur, Jr. *The Imperial Presidency.* Boston: Houghton
Mifflin, 1973.
Scigliano, Robert. *The Supreme Court and the Presidency.* New York:
The Free Press, 1971.
Sickels, Robert. *Presidential Transactions.* Englewood Cliffs, N.J.:
Prentice-Hall, 1974.
Sorensen, Theodore. *Decision-Making in the White House.* New York:
Columbia University Press, 1963.
———. *Watchmen in the Night: Presidential Accountability and Watergate.*
Cambridge, Mass.: MIT Press, 1975.
Strum, Philippa. *Presidential Power and American Democracy.* Pacific
Palisades, Calif.: Goodyear, 1972.
Sundquist, James. *Politics and Policy: The Eisenhower, Kennedy and
Johnson Years.* Washington, D.C.: The Brookings Institution, 1968.
White, Theodore. *Breach of Faith.* New York: Dell, 1976.
———. *The Making of the President 1960; 1964; 1968; 1972.* New York:
Atheneum, 1961, 1965, 1969, 1973.
Woodward, Bob, and Bernstein, Carl. *All the President's Men.* New York:
Warner Paperback Library, 1975.
———. *The Final Days.* New York: Simon & Schuster, 1976.

III. Anthologies Containing Useful Articles on the Presidency

Barber, James, ed. *Choosing the President.* Englewood Cliffs, N.J.: Prentice-
Hall, 1974.
Cornwell, Elmer, ed. *The American Presidency: Vital Center.* Chicago:
Scott, Foresman, 1966.
Cronin, Thomas, and Greenberg, Sanford, eds. *The Presidential Advisory
System.* New York: Harper & Row, 1969.
Halpern, Paul, ed. *Why Watergate?* Pacific Palisades, Calif.: Palisades Press,
1975.
Hirschfield, Robert, ed. *The Power of the Presidency.* New York: Atherton,
1968.
Moe, Ron, ed. *Congress and the President.* Pacific Palisades, Calif.: Good-
year, 1971.
Polsby, Nelson, ed. *The Modern Presidency.* New York: Random House,
1973.
Pynn, Ronald, ed. *Watergate and the American Political Process.* New
York: Praeger, 1975.

Roberts, Charles, ed. *Has the President Too Much Power?* New York: Harper's, 1974.

Tugwell, Rexford, and Cronin, Thomas, eds. *The Presidency Reappraised.* New York: Praeger, 1974.

Wildavsky, Aaron, ed. *Perspectives on the Presidency.* Boston: Little, Brown, 1975.

———. ed. *The Presidency.* Boston: Little, Brown, 1969.

IV. Bureaucratic Politics

Allison, Graham. *Essence of Decision: Explaining the Cuban Missile Crisis.* Boston: Little, Brown, 1971.

Barnet, Richard. *Roots of War.* New York: Pelican, 1972.

Destler, I. M. *Presidents, Bureaucrats, and Foreign Policy.* Princeton, N.J.: Princeton University Press, 1972.

Donovan, John C. *The Cold Warriors.* Lexington, Mass.: D. C. Heath, 1974.

Downs, Anthony. *Inside Bureaucracy.* Boston: Little, Brown, 1967.

Halberstam, David. *The Best and the Brightest.* New York: Random House, 1972.

Halperin, Morton. *Bureaucratic Politics and Foreign Policy.* Washington, D.C.: The Brookings Institution, 1974.

Hickel, Walter. *Who Owns America?* Englewood Cliffs, N.J.: Prentice-Hall, 1971.

Hilsman, Roger. *To Move a Nation.* Garden City, N.Y.: Doubleday, 1967.

Hoopes, Townsend. *The Limits of Intervention.* New York: David McKay, 1969.

Janis, Irving. *Victims of Groupthink.* Boston: Houghton Mifflin, 1972.

Kennedy, Robert F. *Thirteen Days: A Memoir of the Cuban Missile Crisis.* New York: W. W. Norton, 1969.

Lowi, Theodore. *The End of Liberalism.* New York: W. W. Norton, 1969.

Pressman, Jeffrey, and Wildavsky, Aaron. *Implementation.* Berkeley: University of California Press, 1973.

Reagan, Michael. *The New Federalism.* New York: Oxford University Press, 1972.

Rourke, Francis. *Bureaucracy, Politics and Public Policy.* Boston: Little, Brown, 1969.

Weisband, Edward, and Franck, Thomas. *Resignation in Protest.* New York: Penguin, 1976.

Wildavsky, Aaron. *The Politics of the Budgetary Process.* Boston: Little, Brown, 1964.

V. Specific Presidents: Kennedy to Ford

Bradlee, Benjamin. *Conversations with Kennedy.* New York: Pocket Books, 1976.
Evans, Rowland, and Novak, Robert. *Nixon in the White House.* New York: Random House, 1971.
Fairlie, Henry. *The Kennedy Promise.* Garden City, N.Y.: Doubleday, 1973.
Hersey, John. *The President.* New York: Alfred Knopf, 1975.
Johnson, Lyndon. *The Vantage Point.* New York: Holt, Rinehart, and Winston, 1971.
Kalb, Marvin, and Kalb, Bernard. *Kissinger.* New York: Dell, 1975.
Kearns, Doris. *Lyndon Johnson and the American Dream.* New York: Harper & Row, 1976.
Magruder, Jeb. *An American Life.* New York: Atheneum, 1974.
Miroff, Bruce. *Pragmatic Illusions: The Presidential Politics of John F. Kennedy.* New York: David McKay, 1976.
Osborne, John. *The Nixon Watch.* New York: Liveright, 1970, 1971, 1972, 1973, 1974, 1975.
Sorensen, Theodore. *Kennedy.* New York: Harper & Row, 1965.
Wills, Gary. *Nixon Agonistes.* Boston: Houghton Mifflin, 1970.

VI. Political Science Convention Papers

Aberbach, Joel D. "The Development of Oversight in the United States Congress: Concepts and Analysis." Paper Delivered at the 1977 Annual Meeting of the American Political Science Association, Washington, D.C., September 1-4, 1977.
Bailey, Kenneth. "Continuity and Change in Children's Attitudes Toward the President." Southern Political Science Association Annual Meetings, November 1976, Atlanta, Georgia.
Boyan, Stephen. "Prerogative, The Constitution and the Presidency After Watergate." American Political Science Association Annual Meeting, September 2-5, 1976, Chicago, Illinois.
Doig, James. "Corruption in Complex Organizations." American Political Science Association Annual Meeting, September 2-5, 1976, Chicago, Illinois.
Graber, Doris. "Intervention Policies of the Carter Administration: Politica and Military Dimensions." Paper delivered at the Midwest Political Science Association Annual Meeting, April 20-22, 1978, Chicago, Illinois.

Hammel, Robert. "Congressional Responses to Executive Privilege."
    Paper delivered at the 1977 Annual Meeting of the American Political
    Science Association, September 1-4, 1977, Washington, D.C.
Kirkpatrick, Samuel; Davis, Dwight; and Robertson, Roby. "Micro-
    analytic Theory and Group Decision-making." Southern Political
    Science Association Annual Meeting, November 1976, Atlanta, Georgia.
Macaluso, Theodore. "The Presidential Character and Presidential Action
    in Conflict Situations: An Event Series Analysis." Southern Political
    Science Association Annual Meetings, November 1976, Atlanta,
    Georgia.
Minnix, Dean. "The Role of the Small Group in Foreign Policy Decision-
    making: A Potential Pathology in Crisis Decisions." Southern Political
    Science Association Annual Meetings, November 1976, Atlanta, Georgia.
Orman, John. "The Impact of Sexism in Politics: The Macho Presidential
    Style." Southern Political Science Association Annual Meetings, Novem-
    ber 1976, Atlanta, Georgia.
———. "Secrecy, Accountability and Presidential Power: The Case of Gerald
    R. Ford." Midwest Political Science Association Annual Meeting,
    April 21-23, 1977, Chicago, Illinois.
Ravenal, Earl. "Logic or Psycho-Logic? Nixon and Kissinger Move to a
    Balance of Power Policy." American Political Science Association Annual
    Annual Meeting, September 2-5, 1976, Chicago, Illinois.
Simmel, Andrew. "Group Dynamics and the Foreign Policy Process: The
    Choice-Shift Phenomenon." Southern Political Science Association
    Annual Meeting, November 1976, Atlanta, Georgia.
Starr, Harvey. "Images and Belief Systems of Decision Makers: The Study
    of Henry Kissinger." Midwest Political Science Association Annual
    Meeting, April 29-May 1, 1976, Chicago, Illinois.
Thomas, Norman C. "Recent Developments and Accountability: Presi-
    dential Accountability Since Watergate." Midwest Political Science
    Association Annual Meeting, April 20-22, 1978, Chicago, Illinois.
Wattier, Mark. "Presidential Popularity and the Political Process: Public
    Opinion Polls as Linkage." Southern Political Science Association
    Annual Meeting, November 1976, Atlanta, Georgia.

INDEX

About the Author

John M. Orman is Assistant Professor of Political Science at Fairfield University in Fairfield, Connecticut. His articles on politics in America have appeared in *Presidential Studies Quarterly*, among other journals.